Books by Simon Winchester

IN HOLY TERROR
Reporting the Ulster Troubles

AMERICAN HEARTBEAT
Notes from a Midwestern Journey

THEIR NOBLE LORDSHIPS

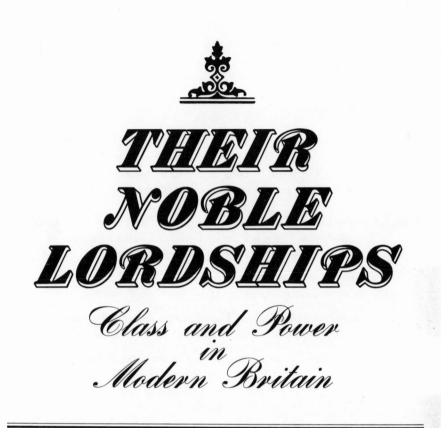

THEIR NOBLE LORDSHIPS

Class and Power
in
Modern Britain

Simon Winchester

RANDOM HOUSE   NEW YORK

*Grateful acknowledgment is made to the following for
permission to reprint previously published material:*

Weidenfeld & Nicolson, Ltd.: Excerpts from *No Regrets*
by Lord Carnarvon. Reprinted by permission.

Library of Congress Cataloging in Publication Data
Winchester, Simon.
Their noble lordships.
Bibliography: p.
Includes index.
1. Great Britain—Nobility.   2. Power (Social
sciences)   I. Title.
HT653.G7W54   305.5'2   81–48273
ISBN 0–394–52418–7   AACR2

Manufactured in the United States of America
9 8 7 6 5 4 3 2
First American edition

FOR JUDY

CONTENTS

AUTHOR'S NOTE

To avoid confusion, two points need to be made in considering just who this book is *not* about. There are quite a few men and women with titles in Britain; not all of them fall into the specific category of the hereditary peerage, which is the subject of *Their Noble Lordships*.

Hereditary peers are those whose titles pass inexorably onward from generation to generation, according to a cumbersome set of rules of considerable antiquity. There is, however, a relatively new type of entitlement known as the *Life Peerage*. This is a phenomenon of the age—it was invented in 1958—that came about in an attempt to bring some faint trace of responsive democracy to the House of Lords, which until then was entirely filled with hereditary peers. A Life Peer—the breed was termed "that life *rubbish*" by one particularly cantankerous old Marquess who loathed pretenders in any shape or form—holds his or her title only for the duration of his or her life. Life Peers are not included in this book, and their standing is not amenable to the arguments I attempt to advance. Readers are advised to dismiss them from their minds.

It will be more difficult for readers to apply the same sanction to a much smaller but infinitely better-known assemblage of British aristocrats who are also beyond the scope of the book—the Royal Family. Each member of the Royal House of Windsor carries a string of hereditary titles of great age and distinction. The Prince of Wales's titles would fill a page of this book: the Dukes of Kent and Gloucester are similarly well-endowed; the Duke of Edinburgh, as Queen's Consort, is magnificently entitled. But the Royal Family is beyond—and, one might say, above—the coarser debate about the future of true hereditary aristocracy, and to the extent it is ever possible to expunge them from the mind, it would be, in reading this book, prudent so to attempt to do.

References throughout this book to members of the peerage by titular description are to those holding such titles at January 1982, the date upon which the typescript went to press.

We spoke of the numbers of Peers at the Coronation which, Lord Melbourne said, with the tears in his eyes, was unprecedented. I observed that there were very few Viscounts; he said there *are* very few Viscounts; that they were an odd sort of title and not really English; that Dukes and Barons were the only real English titles; that Marquises were likewise not English and that they made people Marquises when they did not wish to make them Dukes.

—Queen Victoria, from her Private Journals, 28 June 1838

PREFACE

Alone in all the world, Britain still looks to accident of birth as a convenient means of selecting those who will help write the nation's laws. Not for Britons the unseemly and doubtless vulgar practices of universal adult suffrage or proportional representation—at least, not when it comes to the Upper House of what is proudly known as the "Mother of Parliaments." Instead, a system has been refined over the last seven hundred-odd years whereby the direct descendants, to take one example, of the mistresses who graced the bed of King Charles II still have an inalienable right to enact British legislation. Those upon whom this mantle of rare privilege has so comfortably fallen are the Peers of the Realm—a thousand or more men and women of often ancient heritage and endowed with mystifying responsibility, and whose position in British society is one of unrivalled superiority. Who are these people? How do they live their lives? How do they regard their unique allotments of rights and duties, of power and prestige? Do they see themselves perhaps as a threatened minority, islands of sanity in an ever-declining world?

These questions first came up at a birthday dinner party in Washington late in the summer of 1975. Everyone present that night was British, and while the views advanced in the argument were of a refreshingly varied nature, one undercurrent remained constant: that few of us knew more than the barest and sketchiest details about our noble peers.

We knew, I suppose, that many of them lived in fairy-tale castles and owned vast tracts of land. We knew, too, that a very few were impoverished in tragic and well-publicized ways, and that some eked out what for them must have been miserable existences working as gardeners or police constables or doorkeepers. But most, we suspected, lived unfathomable lives buried in the deepest byways of the English shires and the Scottish glens, lumbering forth only on occasion to see their Monarch enthroned or to take part in the annual ritual of the State Opening of their Parliament. So it was to ferret them from their rural fortresses, to smoke them from their dens, that I first sallied into the Great British Countryside late in the winter of 1976. The discoveries made in many months of wandering from crumbling mansion to grumbling manservant form the central part of this brief narrative of the noble life.

It was abundantly clear, from the very beginnings of this modest and unremarkable project, that many of the peers did not want to be written about. Some were tolerant of the idea that a commoner should scrutinize them: the Dukes of Devonshire and Buccleuch, for example, the Earls of Caledon, Carnarvon and Longford, and Viscounts Brookeborough and Arbuthnott proved delighted allies to the cause, and offered unfailing kindness and courtesy, patience and tolerance. Dozens of others, in ancient homes in Aberdeenshire and in modern *pied-à-terre* in Pimlico, offered me advice and anecdotes, places to stay and people to question. To them, the project was a worthy one, the investigation of privilege and power in today's Britain a necessary task, for which they offered time and trouble.

Others—probably the majority of those with whom I first made contact—were less enraptured by the idea.

"I would not wish to give interviews for any book that would be sold in America," the Duke of Beaufort wrote to me. "On no account do I wish to make known my views," said Lord Ridley. "You may see me on payment of £250 a day," said Lord Bath. (I wrote back respectfully noting that I could not afford a full day, but enclosing a cheque, carefully pro-rated, that would entitle me to a full hour of His Lordship's time. The cheque was cashed: no interview took place.)

In the end I saw about fifty members of the peerage, in their houses from Hastings to the Hebrides; I spent uncounted hours in the House of Lords, I talked to heralds and agents, factors and manciples, butlers and club stewards, sons and daughters and spouses and more distant relations of the titled grandees, every imaginable cog in the vast enginework of hereditary privilege. I sat down in Oxford to write the book, and it was eventually scheduled for publication in London on October 16, 1978. What actually happened had the makings of a brief excursion into nightmare. The peers who had been less charitable about the writing of the book made a determined effort to see that it was never published at all: the manner in which they wielded their not inconsiderable power and influence turned out to be an object lesson in the mechanics of the upper-class survival techniques.

The blow fell three days before publication—appropriately it was Friday, October 13. I was in New York. A cable was dropped on my desk: it was from Charles Monteith, chairman of Faber and Faber, the London publishers. "Lord Mansfield complains about references in book. Having to print erratum slip. Regrets."

The Earl of Mansfield, I had written, was a somewhat conservative figure who entertained strong views about the criminal fraternity: he had wanted the birch and the treadmill brought back for dealing with incorrigible villains.

Regrettably, however, this particular Earl had died; his son—who, thanks to the way the British peerage is established, came also to be called the Earl of Mansfield—was not a man upon whom the sins of his father had been visited, and he decided that the reference to his father defamed *him,* since there was no means for the reader to determine which Earl was which. And, it turned out, he was not to be placated by an erratum slip—one that would simply have added the phrase "the late" before references to the former Earl. Instead he wanted the book banned and pulped. He went before the High Court in London, won an injunction from a Mr. Justice Boreham and, less than forty-eight hours before publication, presented Fabers with the appalling task of retrieving every single copy of the book from every single bookshop in the land—or face suit for contempt of court in the event that a single copy went on sale the following Monday.

News of the withdrawal of the first edition caused a storm in the British gossip columns, and aroused more than a little interest among peers who found their names in the book's index. One by one, other holders of hereditary entitlements wrote to Fabers, demanding that various details written about them be expunged from any forthcoming version of the book. Lord Carrington, for example—later to become the stunningly successful British Foreign Secretary—complained that his expressed views about the more worthwhile aspects of the British class system would cause him embarrassment, and should not appear in print. His solicitors, a firm of impeccable credentials, known as Freshfields, demanded that His Lordship be permitted to vet any future manuscript: when it was eventually rewritten he demanded that every reference to him be taken out. The demand was backed by law—and painstakingly every mention of His Lordship was, eventually, dropped. The lawyers even insisted that a photograph of Lord Carrington inspecting the Life Guards had to be removed, on pain of judicial sanction.

Other peers wrote, via their solicitors, demanding that references to them be bowdlerised. Lord Bristol would have us make no mention of his having plotted to rob a jewellery shop in Mayfair in 1933; we were advised not to talk of a Scottish peer having been fined for assaulting the owner of a service station, of a Marquess having been criticised by a judge for "ungentlemanly behaviour" when he struck a press photographer in 1946, of a Baron being gaoled for interfering with choirboys a decade later. To display the British peerage at all was deemed heretical enough: to display them, warts and all, was quite unpalatable.

There were times when I feared this book would never be published at all. The costs of legal actions and of reprinting a book that had been banned on both sides of the Atlantic mounted to astronomical sums; there seemed little possibility that the innumerable critical observations of mine upon which a newly sensitized peerage were waiting to fall could be reworded in a legally secure manner. "The peers of the realm just don't want to be written about," a Faber's executive commented sadly. "They would rather no one bothered. They just want to be left alone." At each new stage one could almost hear the rustling of ermine as the Dukes and Marquesses, the Earls and Viscounts and Barons rose up once more to do battle with the commoner who had dared try and chronicle their doings.

But then I happened upon an ally—a man with the magnificent name of Sir Iain Moncreiffe of that Ilk, a man who remains the foremost authority on peerage lore in Britain. He disagreed with the thesis of the book, and said so; but he felt it should appear. He agreed to use his skills as a barrister, and the knowledge he had acquired as Scotland's Albany Herald, to turn a legally dangerous manuscript into a book that the Peerage might well still want to have banned, but which, in law, they could merely rail against, and do no more.

This book, then, emerges in no small part thanks to Sir Iain's assistance and advice, and I am delighted to be able to express to him my warmest thanks for his help in what, for him, must have been a somewhat distasteful task. Patrick Montague-Smith, the distinguished and knowledgeable editor of *Debrett's*, and Hugh Montgomery-Massingberd of *Burke's Peerage*, were also unfailingly helpful. But it is to Sir Iain that I owe the greatest thanks: perhaps during all the months when this book was taking shape, nothing was quite so pleasant as sitting at the foot of his old four-poster, away from the snows of the cold Perthshire night outside, drinking good whiskey and listening to all the tales of noble deeds and misdeeds from this splendid old trooper.

My thanks are due to the editors of the *Guardian*, the *Daily Mail* and the *Sunday Times* for their patience and forbearance during this book's prolonged gestation; to Pamela Colman, assistant librarian at Magdalen College, Oxford, for help with much of the basic research; to Charles Monteith and Matthew Evans at Fabers, for keeping the faith even during the darkest moments, when writs were flying like sleet; and, of course, my deepest thanks to my wife, Judy, who typed the manuscript—versions One and Two—in less than a month, each time. By dedicating this book to her I am displaying only a small token of my gratitude.

—Simon Winchester,
Oxford

THEIR NOBLE LORDSHIPS

ONE

EXORDIUM—
Sorts and Conditions

"You should study the peerage, Gerald. . . . It is
the best thing in fiction the English have ever
done."
—Oscar Wilde, *A Woman of No Importance*

"No, no! Indeed, high rank will never hurt you.
The Peerage is not destitute of virtue."
—W. S. Gilbert, *Iolanthe*

Like many a solid and sensible Derbyshire village, the little Victorian
settlement of Beeley snuggles away from winter in a tight fold of the
high sandstone moorland on the fringes of The Peak. In the crook of
sheep-dotted hills where the Beeley Brook chatters its way down to
the more stately River Derwent huddle some sixty buildings: one is a
farm; another a vicarage, smothered in wisteria; a few bear witness to
the momentary fame the hamlet enjoyed as a centre for the manufacture of grindstones for the wandering knife-sharpeners. Most of the
structures, though, are houses—small, rough-hewn, stubby little
dwellings, two up and two down; city houses brought and dumped, it
sometimes seems, in these remote country hills.

Beeley is an easy village to miss, and most of the motorists who
hum their way down the Derwent valley on their way to Matlock
rarely give it a moment's thought. It is a place that displays no more
of note, and no less, than two precisely similar villages named Edensor and Pilsley five miles back north up the valley road. Dour little
cottages of Millstone Grit; a wizened post office; tiny windows shrouded
in nylon lace; empty, windy streets with a curiously impoverished
aspect about them. Only the pub, at which a few knowledgeable

motorists may stop, singles out Beeley as a site worthy of more than casual scrutiny.

The guidebooks describe it as "A stone-built, beamed village inn," and list its Darley Dale telephone number. Travellers will remember that it offers fine country luncheons of good local cheese and beef, of fresh trout and country butter, and that Theakston's ales—even the notoriously strong "Old Peculier"—can be purchased for a reasonable sum in silver. Too few will remark, however, on the name of the pub, though to outsiders it may seem somewhat less than geographically appropriate. It is known by no diminutive or sobriquet: although 200 miles by crow from the sands of Torquay and the granite tors of Dartmoor, this particular public house is known as the Devonshire Arms. Not Derbyshire, in respect of the county in which it lies, but Devonshire, in respect of the ancestors and present majesty of a balding and engagingly shy sixty-one-year-old man who lives occasionally in a large house behind a nearby hill and who happens to own not just the pub, but the three villages too, every single one of the surrounding fields and forests, rivers, streams and mineral mines and—some unkind souls might say—most of the local people too.

The man who has the village inn named for him, and who owns near enough everything that can be seen from the door—indeed from the roof—of the building, is one Andrew Robert Buxton Cavendish: His Grace, as he is known both near and far, the most Noble the eleventh Duke of Devonshire.

The arms that swing and creak above the inn's front door are to be seen time and again in this part of England. Officially, the Heralds in London describe them as "Sable, three bucks' heads cabossed argent," with two "supporters," which, to keep it in the family, are "bucks proper, each wreathed round the neck with a chaplet of roses, alternately argent and azure." To master masons and sign painters, however, bucks are perhaps not the easiest of creatures to carve and draw, and most make do with the heraldic crest that lies curled above the complexities and grandeur of the formal arms: a serpent, knotted in a figure eight. This sign of the snake can be seen in walls, in windows, on writing paper, on merchants' accounts, on gleaming black cars, on dispatch cases and on leather-bound books in nooks and crannies all over this region of the north. To get in or out of the Cavendish lands, one can proceed, if the snowdrifts permit, along the Snake Pass. Once there, one can stay in the Snake Hotel. Fanciful cartographers might ring the thousands and thousands of acres owned by the present Duke with some python-like device; it could fairly be said that the snake, a symbol of employment and security in these parts, holds the people in check, dissuades them from forays of any length of time into the world outside.

For it is true that the villagers of Beeley and its sister settlements are a fixed and contented people, not given to travel or adventure, but happy to remain where they are, generation after generation. Knock on almost any one of the deal front doors, and the story will be virtually the same as that told by Albert and Doris Hodkin, whose address is Brook Cottage, Beeley, and has been for the past thirty years.

"I was born here in Beeley," Albert told me. "My father was born here, and my grandfather too. I was born in 1895, my father in 1870, his father in 1840. All three of us worked for His Grace, whoever he was, for all of our lives. That's the way it is round here. You live and die as part of His Grace's family, sort of." Albert Hodkin, who spends most of his day slumbering before a coke fire that melts the soles of his carpet slippers, was a tenant farmer for the Duke for forty years. He started with thirty acres and a few scrawny cattle, and ended with a hundred acres and a few more cows. He paid his rent on time, he and his Doris, who came over the hill from the railway cottages at Rowsley (in the Duke of Rutland's territory, five miles distant). They made a little butter and cheese and grew their own vegetables and lived fairly well in the rented farm. Then the Duke—or his agent, rather—decided to expand the farms in Beeley and retired Albert Hodkin to Brook Cottage at a rent most townfolk would consider peppercorn. He pays one pound a week for the place, and is utterly content to while away his remaining years, with Doris sitting by his side in the front parlour, listening to the crumbling of the glowing coke and the hurrying of the stream outside their front door and the birdsong that echoes down the valley. That the Dukes of Devonshire may be considered the owners of the Hodkins' lives—in practice, if not in theory; shapers and moulders of three generations of Hodkins, albeit with the voluntary submission of grandfather, father and present Hodkin—does not worry Albert or his Doris in the slightest.

"I remember all the way back to the eighth Duke. I remember his funeral at Edensor—horses draped in black, the dray covered in crepe, the robes over the bier. It was a big event, a very sad one. People came from all over the county.

"And every so often there are events to which us villagers are invited. Quite recently—1965, I think—we all went up to the big house for Lord Hartington's coming of age—that's what they call the Duke's first son. There were tables laid out on the lawns, and there was cold turkey and trifle, and a huge firework display at night. They had three nights of parties for Lord Hartington—a private party for all His Lordship's friends on one night, and then a formal one which Royalty went to, and then the party for all of us. You remember nights like that all your life."

The villagers were asked to contribute whatever they could for a present for Lord Hartington and were pleased to hear he had been given a watch—it cost £350, some said—on their behalf. The Hodkins, and probably all the other villagers, keep His Lordship's letter of thanks safe in a drawer of the bureau.

Though Albert and Doris Hodkin consider travel an exercise in singular pointlessness, and thus do not indulge, and though the farmers and estate workers and most of the other ducal employees in the three villages think along similar lines, it would be wrong to say that no one ventures beyond the boundaries of the Cavendish lands. One man, for instance, makes regular journeys to the West End of London, bent on participating in one of the most secretive operations yet devised by a British peerage that is well versed in secrecy and the unfathomable mystery of inherited wealth.

Derrick Penrose, a one-time dealer in baked beans whose interest in land and property crept up on him some twenty years ago, is the Duke of Devonshire's agent—"the managing director," as he puts it, "of an outfit of which His Grace is chairman." He runs the Cavendish estates with the help of men and women who, were they in American banks or motor-car companies, would sport anonymous and unexciting titles such as Executive Vice-President or Director of Marketing. Mr. Penrose instead has charge of functionaries like the Head Keeper, the Principal of the Domain Department, the Head Forester and the Comptroller, all of whom, working from a converted inn just outside the boundary fence of the big house and park, seem intensely proud of the efficiency with which they manage the ducal fortunes. They preside over an empire worth many millions of pounds: that they manage it with such an ineffable combination of pride and dignified dynamism comes, in all probability, from the fact that predecessors have been similarly managing these fortunes since the seventeenth century, and that what they have now inherited—vast acreages, grand and lovely buildings, whole towns and villages and the lives of hundreds upon hundreds of men and women—is, in an infinitely more tangible way than, say, a shipyard or a biscuit factory, a part of the national character. That Dukes exist at all is due, partly, to the continuing benevolence of a patient and good-natured British people: the Derrick Penroses of the great estates are well schooled in the knowledge that what they manage and control is, while a great privilege, a very public charge as well. And it is partly because of this knowledge that Derrick Penrose and other men, with names like Galbraith and Elliott and James, meet secretly in London, about once every six weeks.

They come down to town by sleeper, or, if they are from the nearer estates in the Home Counties, by car. Their luggage labels suggest their origins: Chatsworth, Welbeck Woodhouse, Drumlanrig Castle, Eaton, Blair Atholl—the seats of some of the most powerful landowners in Britain, some Dukes, some Marquesses, some untitled, some unknown. The men who gather at mid-morning outside the white building at 53 Davies Street, just a little south of the bustle and turmoil of Oxford Street and in the heart of the wealthiest section of the metropolis, are the representatives of the richest and in many ways most influential men in the kingdom. They have come to be known as the Twenty-Five Invisibles, and their mysterious doings will to no small extent dictate just how the peculiar institution of inherited privilege will survive in Britain in the coming years.

"We have come to realize we are no longer a politically acceptable group," explains young Gerald Grosvenor, who has recently inherited the most fabulous peerage title of all, that of the Dukedom of Westminster, and who presides over the Invisibles from the office that houses the nerve centre of the family fortunes. "Our group aims to produce a scheme for assuring our acceptability, for ensuring our survival." The Invisibles prefer that their existence goes unnoticed: the membership is sworn to secrecy about its decisions and operations, and, by and large, keeps its promise. Publicly, such operations as it orders are carried out by a well-known "cover" organization; amidst a political climate which its members variously describe as "hostile" and "marred by the worst kind of jealousies" the prosecution of the battle against extinction is carried out in practised, monastic silence.

A mile or so from the Davies Street office lies a rather more public symbol of the world of title and position. Halfway down a narrow street crammed with stationers to the legal profession, vintners and antiquarian booksellers, is a dignified and cosy old shop with the un-

likely cable address of "Eaglehawk, London." Messrs. Ede and
Ravenscroft, of 93 Chancery Lane, head their writing paper with the
legend "Robe Makers and Tailors since the Reign of William and
Mary in the Year 1689," and no fewer than three badges of Royal
Appointments grace the simplest of communications from the firm.
The Queen, the Duke of Edinburgh and the Queen Mother all pur-
chase their robes here: so, too, do nearly all the 1,148 men and women
whose birth or recent services entitle them to be styled Your Grace,
Your Lordship or Your Ladyship. (Strictly speaking, since every
baronet's wife and every knight's wife is also entitled to be called
"Your Ladyship," the number is far greater than that.)

The front of the shop, a flurry of energetic young men with tape
measures and a quiet eagerness, is predominantly given over to suiting
cloth in grey worsted and black silk for the barristers and solicitors who
haunt these regions of the City fringe. Hanging from hooks in smaller
rooms towards the window marked "Settlement of Accounts and Private
Offices," one sees, and frankly welcomes, an occasional flash of colour
—crimson, maybe, or a rich purple, or scarlet and gold, brilliant white
furs and rich black velvets. These are the first of hundreds of sets of
robes brought to, and usually kept by, the custodians· at Ede and
Ravenscroft, from wardrobes and closets in castles, mansions and
humble houses from Cornwall to Caithness.

In cramped little lofts above the fitting rooms, and in more modern
quarters in an undistinguished warehouse near Cambridge, in damp-
ened air at 40°F, are line upon line of hangers supporting the official
uniforms of the British nobility—the great coronation robes, weighing
forty pounds and worn only a few times each century; and the parliamentary robes of scarlet wool, miniver and gold lace, with the appropriate marks of degree in appliquéd sealskin spots around the back
(so that a Viscount can be distinguished from an Earl, a Marquess
from a Baron, and a Duke from every other mortal), that are worn
by some, perhaps once a year. At the back of each robe is a small flap
of scarlet known as the liripip: underneath this, embroidered on a
fragment of white linen in much the same way as a schoolboy's socks
are identified, is the owner's name. The robes of nobility, like schoolboy's socks can get lost in the scrums in which their owners tend to
be obliged to participate.

The names themselves breathe still more history into a scene already firmly rooted in a half-forgotten era. "Mowbray, Segrave and
Stourton," one label will read; "Bolingbroke and St. John" will be

written on another; "Albemarle"; "Beaufort"; "Grafton"; "St. John of Bletso"; "Fitzwalter"; "Saye and Sele."

Names that tell of ancient battles and the friends of long-dead kings; names that smell of moated fortresses and bloated mistresses, of empires and forgotten philanthropies, of soldiery and glory and the creation, growth and burgeoning of the kingdom. Names from Old England like Norfolk and Somerset, Winchester and Shrewsbury. Names from Scotland—Argyll, Atholl, Erroll, Huntly and Mar. Titles from Irish landholdings that smack of plantation—Donegall, Dufferin, Clanwilliam and Londonderry. Titles that ring with the great sagas of Irish history, like O'Brien, Lord Inchiquin; Butler, Marquess of Ormonde; Dillon, Viscount Dillon; and FitzGerald, Duke of Leinster. Titles from more recent days of union and progress—Nelson, Wellington, Marlborough, Byron, Tennyson and Mountbatten of Burma. Some of the noblest villains and some of the grandest subjects this country has ever produced will have worn the selfsame robes that hang, now sprayed and guarded from all manner of flame, in the warehouse at Cambridge or the dim old rooms of Chancery Lane.

It is unlikely that many of the citizens of the little village of Caledon, deep in the soft, green countryside of County Tyrone in Northern Ireland, will have heard of Messrs. Ede and Ravenscroft, or of the Twenty-Five Invisibles, or, for that matter, of the village of Beeley. Caledon, now a little war-scarred from the latest round of Ulster violence, is not as pure an example of the feudal estate as Beeley: not every house is owned by the Earl of Caledon, whose castle broods from a nearby park; and evidence of the existence of villagers whose lives are quite distinct from the cumbersome processes of the Caledon estates is everywhere to be seen. There are, indeed, a few council houses—one of which, by chance, provided the siting for the very first confrontation of the present episode of the "Troubles." Caledon is considerably less insular a community, much more "normal," in spite of its unhappy siting in the North of Ireland.

Denis James Alexander, whose title as sixth Earl of Caledon was thrust on him in 1968 when an uncle died childless, was little interested during his life in the sordid squabble that proceeds incessantly below the hill. Although a bomb sneaked over the Irish border—which runs at the bottom of his estate—ruined the library in the castle at a fairly early stage of the dispute, and although he employed the sister of one of the principals in that initial confrontation as a secretary, the life of studied ease which he inherited was rarely touched by the miseries of nationalist zeal. True, he used his training in the British Army (his most distinguished relation was Earl Alexander of Tunis, one of the ennobled gallants of World War II) to command a unit of the local Ulster Defense Regiment, but his interests and activities centred fairly solemnly on that which surrounds his castle so extensively and so graciously—his land.

Breakfast on a normal day in his lifetime—he died in 1980—was not served at Caledon Castle until half-past nine. That factory hooters blasted at seven, that London's rush hour had reached its peak at half-past eight, and that most clerks and cobblers are well at work by nine mattered little at Caledon. The Earl was down by a quarter to ten or so, to sit at one end of an immense and highly polished oaken table and open his small stack of morning letters with a golden paperknife laid to the right of his breakfast setting. Porridge—which the Earl, unlike so many peers, would eat sitting down—was brought from a heated tray behind. Eggs and bacon, tomatoes, coffee, honey from the comb and warm toast were carried in by a bustling and cheerful lady from Wiltshire who had been with the Caledons for more years than anyone cared to remember. Newspapers—*The Times* and the *Daily Express*—were read patiently and painstakingly, with the births and deaths column of the Thunderer scanned first with that vague apprehension of families of breeding. The ceremony was rarely completed before half-past ten. What, one was tempted to inquire, did the Earl do now?

"Do? Well I suppose I'll pop down and have a look at the deer herd, or go and have a chat with the foresters or wander over to the office in the village and see Miss Beatty. I have to order a case of sherry for my mother, and in a day or so I have to go over to London to see the trustees. But nothing urgent. Nothing ever is."

The acquisition of large chunks of land. The style that accompanies a pedigree of some distinction. A continual attempt to outwit, invariably by means of compromise, or cunning, or both, the harsh exigencies of opposing political views. These three factors, together with the near-ruthless application of the principle of primogeniture, whereby the eldest son of a noble British family inherits virtually everything, and the younger sons and all the daughters inherit virtually nothing, have managed to keep the British hereditary peerage more or less intact and in more or less robust health for considerably longer than 700 years. True, there are peers without land. There are many without style. Some behave in a manner which will never allow a spirit of compromise to exist between their political opponents and themselves. Some have been incautious enough to permit their estates to be divided among their offspring, or have been unlucky enough to see their estates divided because of their inabilities to provide an heir of the right sex at the necessary time. But in general terms the combination of land, primogeniture, style and compromise has maintained "the best thing in fiction the English have ever done" in fine fettle—finer than it deserves, many would say—for nearly thirty generations.

"To write about the hereditary peers is a vulgar idea," grumbled Harold Macmillan one evening at a dinner in All Souls. "The trouble with them is that so many are unspeakably middle-class. Mr. Pitt, for example, created scores of the fellows, many just too awful. To write about the peerage is about as difficult as writing a book about everyone in England whose name begins with the letter G."

The former Prime Minister—and uncle of the present Duke of Devonshire—who had been offered, but had declined, an earldom, was not alone in condemning the notion of writing an account of the peers of the realm today. Several times, the view was put forward that it was unrealistic to isolate the peerage as a group, except in con-stitutional terms.

Mr. Macmillan and the other critics make a fair point: by isolating the peers one could be suspected of hinting that they were all some-how alike, and thus classifiable in the same way one could classify coal miners or Mormons. But their remarks concern an observation any student of the peerage must make almost as soon as he embarks upon his research—that individually those men and women who make up the peerage today are in a multitude of ways quite astonishingly varied. Many are very rich indeed: of the millionaires who die in Britain each year, some three-quarters are ennobled by birth. Most nobles are, by now, firmly established in what one would call the "upper classes"—and all bar perhaps one-tenth of 1 percent are mem-bers of what either the government or social demographers would term the highest socioeconomic groups. Not a few are consciously estranged from, or never have been members of what used to be called "high society." Not all are "gentlemen," in the sense that while any Prime Minister or Monarch can create a peer, only God can endow sufficient gentility to deserve that particular title. Not all were like the Earl of

Caledon, with time on their hands. Not all are like the Duke of Devonshire, with vast acreages, dozens of farms and uncountable wealth. There are policemen peers, at least one market gardener with the good fortune to find himself heir to an earldom; there is an ennobled dentist, and there was a popular television raconteur who, while he preferred to be known as Patrick Campbell, was in fact the third Baron Glenavy, of Milltown, County Dublin. The group is, in sum, so variegated as to make an observation of it fascinating, but yet not different enough to render the selection of the group invalid. And there are other factors that unite the group in a far more realistic way than, say, the simple possession of the same initial letter of their surnames—factors that tend to make Mr. Macmillan's argument seem specious and other such objections simply thoughtless. What unites the peerage is what gives its members its unique position in the society of this island nation.

To begin at the more frivolous level, it must be noted that each member of the peerage enjoys a style of address that automatically goes with this title. His title may be, according to his rank, either Duke or Marquess, Earl or Viscount, or Baron. If a woman, either in her own right or as the wife, widow, mother or former spouse of a peer, she is Duchess, Marchioness, Countess, Viscountess or Baroness. Dukes and Duchesses are called "Your Grace" (though a divorced wife of a Duke—and there are several—is not permitted to style herself so). The remainder—though they keep their style when addressed in writing, or in formal gatherings—are "Lord" or "Lady," "Your Lordship" or "Your Ladyship." Never are those thus ennobled to hear the distressing appellations Mr., Mrs. or Miss—a feature of their lives that, as one small illustration will serve to depict, usually proves to be an advantage.

In 1974 a young Englishman possessed of something like a flair for deception—he had been hauled before the courts for impersonating a policeman and owning an imitation revolver—decided he would change his name from the decidedly prosaic Mr. Michael Burke to the more imposing Jefrey Jess Le Vance De Roath, and see what happened. He soon found that the name itself, adorned by the entirely spurious award to himself of the Military Cross, made life a good deal sweeter, but changing his name once more, and elevating himself to the temporal peerage with the style and title of Lord De Roath, finally did the trick. Gillian Lipscombe, a girl with perhaps more gullibility than is desirable these days, decided on His Lordship as a suitable husband, and the young lady became what she thought was Her Ladyship.

But the title was not merely helpful in getting his girl, Mr. Burke discovered. He found that his father-in-law became an easy touch for some £4,000—any natural son, as Burke purported to be, of the quite mythical Lord Sinclair of Cleve and Duchess Katrina De Roath must, poor Mr. Lipscombe supposed, be an honourable sort of fellow. The local bank in Lewes decided much the same, and allowed Mr. Burke the not inconsiderable privilege of a £450 overdraft—the kind of privilege it would probably not offer to hospital porters, chauffeurs or builders, members of trades to which Mr. Burke, before his imaginative rebirth, had actually belonged. And, possibly best of all, British Caledonian Airlines, flattered that His Lordship should choose their humble silver bird to transport the happy couple to Argentina, gladly accepted his cheque without any of the sordid formalities that normally accompany such transactions, and happily let the pair romp in the VIP suite at the airport before the aircraft took off. It was only the impersonal bank computer, with magnetic cards that are rarely gulled by persons without means, whether titled or not, that discovered the fraud.

Policemen, not knowingly ennobled ones either, arrested a thoroughly ignoble man and a soon-to-be-disennobled woman on their return to England in January 1975, and he, under the name of Jefrey De Roath, faced trial for fraud, deception and theft. Most sympathy went out to Mrs. De Roath, who, it was said, had supposed herself to be a titled woman from the moment of plighting her troth. "One can picture her distress when she discovered she was just plain Mrs. and married to a man without a penny to his name," said the prosecuting lawyer, and one could understand him exactly. Mr. Burke was sent to prison for a good, long stretch.

Being a peer of the realm undoubtedly also brings the kind of privilege that means very little, but is sufficient to enrage the unprivileged onlooker. Lord Montagu of Beaulieu, one of Britain's showmen peers, called his study of the changing fortunes of the European aristocracies *More Equal than Others*—and that is about the size of it. In a country still waist-deep in a system of class and privilege there is a rigid caste system that overlies, like the transparent spider-web paper in old photograph albums, the social realities afforded by the acquisition of money or respect. The basic inequalities that place an accountant in a socially superior position to a worker in an abattoir are overshadowed by a kind of super-equality that comes with constant reference to a Briton's breeding. If the abattoir worker were suddenly to be discovered, by some diligent slave at the College of Arms, to be heir to an ancient viscounty, then the overlay would begin to glow more brightly than the underlay. Viscount Abattoir, like Lord De Roath, would assume a position of privilege in a trivial but no less infuriating sense that would place him subtly above the accountant in terms of his standing in society—the latter term meaning something quite specific in Britain, as we shall see later. He would become more equal, in the true Orwellian sense, no matter that he is penniless, empty of all social graces, and quite possibly a thorough dullard.

Baroness Wootton of Abinger, who in normal circumstances would be known as Mrs. Barbara Wootton, but is the proud owner of a life barony, finds the trivial perquisites of a noble life the most enraging. "I occasionally find it irritating," she remarks, "that if I go, say, to a local butcher myself I discover he has fillets of steak. But if somebody else goes for me, he hasn't. I can't stand that sort of thing, and I won't continue going to a shop where it happens."

Lord Montagu, who, as a showman, doesn't object in the slightest to being addressed by his title and getting as much mileage from its use as it is possible to get, maintains that ". . . the only people who have real respect for the title are those in the service industries. That is because they suffer under the delusion that a title means money. Therefore the only value of a title is in booking a table in a restaurant. . . ." Or, as Mr. Burke discovered, obtaining an overdraft, a ticket to Argentina, the VIP lounge—perhaps even a wife.

There are rather more people in Britain who are permitted this luxury—that of a title—than might at first be supposed. The basic numbers, which change only when a peerage becomes extinct (although Mrs. Thatcher says that more hereditary peers may be created, none has been since John Morrison was made Lord Margadale of Islay in 1965), are easy enough to ascertain (and these figures omit the "life peers" created for life only since 1958). The official House of Lords figures for 1981 are as follows: 28 Dukes (including the 3 Royal Dukes: Cornwall, Kent and Gloucester), 37 Marquesses, 173 Earls, 110 Viscounts, 438 Barons and Scots Lords, 19 peeresses in their own right and 71 Irish peers: 876 men and women who enjoy the distinction of entitlement by right of birth—save for 59, who were created peers for more recent services to the Kingdom and are the original holders of the titles; it will be their eldest sons, if they have heirs, who will enjoy titles by right of birth alone.

But these are not all, by a long chalk. Scores more people, by virtue of some connection with the noble 876, are entitled to be called by some other handle than the name by which, for example, they would be referred to in a court of law.

Thus, Mr. Maurice FitzGerald, a pleasant, if slightly reserved, market gardener who lives in the village of Chadlington in Oxford, is quite entitled to style himself the Marquess of Kildare, and does so. He is able to call himself a Marquess simply because his father is a Duke—the Duke of Leinster, the eighth of the line—and as such can sport what is called in the trade a *courtesy title*.*

The Duke of Leinster's late father, the seventh Duke, enjoyed a position that was perhaps unique in the world of titleage, and neatly illustrates the profusion of courtesy titleage. Although he took his own life in 1976, he did live long enough to become a great-grandfather, and he was able to distribute all of his disposable courtesy titles. He was photographed shortly before his death, and the picture of all four generations, each destined to succeed eventually to the title of the next oldest in the family, is a charming if ever so slightly ridiculous example of the benefits of the nobiliary status. The old Duke, bowed by age, stands on one side of a pleasant living room. His son, the Marquess of Kildare, sits beside him. His grandson, Maurice, in those days wielding the title of Earl of Offaly, sits in a well-padded chair, holding in his arms the baby of the family, Thomas, who, though an infant in arms, has the style and dignity of Viscount Leinster. All has changed now, of course: the old Duke has passed on, the Marquess is the Duke, the Earl is the Marquess, and baby Thomas, unlikely at this age to be confused by the mechanics of it all, is now the Earl. Not until he becomes father to a son will the title Viscount Leinster return to the roll of honour.

The gift of a courtesy title is, except for the privileges of service, quite meaningless: the constitutional privileges and prohibitions which are developed upon a principal title-holder never apply to a peer by courtesy—he is not, indeed, a true peer, though he is not quite as brazenly counterfeit as poor Lord De Roath. Yet few offered such

---

* "Courtesy" in this sense actually does mean ordinary politeness, literally "the manner of the royal court."

titles ever refuse them. One who has is Thomas Pakenham, son of
the Earl of Longford; he could easily farm Castlepollard in County
Westmeath with the courtesy title of Lord Silchester, but he finds it
all rather unnecessary, he says, and sticks quite resolutely to Pakenham. This is not altogether a surprising choice, since the name
Pakenham is well known and respected and possibly likely to be de-
valued somewhat by being changed to an obscure peerage title drawn
from a little-regarded Hampshire village. Other peers hold similarly
distinguished names they might be reluctant to drop—the Russells,
say, or the Cecils, or the Howards. Far better to be simply a Cecil,
some might say, than a mere Marquess of Salisbury.

There is another category, too, of subsidiary ennoblement. Only
the eldest sons of highly titled peers are permitted full-blown courtesy
titles, maybe; but the remainder are not forgotten. Brothers and sisters
of the heir enjoy additions to their ordinary names. Aunts, uncles,
cousins—all manner of relations, indeed—seem to like to possess,
either by courtesy or by marriage, and often by both, some prefix that
marks them out as, in some indefinable way, more equal than those
who wear their Christian and patronymic designations quite naked.

Take, for example, the sixth Marquess of Cholmondeley, the Joint
Hereditary Lord Great Chamberlain of England. His son, now in his
twenties, is styled the Earl of Rocksavage. His daughters are Lady Rose
Cholmondeley, Lady Margot Cholmondeley and Lady Caroline Cholmondeley. His brother is Lord John Cholmondeley, his sister Lady
Aline Cholmondeley. His mother is the Dowager Marchioness of
Cholmondeley. An Earl, four Ladies, a Dowager Marchioness and a
plain Lord thus lie in his immediate circle of blood relations, all of
whom are able to take some actual physical comfort from their relationship with the noble and gallant Marquess other than the pure pleasure
of his company. Similarly, the children of the Earl of Eglinton and
Winton encompass one Lord and three Honourables, and his sisters
are both Ladies. Even his half-uncle is the Hon. Roger Hugh Mont-
gomerie, though this is because he was a son of the sixteenth Earl of
Eglinton and Winton, not because he is the peer's half-uncle.

And there is yet more besides. While the eldest sons of the most
senior ranks of the peerage enjoy courtesy titles, *all* the sons of the
Duke and Marquesses are entitled to be called "Lord," and the
younger sons of an Earl and *all* the sons of Viscounts and Barons may
append the prefix "the Hon." before their names. Women, too, get a
distinctive accolade: daughters of Dukes, Marquesses and Earls can

all be called "Lady," whether or not their behaviour merits the some-what prim-sounding style; and all the daughters of Viscounts and Barons can, like their brothers, call themselves "the Hon." (Peers' daughters take the precedence, if not the equivalent title, of their eldest brother.) Thus the sons of the Duke of Buccleuch are the Earl of Dalkeith, the eldest; Lord William Montagu-Douglas-Scott, the second son, who uses the family surname; and Lord Damien Montagu-Douglas-Scott, the youngest son, who does the same. Lady Charlotte-Ann Montagu-Douglas-Scott is the only daughter. The children of Viscount Brookeborough, on the other hand, are all "the Hon.," whether the eldest, the Hon. Alan, or a daughter, the Hon. Susie. The Earl of Mar and Kellie mixes the two styles, as Earls should: his eldest son is Lord Erskine; his younger sons are the Hon. Alexander and Michael Erskine, using the family name. His daughter is, however, not "the Hon.," but Lady Fiona Erskine. As it happens, Fiona and Michael are twins, born in 1956: the byways of peerage form are re-sponsible for one of the two being accorded the rather common style of "the Hon.," while the other wins a title shared with the very highest degree of ennoblement. (Feminists will be delighted to discover that it is the girl who benefits from the arrangement—one of the very few examples of sexual egalitarianism to be found in the rolls of the hereditary peerage.)

All told there are some 7,000 men and women entitled to be called by some name other than their own, or with some additional glory, and that by virtue of the good fortune of birth alone. Reference books display column after column of "peers' sons and daughters, brothers and sisters, widows of sons of peers, and Maids of Honour; also grand-children of Dukes, Marquesses and Earls, bearing courtesy titles." They are listed alphabetically by surname: thus the ordinary name Butler, with all the connotations of a life in service, displays the full flower of noble adornment. There is the Hon. Betty Q. Butler, daugh-ter of Baron Dunboyne. There is Lady Denyne Butler, daughter of the Earl of Lanesborough. Butlers are connected to the Viscounty of Mountgarret, the Barony of Erskine of Rerrick, the Earldom of Car-rick, the Baronies of Jessel, Bayford and Forteviot. There are nineteen Hon. or Lady Butlers listed, before one plunges into the delights, further down the alphabet, of the Hon. Desirée Butterwick or Lady Anne Sarah Alethea Marjorie Hovell-Thurlow-Cumming-Bruce who, in spite of one of the grander names evidently well worthy of a lady-ship, turns out to be the sister of the Earl of Mexborough.

Excluding, as well one might, all the knights and baronets whose marriages bring similarly large numbers of ladyships into the lists, we are left with the not inconsiderable 7,000 who sport some sort of title. Sometimes the fact is no more than a source of mild amusement —that there are just tweny-five Dukes, and nearly twice that number of Duchesses alive today, attests not just to the longevity of wealthy females, but also to the scandalous inability of ducal marriages to attain anything like permanence. Margaret, Duchess of Argyll, is a classic case in point: although divorced from a now dead Duke in 1963 under circumstances that were, to put it mildly, liable to raise a good many even quite stubborn eyebrows, she continues—and is permitted by all the relevant authorities in the field to continue—to call herself a Duchess, to demand to be called Your Grace, and to command from a society which still revels in such matters all respect and position which Duchesses have traditionally commanded. The judge who ruled on the late Duke's divorce action expressed surprise at the woman's behaviour. Yet still she is a Duchess, and as such regarded with no small degree of awe. (The Duchess should, perhaps, not demand the appellation "Your Grace" too stridently. Technically, since she is divorced, she has forfeited the title. Her demand rests purely on the common courtesy of those who still receive her in society.)

Neither this Duchess, nor most of the titled Butlers, nor, indeed, any of those whose titles are held purely out of the generosity of the system, is permitted any of the real privileges of *noblesse*. The frivolous aspects—the fillets of steak, the restaurant table, a more patient Harrods accounts department, an obsequious airline clerk or an instant marriage, yes. The real perks of peerage, however, no.

These days the real privileges are small beer indeed: once they were considerable. Until 1948, for instance, members of the peerage had a right to be tried on allegations of treason and felony by their peers only, in the House of Lords*—it will be recalled that such a trial figured in *Kind Hearts and Coronets*, and that the convicted Duke claimed his right to be hanged by a silken cord, rather than the rough hempen rope that was provided for the violent termination of the

* The right to be tried by a jury of your "peers"—which means, literally, your "genuine equals"—goes back to Magna Carta. It was one of the postwar iniquities that shocked British politicians of all parties, that the Allies violated the Geneva Convention and refused Field-Marshal von Manstein the trial by other Field-Marshals, to which his rank and standing entitled him. Until then, senior soldiers had rights similar to those of members of the nobility.

lives of untitled felons. (A lengthy description of the little-used procedure also appears in *Clouds of Witness*, by Dorothy L. Sayers: another mythical Duke, this time of Denver, is the subject of Their Lordships' interest.) In the trials each and every peer sitting in judgement had to cast an individual and public verdict. He had to utter the words "Guilty" or "Not Guilty," followed by "Upon my honour." No vulgar business with a foreman delivering the verdict reached after secret conclave. In the House of Lords those best suited to assess the guilt or innocence of their peer—their equal—deliver their verdicts severally, possibly inaugurating family schisms thereby that might last ten generations.

Likewise the highest ranks of the peerage have always traditionally claimed right of access to the core of government: Dukes have always regarded themselves as able, on short notice, to approach the Sovereign of the day; many less exalted men of noble blood still think their views carry some weight with members of the Monarch's cabinet. Cabinet Ministers, especially those in Labour governments, rarely agree. But access to the Sovereign is still regarded as an inherent right of those who, on Coronation Day, pledge their allegiance to the new Monarch as representatives of the plebeian masses waiting in the rain outside. It is a right rarely tested these days, but still, by all accounts, in existence.

Some peers claim a peculiar right to remain hatted in the presence of a reigning Monarch. According to the standard reference works, the Barons of Kingsale—an Irish peerage, now enjoying few of the other privileges known to peers of the mainland countries—have long claimed that they could remain covered while waiting before a Monarch. Almericus, the eighteenth Baron Kingsale, "walked to and fro with his hat on his head" in the presence chamber of William III, claiming he was asserting an ancient privilege. He did it three times: the original "hat trick." Lord Forester, who, since he lives in Zimbabwe, would be unlikely to need such a right, has a document that appears to be a license granted at the time of Henry VIII giving all the heirs of John Forester of Watling Street the right to keep a covered head in kingly presence. But it seems there is a somewhat unromantic explanation: both Lord Kingsale and Mr. Forester of Watling Street suffered, it is said, from ringworm, and were possessed of heads that would have insulted the Monarch—or anyone else—had they been revealed; hence the "right" to keep the hats on. One later Lord Kingsale attempted to assert his right before the austere presence of Queen Victoria. "It's my right, Your Majesty," he explained. "Don't be so silly," the Queen replied. "It may be your right to keep your hat on before a monarch, but I am a lady, too. Your action is most impolite. Take it off at once." The privilege has not been tested since.

Peers are exempt from serving on juries—sharing the privilege with convicted felons, lunatics and undischarged bankrupts. Sharing the same company, they are barred from sitting in the House of Commons, although peers with courtesy titles are not—a fact which causes immense complications to those not schooled in this most inexact of sciences, who hear of a Viscount or an Earl reported speaking from the Lower House. The Earl of Dalkeith—Johnnie, to his more intimate friends in the Conservative Party—sat for many years for the North Edinburgh constituency until, in 1973, he was forced, quite suddenly, to retire. His father had died, and he had to relinquish his courtesy title and adopt the far grander name of ninth Duke of Buccleuch and eleventh Duke of Queensberry, and by so doing had forfeited his right to sit in the Commons. Since 1963, peers with an overwhelming urge to pursue a political career among the common folk have been legally able to renounce their title for life: but Johnnie Dalkeith was not going to be denied one of the grandest Dukedoms in the islands for political ambitions (which, in any case, he had always regarded as training for the immense ducal responsibilities that would inevitably come his way).

Members of the peerage have one other curious right which makes them the envy of less fortunate classes of society. Since, according to common law, "the person of a peer is forever sacred and inviolable" it is still taken as read by policemen and magistrates that it is unlawful to arrest a noble or a member of the House of Commons in a civil case for a period of forty days before and forty days after a meeting of the Parliament. A Duke may owe you money, a Viscount may be father of your child, an Earl may have libelled you, or a Baron defaulted on his word—but for forty days before and after a meeting of Parliament he is free to come and go at will. Only for a few days in the middle of the summer can a noble be arrested—but since most are out, well armed with Purdeys, on remote grouse moors in Scotland, capture is doubly difficult.

The Heralds, who keep an authoritative eye over the families of the peerage, permit perks as well. Only a peer (or, in England, Knights of the Garter and the Grand Cross), they say, may use supporters to stand alongside his arms—the Duke of Devonshire's "two bucks proper, each wreathed with a chaplet of roses" have been Cavendish supporters since the family was first given a grant of arms 400 years ago. But only the Duke and Duchess may use the bucks proper; the arms of the Marquess of Hartington, their eldest son, will merely use the three bucks' heads cabossed, together with the well-known serpent overhead. No supporters at all. Only the reigning peer may prop his coat, though he should need support far less than his heir. Certain Scottish chiefs, and holders of territorial baronies that were granted before 1592 are also permitted to sport heraldic supporters, even if they are not peers. And also in Scotland, peers' heirs may use the devices if they want.

A bewildering variety of other oddities attend the noblemen: the Duke of Atholl may maintain a private army,* some Earls have a traditional right to the "third penny" of taxes collected in their shire. And there are innumerable objects of fealty: a rose here, a peppercorn there, three bullocks, a swan, the local venison or the first grouse of the season—the cornage and the horngeld—that the commonalty have for centuries paid to the local Lord. These, though, are privileges accorded to the individual by way of some creaking local ordinance: the rights to supporters, exemptions from jury service (which applies to Members of Parliament and others, like barristers, as well), access to the Sovereign and that chief delight "freedom from attachment," apply to all.

Two others remain: one, an infringement, it could be thought, of the basic right of the peers; the other, it is not infrequently argued, an infringement of the basic rights of this democracy. A reigning peer is not permitted to vote in parliamentary elections. And a reigning peer is entitled to sit in, and take full part in, the premier legislative assembly of the country, the House of Lords. It should be noted that certain restrictions apply, as we shall see. The reigning peer's title must be granted in England, Scotland, Great Britain or the United Kingdom —holders of Irish peerages are not so entitled. And the peer must be over twenty-one, he must not be bankrupt and he must not be a lunatic.

As with jury service and their exemption from the right to sit in the Commons, the withholding of suffrage from the noblemen and women places them alongside aliens, lunatics, idiots, prisoners serving

---

* The Atholl Highlanders—the Duke's "army"—are regarded locally as "colourful fun" for volunteers among the local people of Atholl, and nothing more.

sentences for felony of more than twelve months' duration and men and women disqualified upon conviction of corrupt election practices. Few complain too loudly at the missing right: perhaps because in substitution they are permitted a voice in the last remaining legislative assembly in the civilized world for which the membership's sole qualification (at least until the invention of the life peer) is the lucky accident of birth. Spain lost the hereditary element in its government after the Civil War. The House of Peers, to which the Japanese nobles elected some 215 of their number to serve as the architects of that Empire's laws, vanished in 1946. Only the United Kingdom preserves, and indeed, stoutly defends, the absolute right of the Royal Princes, and hereditary peers, a selection of life peers and the Lords Spiritual of one selected religion to have a direct influence on the nation's laws. The chamber in which these distinguished worthies sit, an eighty-foot-long and fifty-foot-wide Gothic extravaganza, is, of course, the House of Lords. Its future is once more under close scrutiny; many feel that it is now approaching the end of its useful life.

"A Young British Peer," a copy of the 1812 edition of *Collins's Peerage* pronounces, "who cultivates his mind and refines his manners; who studies the public affairs of his country; and takes a virtuous part in them, is in a situation as desirable as a chastened and enlightened ambition can form a wish for.

"His rank will procure him respect, and a due attention to all his suggestions. And without being liable to the caprices and expenses of popular elections, he may pursue the dictates of an honest mind, unwarped and uncontrolled. And glow with the inward satisfaction of living for others, and the daily discharge of patriotic duties."

Such was the vision of the House of Lords in 1812, some twenty years before the first murmurs of reforming zeal (which suggested in those days, and rather timidly at that, that Bishops should be excluded from the House). There would be few who would now agree with many of the sentiments except, maybe, that to be a British peer is "a situation as desirable . . . as ambition can form a wish for." That the House of Lords is made up of men and women who, by virtue of their birth, have already fulfilled that "dearest ambition," is, in no small part, one of the reasons why the institution is under fire today.

TWO

"THE GAUDY CENTREPIECE OF THE NOBLE ART"

A severe though not unfriendly critic of our in-
stitutions said that "The *cure* for admiring the
House of Lords was to go and look at it."
—Walter Bagehot, *The English Constitution*

Public opinion has decided that the duties of an
English legislator are such as, on an average of
human capacity, may descend from sire to son.
—Benjamin Disraeli, 1835

Wednesday, 2 February 1977, was a wet and blustery winter's day
in London. Motor-car dealers were whipping the dustsheets away
from the new Ford Fiesta and promising the creation would bring
blessing to an ailing industry; there was much relief expressed at the
discovery of a missing plane in remote bush country in Sudan (a
news story nicely enhanced by the presence among the passengers of
an English Countess); and there was criticism of the Labour Government's admitted "impotence" to do much to ease the plight of Britain's
unemployed. Out in the real world it was a fairly standard day, the
realities perhaps not quite as grim as usual.

Inside the chamber of the House of Lords, the gaudy centrepiece
of the nation's peerage, the reality of the outside world, was, for a
few extraordinary minutes, banished and subjugated to the necessities
of history. Some 200 of the peers of the realm were gathered in the
sanctum that afternoon to watch, and revel in, the bedizened pomp
whereby a common man is admitted to the exalted state of ennoble-

ment. "At half-past two o'clock," the Notices and Orders of the Day proclaimed, "The Lord Glenamara will be Introduced."

It is possible to enter the House of Lords from the west, through the Peers' Entrance; or from the east, by way of the Central Lobby. In both cases the sensation is rather like passing through a number of airlocks into some antique submarine, or spacecraft: as each successive set of heavy doors is opened, then closed behind one, so the hubbub of popular existence fades away, and the world seems to consist of little other than stained glass and scarlet leather, candles and solid brass gewgaws, men in strange clothing and charged with an air of somnolent grace.

From the west, the sensation of entering a Looking Glass universe comes as rapidly as from an anaesthetist's needle. A grave policeman with a powerful sense of his place in the order of things stands at the outer door, opening it for elderly men and powdered women who stroll in from the car park. Inside there is an ex-soldier, kitted out in full livery with shiny metal buttons, and with the polite air of a gentleman's gentleman, who ushers the visitors through what appears very much like a school cloakroom. Rows of thick brass coatpegs stand in serried ranks above worn oaken benches; yellowed bone name plates above each Gothic hook list all the Royal Princes and Dukes eligible to sit in the House—Wales, Gloucester and Kent—and then, in alphabetical order and with no regard for seniority, peers from Aberconway to Zetland, with rank signified by a single letter. Thus Zetland is an M, Somerset a D, Brookeborough a V, Breadalbane and Holland an E, and the scores upon scores of mere Barons just L, for Lord. The coathooks go well with the names beneath the liripips: the impression of an orderly and expensive school vestry is a powerful one.

By this time the traffic noise has faded; no more policemen are to be seen—such stewards as there are wear tails and white bow ties. Large brass objects dangle from the necks of a few of the more distinguished members of the fraternity, giving them the appearance of sommeliers at a fancy restaurant. The suggestions one could make about the appearance and atmosphere of the place—from submarine to public school, cathedral to gentlemen's club, from rocketship to expensive restaurant—are not entirely frivolous. The fanciful can conjure up all manner of fantasies: about the only suggestion that seems perfectly ridiculous is that this antique chamber is in any way connected with the manufacture of laws for the teeming masses outside its doors. That this sleepy and magnificent jewel has anything in common with the democracy that ticks on elsewhere seems faintly absurd.

The impression is reinforced by the sight of the chamber itself, and by such ceremonies as the Introduction of Lord Glenamara, for which the House might well have been solely created. From the galleries—to which a retired military officer in black coat and knee breeches, and sporting the title of Gentleman Usher of the Black Rod, will have permitted entrance—the visitor looks down into another century, into a well of the finest example of the Victorian romantic style. It is, at first impression, oddly small—only twice as long as the average drawing-room of the kind of country house with which many peers would be familiar. No doubt if every single member entitled to come to the chamber did so it would rival the Black Hole of Calcutta for discomfort: luckily the benches are rarely more than half filled.

The light is tinged blood red, such is the filtering effect of the deeply stained glass and the reflective effect of the scarlet morocco leather on the ten rows of benches that run most of the length of the eighty-foot chamber and across the end. Paneling and ornately carved walls, with coats of arms inlaid in gilt and painted enamel, gleam dully from above. Tall statues of the eighteen Barons who forced King John to accept Magna Carta—but which are often mistaken for saints, such is the churchly atmosphere of the place—glower craggily down on the assembled membership. Between the two facing rows of benches and choir stalls is a large and untidy old desk, littered with books on procedure and history and other necessities of the Clerk's trade: a giant egg-timer, by which the length of noble speeches is measured (in five-minute units), bottles of pinkish glue, inkpots, paperclips and wooden penholders, and stacks of official writing paper. Behind the Clerk's Table, at which two men in wigs sit and write, or listen to the proceedings, is a smaller and far humbler table providing accommodation for the official reporters: this often has to be removed altogether for ceremonial, which—since ceremony is such a common feature of the House of Lords—must prove an inconvenience to those charged with recording the spoken words of the assembly.

In front of the Clerk's Table is a great oblong sack, about five feet long and three feet high. It is covered with plain, deep red cloth, and has a low backrest constructed halfway along the topside. It looks like a bale of wool and that, of course, is precisely what it is: the Woolsack, filled with twists of wool from sheep in every quarter of the Commonwealth, and providing the traditional seat of the Lord

Chancellor, uncomfortable though it may look. Lord Chancellors, well schooled in stoicism, are rarely known to fall asleep and tumble off the Sack, though it looks designed for such an accident.

Beyond the Woolsack, the focal point of the working House, is the most magnificent carved screen, an immense golden canopy straining twenty feet up against the western wall of the chamber. Five carved golden knights stand above it, directly over the Royal coat of arms: one hugely solid golden throne stands dead centre, on top of a richly carpeted ascent of three broad steps that rise from the light blue carpet of the chamber floor. Two great candlesticks stand sentry to the throne, each with twenty-five candles, a foot long, arranged in three tiers.

On this particular February Wednesday the throne was empty and covered, and would remain that way until the next occasion the Queen arrived to open a new session of Parliament; and so on this, as every working day, such ceremonial as did occur centred around the Lord Chancellor. Only the nervous figure of Lord Glenamara, waiting in the Robing Room, was to add to the dignity of the occasion.

At half-past two, white-tied attendants in the Lords' Lobby boomed their warning: "Make way for the Lord Chancellor's procession," and slowly, looking perhaps a little embarrassed by it all, a train of men filed past the brass rail of the House and into the chamber. The Great Mace was carried by the Serjeant at Arms; a functionary known as the Purse-Bearer held the Lord Chancellor's handbag (it used to contain the Great Seal of State, an immensely heavy device that once, dropped by an elderly Lord Chancellor during just such a procession, broke a bone in the poor man's foot); the Chancellor himself, dressed in robes of black and gold, and a Train-Bearer walked behind; Black Rod brought up the rear. Various of these filed away as the procession moved on—Black Rod, an elderly sailor, Admiral Sir Frank Twiss, clambered into a little enclosure known as Black Rod's box—until the Lord Chancellor himself, a Labour Party life peer, Lord Elwyn Jones, eased himself up on to the Woolsack, called for prayers and permitted the day's proceedings to begin.

On this particular day the urgent business for which the scattered groups of nobles had arrived was to be delayed. The impression that an event of great moment was about to take place was given by Lord Elwyn Jones who, to the amusement of a small group in one public gallery, placed a black, three-cornered cap on the very top of his full-bottomed grey wig, the effect being similar to the judge placing the black cap on his head before passing the death sentence on some hapless murderer. Today the Lord Chancellor was not in the business of ordering destruction of life: instead he was about to begin the process of creating a brand-new peer of the Kingdom.

Until shortly before, the tall, white-haired man in the Robing Room had been Edward Watson Short, a sixty-five-year-old Geordie who had ably represented the Central Division of Newcastle-upon-Tyne for the Labour Party since 1951. His progress in the party hierarchy had been unspectacular but steady, and had culminated, after a short spell as Education Secretary, in his appointment as Leader of the House of Commons. However, in 1976 he decided to retire from the House and accept the post of part-time Chairman of Cable and Wireless, a nationalized industry. (He has since retired.) The Labour Party, though, had no wish to deny itself of Mr. Short's not inconsiderable parliamentary talents; the managers were, in fact, keen to ensure that an ageing party loyalist should continue to play an active part in politics, well away from the brouhaha of the democratic process. Consequently, the Prime Minister—via the Queen, who is traditionally supposed to be the "Fount of all Honours"—announced that Mr. Short was to be made a peer of the realm for the duration of his life: by such a process does this style of democracy function.

Accordingly, Mr. Short chose his title, after consultation with the College of Arms, and was now ready to be presented to the Lord Chancellor. By half-past two on that rainy Wednesday he was fully equipped with scarlet parliamentary robe, trimmed with two bars of miniver and gold lace on the right-hand side, tied up with black ribbon, and was carrying a black cocked hat—not a tricorn like the Chancellor's, however—in his hand. With a group of men seemingly plucked straight from the mediaeval, the erstwhile Mr. Short began his march towards Introduction.

First, Black Rod, his legs, in knee breeches, looking barely thick enough to support his weight, walked slowly up the House, keeping to the Temporal side (the side on the Lord Chancellor's left, so-called to distinguish it from the side of the House where the Archbishops and the Bishops—and the government of the day—sit, and which is known as the Spiritual side), and bowed at the tableau behind the throne known as the Cloth of Estate. Black Rod was followed this day by a distinguished Canadian historian, Dr. Conrad Swan, who, for the weeks he is on duty at the College of Arms, is known as York Herald—or "York" for short. (Since Mr. Short was a north-countryman, taking his title from a valley in the County of Westmore-land, so the relevant Herald from the northern parts of the realm was chosen to advise him on his choice of title and lead him for his presentation to the Woolsack.) York wore the heavy mantle of his station—a short tabard of satin, with lions and fleurs-de-lis in red and gold woven all around—and looked as though he should be blowing a fanfare on a long golden horn for the entry of some fabled Monarch to an ancient palace, rather than carrying Lord Glenamara's official peerage papers to the Woolsack. Seeing the Herald amidst the glue bottles and paperclips dramatically underscored the oddity of it all.

Behind York, and also dressed in full robes, walked Lady Llewelyn-Davies, a life peeress from the same degree and same political party as Mr. Short. Then came Short himself, carrying documents that summoned him to the House; and finally Lord Shepherd, a senior peer and a colleague of the former MP. As they entered, they all bowed before the Cloth of Estate; they they reached the Clerk's Table they all bowed again; and once again at the rim of the Woolsack, where a jovial Lord Chancellor was sitting. Black Rod nipped round the back of the Woolsack and stood in the Spiritual aisle, just in front of the little Bishop's Box. York Herald whipped round smartly so that he faced Mr. Short and his two colleague peers, and, with true clerkly efficiency, a Reading Clerk—normally John Sainty, who has the right sort of voice for these occasions—slipped from the rails to the Throne, and waited by the Lord Chancellor.

York Herald handed his copies of the official summons to Mr. Short. Mr. Short handed them to the Lord Chancellor, kneeling on one knee as he did so. The Lord Chancellor, playing what looked like a game of pass the parcel, handed the sheaf of papers to Mr. Sainty, and Sainty retired with them to his table. The peers then trotted off to the table to listen to Mr. Sainty while he read out the details on the Letters Patent and the Writ of Summons—language which included such protestations from the Queen (who had written the documents—or so it was meant to seem) as knowing how difficult it was for Mr. Short to come to the House of Lords and so on, would he kindly do so, and "treat and give counsel" to Her from time to time as a member of the gathering. Mr. Short then took an Oath of Allegiance, and became, in the wink of an eye, Baron Glenamara of Glenridding, to be addressed by the Queen, if ever she happened to meet him, as "Our right trusty and well-beloved Counsellor." (No-where near as intimate, though, as had he been created a Duke: a

Monarch, bumping into one of that exalted breed, is supposed to cry out "Right trusty and right entirely beloved cousin," implying some blood relationship which, given the degree of interbreeding between the higher ranks of the peerage and the Royal Families of England, might not be surprising.)*

Once the Oath was over there was much taking on and off of hats; the new peer was taken to his appropriate bench at the back of the chamber; the trio stood, sat, stood, sat, stood, sat three times: Lord Glenamara went up and was shaken by the hand vigorously by a now thoroughly excited Lord Chancellor; and then the whole party— Black Rod, York Herald and the three peers—left, the polite cheers of those remaining in the chamber echoing behind them while they took tea (with, no doubt, the square crumpets that are entirely peculiar to the Tea Room at the House of Lords).

As the circus stilled, one final formality had to be completed: a young man, newly acceded to the earldom held until a few weeks previously by his now dead mother,† stepped forward to shake the hand of the Lord Chancellor and take his seat in the assembly. There was no need for him to endure the mechanical complexities that attended Lord Glenamara: there is but one ceremony for every peerage —not every peer—and his earldom had been created 526 years previ-

---

* Not surprising at all, in fact, since originally all Earls were sons or cousins of the Sovereign. The rank of Duke was eventually introduced to place younger sons of the Sovereign before their increasingly remote cousins the Earls. But in actual fact there was no interbreeding between the higher ranks of the peerage and the Royal Family between 1515 (when the Duke of Suffolk married the sister of Henry VIII) and 1871 (when the Duke of Argyll married the daughter of Queen Victoria). This, of course, leaves out Royal Consorts like Anne Boleyn and Anne Hyde, where the descendants are extinct.

† Normally peerages descend through the male line only. In certain cases, however—as with *all* Scottish peerages, such as the Earldom of Erroll, and with a number of very ancient English titles, the male and female lines can accede. This is the reason the new young Earl of Erroll acceded to a title previously held by his mother, who was Countess of Erroll *in her own right*, and not because she was married to an Earl.

In cases where a peer whose title passes through the male line dies, it is common for the oldest male child to inherit the title, but for the widow—who then retains a title *by courtesy*—to retain the estate for the duration of her life. This may not always be true, of course—often a widowed peeress, who becomes known as a Dowager peeress, may be banished to a tenancy on the estate whose ownership has now passed to her son: her house is then known as the Dower House.

ously. Generally speaking, the date of the creation of an ancient peerage and the date of its formal admission to the House of Lords, would be one and the same, allowing for the space of a few months for organizational purposes, perhaps. In the case of this specific instance, the admission of the young Earl of Erroll, the fact that his was a Scottish peerage caused some divergence from tradition. His peerage would not have been granted formal admission to the House as a matter of right until very recently: before the Scottish peers were admitted by election only. Thus Lord Erroll's peerage would have been admitted during his mother's lifetime, about 500 years after its creation. The general point, though, that newly acceded peers have only to shake the hand of the Lord Chancellor, because their peerage had been admitted at more or less the same time it had been created, is a valid one. Scottish peerage law, as we shall see, introduced testing complexities into an already confused system of governance.

Then, and only then, could the process of government—or, rather, that slim prerogative of government still retained by the House of Lords—begin again. On that Wednesday, while the Fiestas were sold and the snow lay thick on the ground in Buffalo, New York, the House of Lords turned its venerable attentions to the release of Cabinet papers relating to British postwar activities in Palestine; the possibilities of prosecuting speeding Northern Irish drivers as they pass through southern Scotland; the problems of retirement; and the education of children in Madagascar. Questions of inflation, the redistribution of income, the decline of sterling and the shortage of housing were not touched that day by the House. As Lord Arran noted on one memorable occasion: "I myself introduced two Bills in the House of Lords, one on badgers, the other on buggers. On the whole I think their Lordships were rather more interested in the badgers."

Cramped though the House may be, and though dripping with ceremonial that must verge on the tiresome, there can be few Lords who do not cherish the place as—even though the comparison is well-worn—one of the most well-mannered and congenial clubs in the world. Since 1958, when the government began the introduction of the life peers, the exclusivity of the club has diminished: White's and Brooks's and the Turf are still the favourite watering holes of men who want to mingle only with their equals, both in standing and in sex. But, as one writer heard, while researching a thesis on the House, the membership is not ready to complain about the falling standards.

"A good library," said one. "Very agreeable. All the books and news-papers you could want." "I feel I'm *liked*," said another. Yet others: "Everyone is here to help you, as the Doorkeepers said when I first came in." "Intelligent and congenial people to talk to . . . and the best restaurant in London."

Those who have eaten in the restaurants might not agree with the last quoted—though peers, being largely from the public schools (by which the British mean, of course, private schools), have palates less well educated than most. Certainly formal critics of the catering are not ones to heap on the praise. "The consommé en gelée," reported one writer in a popular magazine, "betrayed a canned provenance." The Peers' Dining Room, where the service is "mainly Irish," is, according to one Lord, "even worse" than the Guests' Dining Room, where Lords and commoners can meet and moan together. That restaurant "feels like a room in one of the vast English country houses which the National Trust can't afford to take on. People talk quietly and ladies wear hats." And the restaurants lose money, though they do not care to admit it.

The library, one of the finest in London, reinforces the club atmos-phere of the place: fine octagonal writing tables; paper and envelopes standing erect in wooden holders in the centre; ashtrays and pen-holders all crested and silver; the comfortable leather armchairs in which Bishops snooze and, as in the Athenaeum, ennobled gentlemen of distinction lie buried under copies of *The Times* that rise and fall gently with each breath; thick carpets with warm Pugin designs; book-lined shelves; whispering assistants in half-moon glasses; ancient stencilling on the ceilings. It is a place that exudes gentility from every beeswax-rubbed piece of wood, the kind of library one would pay a fortune to subscribe to, and be happy no matter what the cost.

But the quite extraordinary thing is that all this magnificence— the ability to buy "House of Lords" cigarettes in the bar (more ex-pensive than most equivalent brands), to sit in the warm sun on the terrace and listen to details of elderly men's ailments ("You see, this is a kind of hospital," one peer told Anthony Sampson; "You have to be something of an expert on operations")—not only costs the mem-bership nothing, the taxpayer actually *pays them*. Descendants of the ducal families, recipients of life peerages, the member Bishops and two Archbishops, Earls with vast fortunes in land and Viscounts who com-mute from Basingstoke can all claim, not only their travelling costs to and from the Palace of Westminster, but up to £34.00 for every day they attend.* Those few peers who looked in for a couple of minutes on every single one of the 155 days on which the House sat in the 1976 session (when the rate was only £13.50) could have drawn £2,092.50, without the need to pay any income tax at all—the equivalent of a salary of about £3,000 a year, for what could be less than a full day's work. In 1981 a similarly dedicated noble could draw some £5,000.

Of course it is by no means true that peers just pop into the House whenever they happen to be in town, simply for the purpose of claiming their allowance: most members who do go tend to stay for at least an hour, and probably more—though the comforts of the rooms surrounding the actual chambers where the work is performed generally tempt most of them away from some of each day. On average, the peer who claims—and not all do—spends a good half-afternoon of each day visibly performing the duties expected of a legislator: he may well, of course, spend many hours performing the less apparent, but by no means less important work that he regards as his constitutional *noblesse oblige.*

In addition to an attendance allowance, the peer is also encouraged to claim his travelling costs: thus the Earl of Kintore, who lives in a crumbling mansion some dozen miles from Aberdeen, is enabled to travel about once a month to make an appearance in the House. He takes the overnight sleeper, first class, from Aberdeen to London; stays at his residential club; visits the Lords for the afternoons of Tuesday, Wednesday and Thursday; lunches at the Beefsteak Club in Leicester Square; catches up with the gossip of the metropolis; does some shopping for his wife; takes the Thursday-night sleeper for home and arrives back at Keith Hall.

The good Earl, though, is far from being ". . . a nation's curse. A pauper on the public purse . . ." as a satirical poem on the nobility put it, back in 1842. He takes his responsibility of participation in the process quite seriously—he is also an extremely assiduous member of a number of important boards and committees in his native Scotland. When he was the mere Viscount Stonehaven, of Urie, he wrote a paper on his responsibilities, which was published in the *Aberdeen University Review.* It was before the days of the attendance allowance,

---

* In July 1980 the 1977 figure of £16.50 a day was altered so that peers could claim only £11 for each day that they attended, but in addition up to £23 if their attendance involved staying the night.

which accounts for his reference to the average attendance of around 100 (in 1976 it was 275, reflecting the only fairly recent introduction of payments in 1957). "There is an expert available in the House of Lords on almost any conceivable subject," he wrote. "There are peers who have lived in the Arctic and built igloos, tropical peers who have run irrigation projects, prospectors, qualified divers, airmen, seamen, racehorse owners. It is absolutely fatal to make a speech or a statement in the House without first checking your facts. If you have not and make a rash statement, up jumps an expert and confounds you.

"On account of the available personnel it has become the custom for only experts or at least people with considerable knowledge to speak on specialized subjects. This leads to a very high level of debate. It is nearer true of the House of Lords than of any other institution that the members have no axe to grind. You cannot be turned out. You cannot be rewarded. You have no electors to please. There is no strict toeing of any party line. Divisions seldom take place and when they do peers vote according to their conscience." Such is the classic argument by the hereditary peer for retaining the House: not everyone, as we shall see later, agrees.

If the atmosphere of the House encourages gentility and courtesy, the quaint traditions of procedure in the chamber reinforce all the gentlemanly virtues. The hours, for example, are far from tiring: the House meets only three times a week, save in the most extraordinary circumstances—and virtually only the declaration of hostilities can persuade a Lord to gather with his colleagues at Westminster on a Friday. The last day of the week is reserved for the arduous process of returning to the country, as it presumably is for all those other fortunate metropolitan souls who have farms or homes in the shires. The curious point is that while businesses—and even the House of Commons—manages to function on Friday, the Lords have chosen to institutionalize their exodus, by declining to permit their place of business to open, save under the direst of emergencies. (This habit is now on the decline, the House reports.) It only takes three peers, including the Lord Chancellor, to make up a quorum, and on occasion a stranger walks into a gallery to find only the bewigged Chancellor on his Woolsack, an ageing Lord fast asleep on one of the benches and a tedious man in a tweed suit intoning about some arcane topic from the opposite side. It is usually after occasions such as these, when the peers cannot be interested in anything in particular, that the

Lord Chancellor leaves the chamber and the television annunciators tell the remainder of the hard-working Palace that the House is "Adjourned During Pleasure." The phrase proves suggestive to bored men in the Commons with more fertile imaginations. "Visions of girls in black leather underwear with whips, lashing wrinkled men in coronets, vanish when one looks in at a group of normal-looking chaps wolfing down suet pudding and gin," one wrote.

While they are at work, every detail of their functioning positively drips with good behaviour. "Let the other place [the Commons] go on its loutish way," wrote Lord Lovell-Davis in a comic account of his time as a Lord in Waiting, "yah-boohing each other while we, quietly and with dignity, sort out the problems that are afflicting the serfs." Quiet, broken only by the occasional bellow of laughter—or from time to time, amplified horrifyingly by the electronics recently installed, a snore—dominates the proceedings, and Standing Orders make very sure it stays that way. "Any Lord," the rule book observes, "may call the attention of the House to any breaches of order or to any undue laxity in observing the traditional customs."

Customs like bowing to the Cloth of Estate whenever entering the House ("Court Bow" only, mind, and not a ceremonial ditto from the waist); never passing between the Woolsack and the Lord who is then speaking, and never walking between the Woolsack and the Table. Never moving out of place "without just cause, to the hindrance of others, that sit near . . . "; Never bringing books and newspapers into the chamber, and never leaving a debate in which you have taken part before "the greater part" is over. That is the decent thing about the rules of the House: almost every one can be bent to one's own personal interpretation. If you consider "the greater part" of the debate is over, and you have earned your £34.00, then you can leave without feeling you have uttered a slight; similarly you can of course bring in the *Daily Telegraph* and polish off the crossword if you can somehow relate the activity to the debate—by, say, insisting that it keeps your mind in fine fettle should you be called upon to speak.

It has always been considered rather bad form to read your speech from a text, though, bending the rules again slightly, "some speakers may wish to have 'extended notes' from which to speak, but it is not in the interests of good debate that speakers should stick too closely to a prepared text." Likewise, it is thought a bit odd if you ramble on for more than ten or fifteen minutes, even though in the Lords, unlike the Commons, there is no fear of guillotines or closure votes to shut you up. The Procedure Committee had some clocks installed at points in the chamber, but these, it seems, have been deliberately designed to blend into the woodwork and, in consequence, have been easy to overlook. So not a few speeches take half an hour or more, with the result that all those still awake troop out to the Tea Room until the television annunciator informs them that it is over.

The ultimate sanction against a Lord who is too windy or who offends too many of the traditions of the House is for an irritated peer to rise and, with as much testiness in his voice as possible, deliver the formula "that the noble Lord be no longer heard." That usually wraps it up—though it very rarely has to be used. The last time is believed to have been in May 1960. Another rare device is for the aggrieved listener to ask that the Clerk at the Table read the Standing Order on Asperity of Speech—but since that, like asking that the Lord be heard no longer, is a motion for which there has to be debate, few either risk its delivery or insist upon the debate. Heat is not often the consequence of a group (though they are of all ages: one of the advantages of the hereditary system) distinctly lacking in fire: about all they ever produce, an unkind critic might not unfairly say, is hot air.

Note, incidentally, that even in uttering the grave words "that the noble Lord be no longer heard" the dignity of the occasion is not forgotten. There are very precise rules laid down for references to members of the House who, after all, have no constituency, but only rank. While in the Commons, references are made to "The Honourable Member for Barsetshire," in the Lords one has to have a ready knowledge, not of place, but of degree. It is easy enough to spot an Archbishop, who will be referred to as "The Most Reverend Primate"; easy enough, too, to know the faces of the three Royal and the twenty-five non-Royal Dukes likely to attend: they are called simply "The Noble Duke." (The Royal Dukes are those of Cornwall, Gloucester and Kent. The Duke of Edinburgh is, within the House, considered the holder of a non-Royal dukedom, since he is not a blood relation of the Monarch.) But one can be thrown with great facility by having to know the precise differentiation between "The Noble Lady" and "The Noble Baroness" (the former being Scots), and when to say "Noble and Gallant Lord" (when the peer is an Admiral of the Fleet, a Field-Marshal or a Marshal of the Royal Air Force); when to address a speaker as "Noble and Learned" (the Lord Chancellor wins this accolade, as do Lords of Appeal in Ordinary, Law Officers of the Crown and Judges of the Superior Courts); when to say "Noble and Right

Reverend Lord" (to an Archbishop or Bishop subsequently created a peer); and when, if ever, it is all right to call a party colleague "My Noble Friend." Only one device is really easy: "My Noble Kinsman." That you say if you recognize the speaker as—it often happens—a member of your family.

One has only to read the bound volumes of Hansard ("sent to those Peers who intimate their desire to have them," and free of charge at that) to feel the flavour, a heady cocktail of *politesse* and earnest pointlessness, of the exchanges.

For example, consider the occasion on 19 November 1976 when Lady Sharples rose to ask Her Majesty's Government whether the spread of beech bark disease was likely to cover the whole country, as happened with Dutch elm disease. The subject is one on which peers often wax lyrical—trees, fishing, the breeding of deer and the advantages of tied farm cottages are all dear to their hearts—and on this particular day one noble became so enwreathed with ecstasy that he quite forgot that this was Question Time, and not a period for the making of speeches.

"*Lord Strabolgi*: 'My Lords, I think that this disease cannot be compared with Dutch elm disease. As I have said it is endemic. It is widely scattered over the country. Recent major outbreaks have occurred mainly on the chalk downlands of Southern England, but it does not spread as quickly as Dutch elm disease. I agree that there are no grounds for complacency, but we have had this disease for 100 years, I regret.'

"*Lord Davies of Leek*: 'My Lords, may I, finally, from this side of the House, put forward the plea for the Government to look deeply—'

"*A noble Lord*: 'Question!'

"*Lord Davies of Leek*: 'I have already said "May I." What is the matter with the House? As an interspersion I should like to say that it is rather nice that we finish in difficult times, like this, this morning. May I ask my noble friend whether he will press upon the Government the need to look in depth into the problem of our national forestry, which is one of our great assets . . .?' "

And so the debate stumbled along. A few moments later there was the following speech by the Parliamentary Undersecretary of State at the Department of the Environment, Lady Birk:

"My Lords, I beg to move that the Commons Reasons for disagreeing to certain of the Lords Amendments, Commons Amendments in lieu of certain of the Lords Amendments and Commons Amendments to certain of the Lords Amendments be now considered.

"Moved, That the Commons Reasons for disagreeing to certain of the Lords Amendments, Commons Amendments in lieu of certain of the Lords Amendments and Commons Amendments to certain of the Lords Amendments be now considered.

"COMMONS REASONS FOR DISAGREEING TO CERTAIN OF THE LORDS AMENDMENTS, COMMONS AMENDMENTS IN LIEU OF CERTAIN OF THE LORDS AMENDMENTS AND COMMONS AMENDMENTS TO CERTAIN OF THE LORDS AMENDMENTS.

"References are to Bill (303) as first printed for the Lords.

"Lords Amendments: (1) Page 1, line 9, leave out sub-paragraph (i); (2) line 17, leave out 'grazing, meadow or pasture land or' . . ."

It turned out to be the political hot potato of the moment, the legislation concerning farm buildings. Only the existence of the House of Lords, critics say, could lead to such preposterous complexities as those which poor Lady Birk had to shepherd through the House that day.

Whenever the House divides over an issue—something of a rarity, and itself as magical a fantasy as everything else, involving as it does men with white wands strolling about the chamber tapping people on the shoulder as if they expect them suddenly to disappear—the question is not whether to vote Aye or No. It is, in this House alone, whether to vote "Content" or "Not Content"—a wording that, like so much else, is of vague origins. (The peers used to be polled by the Tellers, from the most junior Barons upwards, as to whether they gave their "consent," or not. Whether the word has become bastardized no one is quite sure.) Whatever the origins of the cry, it is an apposite one. For more than a century—before, in fact, the building of the magnificent structure in which the House is lodged—politicians have been expressing their lack of contentment with the powers and responsibilities of the House of Peers. Today the institution, its powers already circumscribed almost to the point of legislative impotence, is under withering attack once more: leaders of both major political parties want it either demolished or more radically changed than by any reform measure of the past.

And yet Their Lordships stand fast—the motto, as it happens, of one of their number, the Baron Strathspey. Land, style and primogeniture have maintained their position in society; by the relentless pursuit of courteous compromise they have also maintained their position, uniquely on the face of the globe, in the machinery of the legislature. Can they survive the new onslaught? Do they deserve to stay? Which reforms mesh most comfortably with their own ideas for compromise? Is it possible that this single greatest privilege—the right to make the laws of the kingdom*—will soon be taken away completely? Before considering these questions we should look a little more closely at the monstrous enginework that keeps the very idea of a peerage alive in this society in the latter quarter of this century. If Bagehot's friend recommended that the best cure for anyone admiring the House of Lords was just to go and look at it, he would also recommend that just a few moments be spent listening to the sound of the machinery that keeps nobility alive, to curb any unbridled admiration directed to that quarter.

* In fact the House of Lords no longer *makes* the laws of the Kingdom, as will be seen. It simply acts as *jury* with powers to correct or delay legislation emanating from the Lower Chamber. "Can't you see the danger in removing this brake on unbridled legislative power in a demagogy, before it's too late?" asked one defender of the Upper House.

THREE

"THE FIDDLE-FADDLE OF NOBILIARY ENROLMENT"

Ye butterflies, whom kings create:
Ye caterpillars of the state:
Know that your time is near!
This moral learn from nature's plan,
That in creation God made man;
But never made a peer.
—Anon., published in the *Northern Star*, 1842

A clumsy Irish padre and an heroic member of Britain's gilded youth conspired with Fate one March day in 1916 to trigger one of the oddest sagas ever in the long history of the European nobility. It is a saga that illustrates many of the features of noble—and ignoble—behaviour: a tale of profligacy and ambition, pomp without circumstance, mental instability and money. It illustrates, too, the strange desire that grips ordinary mortals from time to time to become titled, and the lengths to which they will go to seek enrolment in the lists of the Lords Temporal. It all began in the unlikely setting of a practice trench way behind the British lines in northern France, on 3 March 1916.

According to the regimental lore, the company padre of the Irish Guards was with a group of soldiers that day learning the complexities of properly throwing the newly invented weapon, the hand grenade. Perhaps the Almighty had not wanted one of His chosen servants to engage in such sport; the padre, pulling the ring from the weapon as he was told, accidentally dropped the beast, leaving it to roll among the thicket of legs of the other Guardsmen standing in the trenches.

The officer commanding the grenade practice was the twenty-eight-year-old, twice-decorated Major, Lord Desmond FitzGerald. Without pausing for thought he hurled himself on top of the grenade with a second to spare, and was blown to pieces. All the men in the trench were saved: Lord Desmond was killed almost instantly, one of the great unsung heroes of his time.

Lord Desmond was one of three sons of the very wealthy fifth Duke of Leinster, a member of a family that had built the great Maynooth Castle outside Dublin, had owned Leinster House, where the Irish Parliament now sits, and had constructed Carton, a superb Palladian mansion in County Kildare that still ranks as one of the finest examples of its period in the British Isles. Thanks to a tragic genetic accident Lord Desmond was the almost certain successor to the dukedom, even though he was the second brother.

The first brother, Maurice, who had in fact acceded to the title in 1893, when only six years old, was severely mentally ill. Some say he had a tumour on the brain, others that he was unbalanced for less easily fathomable reasons. (Those cynics who might suggest that insanity is often to be found among the peerage because of the high rate of inbreeding would do well to consider that the eight great-grandparents of the afflicted sixth Duke of Leinster were as unrelated as it is possible to be in so small a community as the British Isles. They were Augustus Frederick, third Duke of Leinster; Lady Charlotte Stanhope, daughter of the third Earl of Harrington; the second Duke of Sutherland; Lady Harriet Howard, daughter of the sixth Earl of Carlisle; the second Lord Feversham; Lady Louisa Stewart, daughter of the eighth Earl of Galloway; Sir James Graham, Baronet; and Fanny Callander, of Craigforth, the daughter of a local colonel. A varied selection of noble antecedents, and not one of them related to another. The insanity of the sixth Duke of Leinster, if that is what it was, must have stemmed from another cause.) Whatever the cause, he had been kept under constant medical observation and was at times admitted to Craig House, a dour establishment on the outskirts of Edinburgh, almost from the moment he came of age in 1908. He made a will in the year he first entered the hospital and from that moment on, little, if anything, was heard of him by the general public. According to the official records he died, unmarried, on 2 February 1922 (although some sources claim he died on 4 February); newspapers did not get around to recording the demise of one of Britain's wealthiest peers until 6 February. Unusually for members of the nobility, no mention of his passing was made in the personal columns of the Establishment's notice board, *The Times*. With his death, and owing to the tragic fall six years before of his younger brother, Lord Desmond, the dukedom passed to the youngest brother, Lord Edward. Fate had dealt Ireland's premier dukedom, marquessate and earldom— for Leinster held all three—a cruel blow.

Edward FitzGerald was one of nature's sadder specimens. The fact that he was only eighteen months old when his father died may have contributed; the rigid application of the principle of primogeniture may have unshackled him from any of the restrictions of rank. Whatever the cause, Lord Edward threw himself into the waters of the Edwardian era with all the wanton zeal of the true saturnalian. He married, as did so many of his contemporaries, an actress—a Gaiety Girl named May Etheridge with whom, as he was to claim later, he had never been remotely in love. The union was made in the Wandsworth Registry Office, in 1913; May gave birth to a son, Gerald, in 1914; the couple moved apart a year later and by 1930 were divorced. It was a sad marriage, but not untypical of the era.

The First World War provided a stage for a brief period of distinction for Lord Edward, though perhaps the death of Lord Desmond gave his hedonistic habits a fresh boost, since he knew that when his brother died he would inherit. As a result, despite the entreaties of the trustees, he spent his way around Europe and ran up the most gigantic set of debts. By 1919 a receiving order was made against him as a bankrupt, and turned him to the fateful decision that has since depleted the Leinster fortunes and turned a grand dukedom into really rather an ordinary one. Young Lord Edward decided he would sell off his life interest in the Leinster estates to a wealthy businessman named Sir Harry Mallaby-Deeley, the founder of a chain of clothing shops, The Fifty Shilling Tailors. For £60,000—a sum which would cover his debts and satisfy the receivers—Lord Edward would give Sir Harry and his lawyers all and any income due to him from the estates. Since the mentally unstable Duke was still alive up in Edinburgh, and since the income from the estates was minimal, Lord Edward decided it was a fair deal: whatever happened in the future he would deal with then; Sir Harry's scheme helped him out of an immediate jam.

But Lord Edward had gambled on his brother living out his years in Craig House. In fact he died, as we have noted, some time in

February 1922, the year after Sir Harry's deal was closed. Lord Edward became the seventh Duke and as such was entitled to no less than £80,000 a year from the settled estates. Under the terms of the contract Sir Harry was to get that money, the new Duke nothing. It was the most ghastly situation.

As befits the shrewdest of businessmen, Sir Harry's lawyers had made the contract watertight. So long as the new Duke lived, all his property belonged to the Mallaby-Deeleys. He could not buy back the inheritance, and no sum of money short of £400,000, which the trustees did not have, would persuade Sir Harry to back down. The lawyers had even inserted a clause preventing the Duke from subjecting himself to unusual dangers, and thus denying Sir Harry the pleasure of the income for what promised to be a goodly period. Lord Edward FitzGerald had ruined his inheritance: all he managed to win from the Mallaby-Deeleys was a grant of £1,000 a year—the proverbial Fifty Shillings, with noble overtones. Frantically he tried to make money on the side, but every inelegant twist and turn was scrutinized under the harsh glare of popular publicity: he foundered under a bankruptcy order, was hauled before the courts for obtaining credit on false pretences and then departed for a short while to America. He married three more times, became bankrupt twice more, took his seat in the House of Lords for the first time in July 1975, when he was eighty-three (sitting as a mere Viscount: the dukedom is an Irish title, and did not entitle him to a seat), and took his own life in a flat in March of the next year. All who knew him spoke well of him—a gentle, kindly old man, a trifle dotty, easily gulled into the wildest schemes, truly pathetic but very, very decent.

Gerald, the child born out of the unhappy union with May (who died of an overdose of a sleeping draught in 1935), succeeded at the age of sixty-two. He had worked hard to make himself a living—he is perhaps the only Duke to be engaged, full-time, in commerce*— and had built up a small flying school outside Oxford to one of the best and biggest in Europe. By the time the dukedom came his way—though shorn of most of the property once due to him (Carton,

* The new Duke of Norfolk, formerly a Major-General who was about to become the Head of Military Intelligence, went on to become a first-rate merchant banker in the years before he succeeded to the dukedom. The Duke of St. Albans, too, has something of a commercial background, though none too successful.

which had been sold by the Mallaby-Deeleys, was sold once again in 1977 for more than one and a quarter million pounds)—he was just about financially equipped to manage the title. The secretaries in the office were just getting used to calling the little bespectacled flier "Your Grace" instead of "Your Lordship" when the Lord Chancellor's office came through: the Writ of Summons, the document that calls the new peer to attend the House of Lords, was being held up. *There was another claimant to the title.*

In truth, Gerald FitzGerald had expected the news. Two years before his father died his stepmother had a letter from California, from a certain Mrs. Roberts in San Francisco. Her brother, by name Leonard FitzGerald, was, she claimed, the rightful heir to the dukedom, and the Marquess would have to look out when the time came for the succession to be claimed.

The claim was not, or so a respected firm of London lawyers felt, entirely frivolous. It was based partly on the circumstances surrounding the death of the sixth Duke. According to Leonard, a schoolteacher, the Duke never did die in Scotland. Instead he ran off to tour the world when he came of age in 1908. He settled in Canada, served with the Canadian Army in the First World War, led a varied career as a rancher, broncobuster and stockbreeder in the Western Provinces and finally settled in California. He died in San Rafael in 1967, aged eighty. Leonard, his eldest son, was his rightful heir; he and his father had been cheated of both their title and their inheritance by a cabal of wicked uncles who, when Maurice left the country on his world tour, invented the story of his condition, procured a surrogate "Maurice" who was treated as mentally unstable, was persuaded to draft a "will" and was finally allowed to "die" thirteen years later. Circumstantial oddities—the lack of the announcement in the deaths column, missing burial records, inconsistent reports about the actual date of his "death"—all conspired to make the FitzGerald children in North America believe firmly in their father's tale that he was the rightful Duke, that they were his heirs and Leonard his successor in title.

The flying-school peer dismissed the tale as "rubbish." He found that a certain "M. F. FitzGerald" might have once been employed as a labourer at Carton, and wondered out loud whether this man had gone off to Canada and then, realizing the distinction of his namesake, concocted the story and presented himself as a Duke in exile.

Correspondence indicates that the Canadian "M. F. FitzGerald"—Maurice Francis—had assumed himself to be titled in 1964: his children remember him telling them he was a Duke for years before that. They all believe the veracity of his story implicitly, and no one engaged in sorting out the complexities of the case ever accused Leonard or his sister of improper ambitions.

For case it did become. One of London's most respected firms of solicitors, Theodore Goddard & Co., took up the Californian's claim, saying that it was by no means totally absurd. The firm got in touch, as the law requires, with the Crown Office at the House of Lords—the bureaucracy that is the reality behind the phrase "The Queen," when talking of ennoblement. The Clerk of the Crown, Sir Denis Dobson, delayed issuing the Writ of Summons to Gerald. Men with peculiar and little-known official functions, working from within the bowels of the Lord Chancellor's office, delved into the affair. Were there in fact inconsistencies surrounding the "death" of "Maurice" in 1922? How did the California FitzGeralds come to know so much, as their letters indicated, of the personal details of the Leinster life and fortune? Was there ever a fourth, perhaps bastard, son born to the fifth Duke?

More was at stake than the mere title, grand though that might be for a teacher of nine-year-olds in the San Francisco suburbs. If it turned out that Lord Edward had never been the rightful heir to the dukedom, then his deal with Sir Harry was consummated under mistaken circumstances and, put to the legal test, might well fall flat. The Fifty Shilling Tailor magnate and his successors might have to repay as much as ten million pounds (the sum they got in exchange for the £60,000 "helping" hand to the hedonist heir); Carton might become the centre of an explosive legal tussle. A mess of truly noble proportions seemed in the offing.

Then the Crown Office made its decision. On 7 September 1976 Gerald was sent his Writ of Summons. Copies of Lords Hansard began appearing in his office, sent to him by right by the imperturbable clerks of the Palace of Westminster. Leonard FitzGerald and his lawyers stilled their claim, and the ambitious sister stopped writing. Gerald finally took his seat on 21 October 1976.

A note of finality to the proceedings was briefly jotted into the Lords Minutes on 5 March 1977. These read:

"2. Dukedom of Leinster—Report made by the Lord Chancellor

that Gerald, Duke of Leinster, has established his claim to the Dukedom of Leinster, and ordered to lie on the Table."

From his office at Oxford Airport, the eighth Duke said happily
that this sounded very uncomfortable, but was very satisfactory all
the same.

One of the reasons for including this long tale, aside from its inherent
interest, is to allow mention of the offices and institutions that regulate
and direct the creation and duration of the British peerage. Possibly
few branches of government work as well as do the Crown Office and
the Committee for Privileges. Bodies like the College of Arms and
Lyon Court in Edinburgh are models of scholarly efficiency. Britain
looks after the mechanics of ennoblement with considerably more
care than some of the more common features of twentieth-century life.

It has been notoriously simple for the Prime Minister of the day
to award peerages, even though, in theory, they are for the Monarch
to give after consulting with his or her advisers. Pitt, as Mr. Macmillan so scornfully pointed out, handed out titles as frequently and
with as little discrimination as a modern American president hands
out ballpoint pens: of those titles existing today, seven marquessates,
five earldoms, one viscounty and eighteen baronies* were created by
the obsessed Premier. He promoted Viscount Weymouth to the
Marquessate of Bath. To the seventh Earl of Salisbury, already a
Fellow of the Royal Society, he also awarded a Marquessate of the
same Wiltshire city. The fourth Earl of Bute, a far-sighted town-
planner (of Cardiff), was also promoted a degree. Still others, like
Lords Berwick, Somers and Lilford, were plucked from the obscurity
of the Commons to be gilded with the fifth degree of the peerage;
and the man who fashioned many of the south Birmingham suburbs
was made Lord Calthorpe by a Pitt eager for his political support.

In more recent years the practice accelerated, spurred on, perhaps,
by the apparently firm decision to abandon the creation of hereditary
titles in 1965. Harold Macmillan, despite being critical of the social

---

* Among the marquessates Pitt awarded were Landsdowne, to a retiring
Prime Minister; Townshend, to a former Lord Lieutenant of Ireland; Hertford,
also a former Lord Lieutenant of Ireland; and Abercorn, the greatest magnate
in Northern Ireland.

The viscounty he awarded was to Admiral Hood, for his brilliant services
against the French Navy in 1796.

standing of the peers created by Pitt, handed out honours of one kind or another to almost every elderly Conservative who still showed signs of life. Between entering office in January 1957 and leaving it in October 1963 he showered upon the nation no fewer than sixteen hereditary nobles; adding to these all the knights and baronets (the latter a hereditary knighthood, originally sold to help James I finance his Irish wars), Macmillan was dishing out honours, in the name of the Queen, at the rate of one a month. There was no suggestion, as forty years before during the heyday of Mr. Maundy Gregory and his adept title salesmanship (£6,000 for a knighthood; £150,000 for a peerage), that honours were actually then to be bought. There was, after all, an Act specifically designed to prevent abuses of the system. But it remains an undeniable fact that honours were seen more as rewards for faithful party service in the interests of Conservatism than for any less partisan service to the nation as a whole. Now, though, the practice is said to be over. No more hereditary peerages at all. The Establishment grumbled. "The consequences could be grave," wrote one authority, "not only for an isolated defenceless Monarchy, but also for the titled Aristocracy, which can only become a closed corporation doomed to decadence and eventual extinction." The words were written in 1975: astonishing to those who felt the days of literal Aristocracy had passed by many years before.

A spirited correspondence in *The Times* developed early in 1977 after a Conservative MP wondered in print whether it was not constitutionally improper for Prime Ministers to fail, as they had for the previous twelve years, to advise the Queen to create more hereditary peers. Was not this "constitutional change by stealth"? Would it not leave the Monarchy "ripe for the republican picking"? Was not the peerage one of "the greatest assets England has"? Writers with magnificently orotund names—Hugh Montgomery-Massingberd, Charles Fletcher-Cooke, Iain Moncreiffe of that Ilk, H. B. Brooks-Baker—writhed literate agonies at the deliberate defaulting of Harold Wilson, Edward Heath and James Callaghan: Sir Iain came up with a compromise plan, that, as in the reign of Elizabeth I, peerages should be created for real merit, and very sparingly indeed. She created only eight peerages during the entire fifty-four years of her reign: in the fifty-four years up to the creation of Lord Margadale's title no fewer than 359 were made—a ratio of nearly forty-five to one—even though these are said to be more egalitarian times. Possibly the peerage is under attack as a direct consequence of just that kind of excess.

All manner of advantages come wrapped in the bundle of scarlet and ermine of a hereditary title, as we have seen. The most ancient complexity—and yet one not quite forgotten in a few homes, in Royal circles and in the magical mystery tour of domestic protocol—is the matter of Precedence: no doubt it was the delights of British Precedence, as much as the possible ten million pounds, that spurred on Leonard FitzGerald in the pursuit of his peerage, and a dukedom at that.

"God made them high and lowly/And ordered their estate," it used to say in *Hymns Ancient and Modern*. Few more rigidly ordered societies can be found anywhere in the world than in Britain—even now, the caste system is only slowly and painfully being dismantled.* Dozens of pages in the various annual guidebooks to British society tell precisely where everyone of note stands in rank—useful for arranging processions, for seating people at formal dinners, for knowing whom to introduce to a visiting Head of State and in what order, for learning how wide the choice is for a forthcoming marriage, and for gauging how important are those who let it be known they think they are important. The list is headed, of course, by the Queen—"the only person whose precedence is absolute." Her Majesty has the arrangement of the precedence of all others as one of her Prerogatives: she may alter precedence from time to time, though not drastically; she may well bow to the realities of any situation and permit temporary alterations, since "it not infrequently happens that, in the relationship between hosts and guests, the requirements of courtesy and hospitality override any strict order of precedence."

It would be tedious in the extreme to recite in any detail the nature of the Official Tables: it is almost sufficient to say they exist. But in general terms, the Tables have always placed, and always presumably will continue to place, Dukes of England at the very top (behind a score of official office-holders, such as the Archbishop of Canterbury, the Prime Minister, the Lord High Constable and the Master of the Horse) and Labourers at the very base of the prece-

---

* Defenders of the Order of Precedence say its purpose is quite the opposite. "It puts the *really* mighty down a peg or two so as to make them realise they are only part of the historical perspective."

dential pyramid. Since the regulators of Precedence no longer recognize a specific Order of Procedure for people below a certain rank, it can justifiably be said that to suggest that Labourers still occupy any officially lowly position is tendentious. But the fact remains that the attitudes that regarded Labourers as worthless drones unsuited for grander designs persisted, officially, until very recently. The legacy of those attitudes remains with a significant proportion of British society even today, though it is officially discountenanced.

From a 1909 edition of *Dod's Peerage, Baronetage and Knightage* one can see how the lowly orders were once recognized. Labourers were lower than Artificers; above them were Tradesmen-who-are-citizens. Higher still were Yeomen, Professional Gentlemen, Subaltern Officers of the Army, Barristers, King's Counsel, Clergymen, Bachelors of Medicine, Bachelors of Law, Bachelors of Divinity, Doctors of Medicine, Doctors of Laws, Doctors of Divinity and then, at long last, at position number 162 in the table—Younger Sons of the Knights Bachelor. Not quite descendants of the ennobled maybe, but the offspring of the lowliest group to have made contact with the Monarch in his (in 1909, of course) function as the Fount from which all Honours spring. In that same table one still has to struggle upwards through a bewildering variety of dross—Elder Sons of the Knights Commander of the Star of India, Masters in Lunacy, Companions of the Bath, Knights Grand Cross of the Order of St. Michael and St. George, Knights Banneret (now defunct), Baronets (a fierce squabble took place between the Society of Baronetage and the Palace because of the Sovereign's apparent desire to recognize Children of Legal Life Peers as of higher precedence than Baronets—the Baronets lost) and others with similarly sonorous titles, before the first of the real peers is reached. The lowest rung on the ladder of ennoblement is held by that unworthy creature, the Baron of the United Kingdom.

The precedence of peers then runs up from Barons, to the exalted heights of Dukes of England, some 355 of the former, eleven of the latter (if you count the Duke of Cornwall, the oldest English dukedom of them all, but "of the Blood Royal"). In between are the Dukes of Scotland, Great Britain, Ireland and the United Kingdom since the Union; Marquesses in the same order; Earls ditto, Viscounts ditto and the Barons, arranged in the same manner. In between are the offspring, arranged in a marvellously impertinent scheme, so that fifteen-year-old sons of impoverished Irish Marquesses may take precedence in the land over Bishops, and younger sons of Dukes of the Blood Royal may stand technically senior to Secretaries of State and Lords Commissioners of the Great Seal. There is a cartoon in Nancy Mitford's incomparable *Noblesse Oblige* showing a chinless young man walking haughtily in front of an enraged Sir Winston Churchill. "Younger son of an Earl taking precedence over Knight of the Garter," it says and one can understand Churchill's irritation at the child's contumely. (Though he would have had only himself to blame, from all accounts: he was offered the Dukedom of Dover—the first non-Royal dukedom to be made since 1874—but turned it down.)

There are all kinds of lists for all kinds of classifications of Britons— and foreigners, who are tartly reminded that "no foreigners whatever are *entitled* to precedence in this country . . . but all foreigners *enjoy by courtesy* some share of distinction in mixed society. A foreign Count is often really of lower position than an English country gen- tleman, and his wife is no Countess in the English sense of that word." Thank goodness the same guide that included those acerbic remarks did not go on to chronicle precedence in foreign countries—as one true snob remarked, everyone above the Americans, except American women! Such things have a habit of starting wars.

There are long Tables of Precedence for females: Wives of the Sovereign's Uncles, for example, coming above English Duchesses, and Wives of the Eldest Sons of Dukes coming above Daughters of Dukes. That, one imagines, would be doubly galling for a liberated British noblewoman, of which there are perhaps too few. To be re- garded as totally inferior anyway, even though your father is a Duke, must be unpleasant; to find your brother, who could be, perhaps, younger than you, marrying a wench who then assumes higher prece- dence than you—enough to make you go and marry a commoner!

And concern about Precedence goes on apace. In Northern Ireland, for example, there used to be a complete Table (as there was in the East Indies, placing the Commissioner in Sind above the Recorder of Rangoon); but with the onset of the "Troubles," and the conse- quent shifting around of the offices of government, "The Official Table requires considerable amendment. . . . the Queen has not approved a new one. . . ." Presumably an official at Buckingham Palace is wearing out pencils trying to think whether the Secretary of State comes above the Archbishop of Armagh, and whether, on the occasion of an official visit by dignitaries from the Irish Republic, the Knight of Glin comes above the Macgillicuddy of The Reeks, or vice versa. Certainly Younger Sons of Earls come above the High Sheriffs of Belfast and Londonderry, for which the same Younger Sons must be well pleased. The Legislative Draftsman of Northern Ireland has his own spot, too, about four from the bottom.

Patrick Montague-Smith, who brought out a second, revised edition of *Debrett's Complete Form* in 1977 as one of his contributions to the Jubilee—he wanted punctiliousness to continue to reign along with the younger Elizabeth—tries, not always successfully, to apply pragmatism to the ancient formulae. "Common sense must none the less be used in deciding the precedence to be accorded to peers, peeresses and their children. It is often necessary to take age and other factors into account. For example, it is usually unwise to seat the younger son of a Marquess above a Baron simply because this is how he ranks in the Table of Precedence, when the former is a youth of eighteen and the latter an old gentleman of eighty. Again it may be best to sit a high-ranking officer in the Armed Forces, or the Chairman or Managing Director of a large firm, with a low place in the Table of Precedence above a peer who, although he has a much higher place in the Table, is only a junior officer or employee." In fact, that is what usually happens, though not all would have it that way.

Sir Iain Moncreiffe of that Ilk, as a Herald, is a great stickler for exactitude of rank. He regards it as "partly a jumble of nonsense," but since it is all "great fun" as well, and does no harm, he is all in favour of normally applying the rigid precedential rules at table and watching the results. His view is that pompous precedence geared meticulously to real importance, as in some countries of the Eastern bloc, tends to become intolerable as one is always preceded by a rival who has "pipped one to the post." To him, the British system is a fascinating blend of history that mitigates real importance salutarily but just sufficiently to remind ministers, for example, that the word means public "servants." It harms nobody that a boy of twenty, the representative of some Victorian Cabinet Minister who became a Viscount, should go in to dinner before Lord Home, a former Prime Minister. It also amuses him that the wife of a life peer's son precedes a baronet's lady: thus the Hon. Mrs. Zuckerman ranks above Lady Moncreiffe. He recounted how his old friend the late Duke of Alba, when Spanish Ambassador in London, caused some seating problems when dining with Sir Iain as Captain of the King's Guard in 1945. Since the Duke was a representative of the Spanish Head of State, it seemed safer not to invite him at the same time as King Peter of Yugoslavia in exile or the Regent of Iraq, but such exquisite dilemmas were further complicated by the entitlement of the household cavalry's Officer Commanding the King's Life Guard to sit on the right of the foot guards' Captain of the King's Guard anyway. Some enjoy the humble crossword: to Sir Iain Moncreiffe, a seating plan has all the allure of backgammon with the subtlety of chess and the historical charm of mah-jong. He defends the use of our precedence as a basis for seating people at dinner. At American dinners, he is told, the guests of honour are placed in the centre and the crashing bores to the flanks, displaying conversational peaks and troughs: a Moncreiffe-made table would spread fascination, family and friends equally across the board, with resulting intercourse of memorable satisfaction.

Debrett's Correct Form, scarlet-covered with an embossed coronet and 422 pages long, is one of a number of similar-looking, but much thicker works that adorn the library shelves of most members of the peerage, telling them with all the gravamen of historical authority the fine details about their titles and their standing. The stud books of the British nobility are a subindustry in themselves, incomparable and incredible, yet bowing slowly to the same pressures that are prompting the new decline of their subjects. Thousands of pages long, the books are more massive than the weightiest of telephone directories, more costly than encyclopaedias: quite probably some editions of the grander of their number must rank as the largest single-volume works in existence.

Pre-eminent among their number is a massive, nine-volume work, *The Complete Peerage*, the nearest thing to an official compilation of the histories of titled families. It was written by an eminent genealogist, George Edward Cokayne—no better name, perhaps, could have been chosen for the author of a book about the people of some fabled land of luxury and delight—who was employed as a Herald—first Rouge Dragon Pursuivant (of which post later), then Lancaster Herald and finally Clarenceux King of Arms. *The Complete Peerage* was his intended memorial, and it is still referred to, by those few who could afford to buy it before it disappeared, as "GEC." Its thick, rough-edged pages and clear, nobly sized type, make it still a joy to read: its footnotes and appendices abound in the most delightfully recondite details.

Sadly, though, "GEC," like its author, is dead. A supplement was issued in the 1950s to record details of the peerage creations between 1901 and 1938, and the nine volumes haughtily, but correctly, claim total accuracy for every single creation from the thirteenth century to the outbreak of the Second World War. But now no one can afford the time and trouble, it seems, to write any more: no further volumes are likely to be published, even though peerages are still created and a new volume could be filled with consummate ease. The massive tomes sit in a few well-endowed libraries, gathering dust. All the paperwork is kept by the Clerk of the Records at the House of Lords.

World War II also very nearly claimed the life of that other stud book of the blue-bloods, *Burke's Peerage*. Until then the monstrous, scarlet, gold-blocked volumes had thundered down from the printing presses almost every year, to stand alongside *Who's Who* and *Crockford's Clerical Directory* as the standard book ends to prop up the gardening magazines on the roll-top desk. These days *Burke's*, a century and a half old, comes out at irregular intervals: it had been printed each three or four years, but now will appear at intervals of about a generation. The next will appear, ominously, soon after 1984, if any peers remain.

Burke's is a truly splendid book, if only as a gallimaufry of oddities and a treasure house of material for the aspirant bore. Those who deride it as a "snobs' bible" might have been right half a century ago—in those days mothers of marriageable daughters probably did flick through the pages of the *Peerage* and its sister volume, *Burke's Landed Gentry*, to determine the suitability of various would-be husbands—but these days true snobs dismiss such a necessity, claiming they can tell a young man's suitability just by looking at him and listening to him talk. No, *Burke's* is the kind of book one can delight in curling up with on a rainy winter's day, to marvel in the mysteries of the truly Upper Class. (Though it is often remarked that the *Landed Gentry* is far classier than the *Peerage*; within the three volumes of the *LG* are the true representatives of living history—thanes and sokemen, drenches and radman.) Anthony Powell, listed as a fine specimen of the gentry, quotes an 1852 press review of one *LG*:

"The landed gentry of England are a more powerful body than its peerage. The office of peerage is hereditary, it is true, but when the strict line of succession terminates the Crown substitutes a new family. The new peers are selected from the landed gentry, or from successful adventurers in law, commerce, arms or divinity, who having acquired wealth, contrive to get themselves adopted into the land-owning class. In the identification of the peers with the great land-owning class lies their strength. As an isolated body they could not exist for a year. . . . a mere peerage conveys a very inadequate notion of the position and consequence of peers."

Nevertheless, the *Peerage* does not lack class, as anyone who coughs up his £38 for the work will admit. There are none of the advertisements for Rolls-Royce or Twentieth Century Fur Hire that grace the *LG*, but there are 2,950 fine India-paper pages filled with five-point type detailing the family backgrounds of men and women from Sir Robert Abdy, Baronet, to the eighteenth Baron Zouche of Haryng-worth. Some entries are stupendous: the nineteenth Earl of Moray's, for instance, continues for eleven pages, with details of his extraor-dinary range of ancestors, including Kings of the Scots, a gentleman known as the Wolf of Badenoch and another (an indirect relation) known as the Wizard Earl of Bothwell. The present Earl of Moray shares his membership of the House of Stuart—of which Bonnie Prince Charles is most notorious—with descendants who include the Dukes of Richmond, Grafton, St. Albans, "the British marquessate of Bute, earldom of Wharncliffe and barony of Southampton, the United Kingdom dukedom of Gordon, viscounties of Daventry and Stuart of Findhorn and barony of Montagu, the Irish earldom of Castle Stewart, the Scottish dukedoms of Buccleuch, Lennox and Queensberry, also earldoms of Galloway and Moray, the French duke-doms of Aubigny and the Spanish dukedom of Penaranda; besides several baronetcies." The nineteenth Earl was a colonial farmer in the grand manner and married one Mabel Wilson, the only child of the late Benjamin "Matabele" Wilson of Battlefields, Southern Rhodesia. The twentieth Earl sounds a less colourful fellow, though married into the Earldom of Mansfield (the family that owns Scone Palace in Perthshire).

Other entries, especially for the life peers, whom one imagines *Burke's* rather despises, are short. All, however, are introduced with a splendid engraving of the family coat of arms—prompting some assiduous readers to colour in the coats of the peers they have met, a sort of high-flown train spotting practised by the wealthier souls with time on their hands. The language of the *Peerage* is suitably pompous, and is filled with abbreviations that are common knowl-edge to students of the subject, but quite unknown outside. The fact, for example, that a certain Baron "d.s.p.m.s." (*decessit sine prole mascula superstite*) may not seem of great import: in fact, though, since it means he died without surviving male children, it could have a profound effect on the future of his barony. The shorthand of nobiliary Latin can be used to soften the blow of some distant cousin's impotence, as in "Poor Gerald d.s.p. (died without child). Poor chap—tut-tut!" In the same vein "b." means "born," "s." "succeeded," "d." means died and "bur." buried. An awful lot of the flower of the titled youth were "k." in World War I, or perhaps "d.v.m.," died in the lifetime of their mothers. The jungle of *Burke's* abbreviations can be as fascinating as some of the entries themselves.

Strangely enough one short form that occasionally occurs in the conversation of the more socially conscious nobles is the ugly word "colls.," which really doesn't appear in *Burke's* except as the abbreviation for "collector" or "college." To readers of *Burke's* only real competitor, *Debrett's Peerage and Baronetage*, it has an importance all of its own—it means "collaterals" or distant family, and is much used when referring to the provenance of a stranger. "Oh, it's all right, I looked him up in *Debrett's*, and he's in the Duke of Atholl Colls., so he'll do."

Debrett's, though far less detailed about historic ancestry than *Burke's*, is the Bradshaw of the present membership of titledom. It makes no claim to table the deeds and misdeeds of the ancestors of England's great men and women; instead, in 2,256 rather smaller pages, it lists all the living members of the titled families, gives brief notes on their present doings and, ideally for Raffles-style burglars, who subscribe to it, gives their addresses. *Debrett's* is the useful work, invariably well-thumbed, fashioned for hard wear, and a work of commerce as much as of scholarship. The firm that publishes the guide also turns out the *Complete Form* ("An Inclusive Guide to Everything from Drafting Wedding Invitations to Addressing an Archbishop"), and has started a service for anyone wanting a family tree. Most early clients, when the service was begun in 1977, were Americans.

Reviews of the 1976 edition of *Debrett's* pointed out its many failings; the surprisingly large number of "Residence ———," suggesting to the mischievous that the peer involved might have been carted off to the local asylum; the indifferent typography; the many gaps in the heraldic coverage; the occasional mistakes, such as that placing the creation of the Moncrieff baronetcy in 685, long before the creation of the institution, rather than a thousand years later. Mistakes, as noted a caustic review in *The Times Literary Supplement* in 1976, "became more serious when we read that a Viscount's daughter who divorced in 1968 and married a Marquess in the following year has issue living '(by 1st m),' a son 'b. 1973'; the Most Honourable's entry fortunately refutes the possible libel."

Unhappily *Debrett's* too, is succumbing to the gradual erosion of fortunes and families, and will appear, the 1976 preface notes glumly, "at longer intervals than previously." The *TLS* reviewer would happily make do with *Who's Who* and *Kelly's;* only Raffles would be unduly put out, one imagines, by the passing of the address book of the very best hoards of national treasure.

There are still other works essential for true snobs. There is another scarlet-bound volume, slimmer than either *Burke's* or *Debrett's,* called *The Royalty, Nobility and Peerage of the World,* with notes on all titled heads from Haakon to Zog. There was the extraordinary *Almanach de Gotha,* filed at the Bodleian as a "foreign periodical," which doubtless the financially harassed Hugh Montgomery-Massingberd and Patrick Montague-Smith (former editors of *Burke's* and *Debrett's* respectively) would wish their publications to be.* The *Almanach* ceased publication during World War II. Its successor, the *Genealogisches Handbuch des Adels,* known unofficially as the Neo-Gotha, is pocket-sized and written in German, and has all the appearance of a racing calendar for Freiherrs and Counts of the turf; in a sense that is precisely what it is.

The Queen may be the Fount of Honour; the Crown Office and the Committee for Privileges may be the guardians of entitlement, and the vast scarlet volumes the records of hereditary glories, but all these august institutions produce, at the end of the day, is paperwork. Impressive paperwork maybe, but only paperwork. The office that translates awards and honours into stylish, dashing, colourful reality is housed in the City of London—the College of Arms. Into this

---

* The old original *Almanach de Gotha* was written in French, included the Royal Houses and European Dukes and Princes—though not the Spanish—and a great deal of diplomatic and statistical information. Later there were separate volumes in German for German and Austro-Hungarian Counts and Barons, and for the German untitled nobles.

office have strolled scores of anonymous and common starlings, and out have strutted an almost equivalent number of proud and ennobled peacocks.

It is the College of Arms, and its quaintly titled officers, who advise a man on his choice of title, the design and colour of his coat of arms. Alun Gwynne-Jones, a soldier from South Wales who gained a reputation as a snappy dresser and a smooth talker, and who ended up as a writer on *The Times* and a Labour minister, was ennobled in 1964 and, feeling pretty grand, decided he would tell the Heralds at the College of Arms that he wanted some title like Glendower or Llewellyn—a fine old Welsh title, full of battle-cry and national feeling. The Heralds were politely aghast—the offence, they discreetly suggested, might be huge, especially among all the descendants of Owen Glendower and the ancient Kings of the Principality. Could he not think of another site for his title, one that would be somewhat more anodyne? Gwynne-Jones scratched his head and, at the Herald's suggestion, pondered over the various places in which he had lived or where he had worked. Where, the Herald wondered, had he been stationed during the war? Gwynne-Jones named an undistinguished dormitory town a few miles outside London, Chalfont St. Giles. Perfect, the Herald replied—how about Lord Chalfont? And so that is how the translation of Alun Gwynne-Jones to Baron Chalfont of Llantarnam, Co. Monmouth, was effected, absurd though it may sound in the telling.

His coat of arms, propped by supporters, as a peer's is entitled to be, is suitably militaristic, though not especially modern. In the middle is a sword, pointing downwards, with olive branches surrounding it; on each side is a soldier—on the left a South Wales Borderer (Gwynne-Jones's regiment), on the right a Herald with his tabard emblazoned with the same down-pointing sword and olive branches; above the whole lot is the Welsh dragon, holding a black and silver (or sable and argent, to use the Norman French rendering of colours still used in heraldic language) rod in his paw. A fine design, all above the Latin motto *"Cedant Arma Togae"*— "Arms Yield to the Toga," a sort of circumlocutory way of saying that the pen is mightier than the sword.

The College, while not a British government department, is an official body: the officials who man its dusty offices are not civil servants, but they are members of the Royal Household, answerable to the Queen through the holder of the oldest English dukedom, the Duke of Norfolk, in his capacity of Earl Marshal (his best-known duties as Marshal are to organize great ceremonies of state, like the coronations and funerals of Monarchs). Its principal officials are the three Kings of Arms: Garter, the senior; Clarenceux, responsible for grants of arms throughout England south of the River Trent; and Norroy and Ulster, who looks after England north of the Trent, Wales and Northern Ireland. A quite separate office on Princes Street in Edinburgh, run by the Lord Lyon King of Arms, looks after the curious and utterly complicated arrangements for Scottish arms-bearers and clan chiefs.

The six Heralds—Windsor, Richmond, Somerset, York, Chester and Lancaster—and the four Pursuivants—with their splendid titles of Portcullis, Rouge Croix, Rouge Dragon and Bluemantle—take turns as duty officers at the College, to answer the inquiries that come in from new peers, or from farmers out in Indiana who believe they are heir to a Norman bequest, or from old ladies up in town from Shropshire for the day who would like to see their family trees. For most inquiries the Heralds charge fees, all of which are ploughed back into the College, making it a more or less completely self-financing institution.

Walter Verco, the present Norroy and Ulster King—and secretary to the Earl Marshal besides—works in an airy office thick with copies of *GEC* and antique editions of *Collins's Peerage* and *The Genealogist*. Outside, a middle-aged secretary in a thick cardigan sits at a narrow desk, warmed by a small fire. There is no cat, but the air of pleasant domesticity suggests there should be one. The King does not sound like, or behave, like one imagines a King should, but instead is a fussy, busy man, stiff in a shiny white starched collar and a light grey suit, exuding officialdom.

He is a Londoner, no university graduate or untutored aristocrat, but a London Cockney, with a slight hint of accent and the vague trace of the glottal stop. He was a schoolboy when once, running an errand for a friend, he had to go to the College of Arms to make inquiries. "They must have been impressed with the way I asked my questions," he recalls. "The Officer who saw me wrote to my head-master, with the result that I became his secretary—sort of Lady Falkender to the Herald." His rise in the hierarchy, though inter-rupted by a short spell in the RAF, was steady—first a Pursuivant,

doing the day-to-day running of a heraldic office, then Herald, attending the occasional peerage investiture at the House of Lords and
marching in stately pomp at major ceremonies. Now, as a King,
subject in granting arms only to the ultimate authority of the Earl
Marshal, he is at the top of his uncrowded profession, with a
reputation such that the RAF, among others, have retained him to
design their crests and shields of the various Wings and Flights that
remain. He is prouder of these—of mailed fists and propellers and
lightning flashes painted on sleek aircraft and outside bases in the
wilds of outer Suffolk and the north of Scotland—than perhaps of
any other work he has done. It is also very financially rewarding, and
neither he, nor any other Herald, goes to bed hungry.

Some inquiries are answered for nothing. In Brian Masters's study
of ducal histories there is reference to an obscure heraldic controversy
over the rights to adorn coats of arms with an escutcheon known as
the "Flodden Augmentation"—in the lingua franca described as
"(on the bend) an escutcheon Or charged with a demi-lion rampant,
pierced through the mouth by an arrow, within a double tressure
flory counter-flory Gules." The augmentation was granted to the
victor at Flodden Field in 1513, and is proudly sported by his Howard
descendants—Lords Carlisle, Suffolk, Effingham and Howard of
Penrith among them—his co-heirs, Lords Mowbray and Petre and,
above all since the dukedom is the same as that restored to the victor
after Flodden, by his heir male, the Duke of Norfolk, the head of
the whole house of Howard. However, there is some argument over
whether or not the Duke himself is entitled to wear the augmentation—a tricky problem since, in all matters of heraldic judication, the
Earl Marshal's court reigns supreme, and if the matter were to be
put to the test, the Duke would have to preside over his own case
or appoint a surrogate president of the Court of Chivalry. It seemed
a worthy matter for inquiry, so letters were dispatched to Norroy and
Ulster King who wrote back, charmingly, saying he had forwarded
the inquiry to a functionary titled "Maltravers Herald Extraordinary,"
who worked in Sussex. Back came a letter, stiff with the import of
the matter: "I regret that I cannot place great reliance on some of
the statements in Mr. Masters' book," he grumbled. It was, all things
considered, a "facetious suggestion" that Mr. Masters had put forward.
The letter was signed "Francis W. Steer—Maltravers," and written
from the Duke of Norfolk's seat at Arundel, where Mr. Steer was
archivist and librarian. For all this help, no fee.

Once the Heralds, with the King's approval and the Earl Marshal's sanction, have made the grant of arms and have decided upon the title by which the new peer will be known, only one matter remains before the lucky individual is free to supplicate for membership of the House of Lords. He—or she, since 1958—has to pay the mandatory visit to Ede and Ravenscroft, the quaint old shop in Chancery Lane, and let one of the staff exchange quantities of scarlet cloth, ermine bands, gold leaf and appliquéd sealskin for the sum of £600. The robes, packaged in a traditional gold-trimmed scarlet bag with yellow dressing-gown-cord ties so it can be slung casually over the shoulder as the peer dashes for the Aberdeen sleeper, will take a month to make, and will last for ever.

In case a coronation is heaving to on the horizon, a new entrant may also be sold two other marks of rank: a coronation robe and a coronet of degree. Only the Duke, who will probably have a fortune already, will have to produce a coronet made of solid gold: an essentially simple thing, this has eight strawberry leaves round the rim, and fits around a velvet and ermine "cap of estate" that stops the ducal brow from becoming chafed. Other peers have plainer, silver-gilt bands, though rather more complicated—the Marquess having his adorned with four strawberry leaves and four silver balls, the Earl with eight silver balls and eight strawberry leaves, the Viscount with sixteen silver balls. Only the Baron's is truly humble, as befits his station: a mere six silver balls set on the rim of a silver-gilt circlet. Most peers keep their coronets in Asprey's or one of the other London jewellers, though quite a few—those created since 1953—do not possess one at all, and will not until King Charles III has to be crowned. Then, as in 1952, the court jewellery makers will be inundated with orders—and all for pieces that are worn for perhaps half an hour at most, and which many peers will use, as then, to protect their sandwiches and their Horlicks tablets during the interminable wait in Westminster Abbey.

This then, is the basis of the clockwork that keeps the British peerage in good condition—clockwork amply provided with tripwires and booby traps to fault hopeful foreigners who entertain ideas of invading the ennobled ranks. And yet time and again commoners—not only foreigners, but Britons obsessed with some vague idea that a distant cousin's death left them heir to a title, or a fortune, or both— write in, to the Heralds, to the Lord Chancellor, to the Crown Office, to *Burke's* and *Debrett's,* asking for information about or for confirmation of their own entitlement. Few are ever allowed: for although the granting of a title is an often fickle procedure, with appointments frequently frowned upon by the mechanicians (the College of Arms, for instance, is said privately to have thought little of the choices for life peerages made by Harold Wilson), entry into the lists by those who are neither appointed nor clearly related is impossibly difficult. There have been only four cases presented to the Committee for Privileges since the war: the Dudhope and Dundee cases of 1952 and 1953, in which Henry James Scrymgeour Wedderburn of Wedderburn established his claim to the Earldom of Dundee and Viscounty of Dudhope; the 1976 case of the Ampthill barony; and the 1977 case of the Oxfuird viscounty. "It is hard to think of any recent case, or indeed any case at all, that has aroused the same degree of public interest as the Ampthill case," said John Sainty, the Lords Reading Clerk and Clerk of the Journals. It provides a splendidly bizarre episode, illustrative in the same manner as was the Leinster case of the ambitions for title, with which to close this lengthy account of the enginework of peerage.

Burke's records the controversial episodes drily enough. "The 3rd Baron Ampthill (John Hugo Russell, CBE), served in World War I and in World War II, CBE, Croix de Guerre with palms; US Legion of Merit . . . m. 1stly 18 Oct. 1918 (m. diss. by div. 1927) Christabel Hulme, dau. of late Lt. Col. John Hart, Leinster Regt., of Broadhurst, Heathfield, Sussex . . . and has issue Geoffrey Denis Erskine, educ. Stowe . . . He m. 2ndly Sibell Faithfull . . . (d. Sept. 1947); he m. 3rdly Adeline Mary Constance and by her has issue . . . John Hugo Trenchard, educ. Eton." The four characters played their parts—albeit two of them posthumously—in a drama that had all the most bizarre elements a British newspaperman could dream for: virgin birth, family feud, fortunes, curious sexual practices, and the House of Lords. The story begins, appropriately enough, with an advertisement in the *The Times.*

"Lost in the North Sea mist," the advertisement ran, in the agony columns one winter's day in 1915. "Three young midshipmen serving in the Grand Fleet would like to correspond with young ladies." One of the young blades serving up in the lonely fastnesses of Scapa Flow was the Hon. John Russell, oldest son and heir of the second Baron Ampthill, a deputy Viceroy of India; one of the hundreds of girls to reply to the notice was a quintessential forerunner of the Roaring

Twenties, Christabel Hart. She sent a photograph, met the men at King's Cross Station and began a flirtation with the Hon. John that was apparently as outrageous as one would expect of a girl who rode her hunters astride, rather than sidesaddle, and who was by all accounts an eager nightclubber and founder member of the flappers. The war tended to muck things up a bit, of course, but by 18 October 1918 the two, Christabel and the Hon. John, were happily married and settling down to a life of easy bliss. The only trouble was that Christabel, for reasons best known to herself, either didn't care too much for sex, or didn't care too much for the bodily attributes of the heir to the barony. It was separate beds for John and Christabel, from the very start.

Occasionally, however, John's more beastly tendencies did get the better of him, according to hints and whispers from Christabel's maid, and he would creep into his wife's bedroom and engage in a somewhat more physical version of what was then known as spooning. One night, that of 18 December 1920, something occurred in Christabel's bed that she preferred only to describe as "Hunnish practices"—and 301 days later, baby Geoffrey, to Christabel's evident consternation, was born.

Curiously, she did not realize she was pregnant until five months after the "Hunnish practices" had taken place; and doctors who examined her found she was almost completely physically intact. The impending delivery was, so the newspaper later claimed, an example of virgin birth.

The story moves on quickly after this, with an incensed Hon. John suing his wife for divorce on the grounds that, since he had never had intercourse with her, the child could not be his: Christabel was a stunningly beautiful woman, constantly surrounded by admirers, and the Hon. John found no difficulty in claiming two co-respondents. In court, Christabel managed to persuade judges on one occasion that she had not committed adultery, and that young Geoffrey had been conceived as a result of "marital rape" by John; indeed, she said, she never had permitted him to sleep with her, but she had not slept with any others either. The second time around, however, John was granted a divorce and Geoffrey was disinherited. The famous Russell baby case, which gripped a fevered 1920s public for half a decade, was over. Perhaps it was just as well: so lurid was the reporting of the divorce hearings that rules were later introduced to curb the excesses of the most lubricious press.

Although the courts had had their day as far as the matter of divorce was concerned, Christabel battled on to get her son legitimized; eventually the House of Lords agreed. In a 3:2 verdict the Law Lords decided that nobody born in wedlock could be ruled illegitimate by one or the other parent giving evidence of non-intercourse. It was a legal ruling of great precedential importance, and, of course, enabled Geoffrey to resume his rightful position as heir to the barony. Not, one supposes, that he cared very much: at the time he was only five.

After the divorce, the Hon. John duly succeeded on the death of his father in 1935 to the title as the third Baron, married again, became a widower, then married a third time. This wife, with no known fuss or commotion, produced a son for His Lordship in 1950— a half-brother for Geoffrey and, so far as both his mother *and father* were concerned, the first legitimate son to descend from the barony. Was it possible that the new Hon. John, the 1950 son, was the rightful prospective holder of the fourth Barony, and that Geoffrey, by now a rising star in the world of theatrical management, could forget his hopes of succeeding?

A family battle of the most intense kind gripped the Russells for more than a generation: on the one side Geoffrey and his supporters, who aside from his mother, were few (he was once offered £30,000 by the family to persuade him to renounce all interests in the case), and on the other baby John and his allies, who included Lord Ampthill's brothers and his sister.

In 1973 Lord Ampthill died and Geoffrey, obviously ignoring the £30,000 inducement, claimed the barony for himself; in 1975, John, now a successful, if rather less spectacular City of London accountant, decided to challenge the petition and claim the title for his side of the family. Battle royal was set, and joined early in 1976 in Committee Room Four of the House of Lords, before the august majesty of the Committee for Privileges and a representative of the Sovereign, the Solicitor-General, who announced he was there "to guard the rights of the Crown and the Peerage." Under a vast oil painting of the Coronation of George VI, a horseshoe-shaped arrangement of scarlet chairs was laid out to hold Lords Molson, Champion, Erskine of Rerrick, Wilberforce, Beswick, Simon of Glaisdale, Kilbrandon, Russell of Killowen (no relation) and the Earl of Listowel, as they prepared to listen to the kind of claim that makes a lawyer's heart— and wallet—beat wildly. It was to be, a newspaper said, a moment for connoisseurs of litigation to savour.

In the event it proved very nearly as dry as dust. Though some of Christabel's divorce evidence was read into the record and provided a few pearls for news editors to sift from the sand—"He attempted to effect penetration but I did not allow it"—and though the event provided the press with an opportunity to dig out the spiciest of cuttings from their yellowed files of the 1920s, the drama had in effect been over for many years. True, it was fun to see the stiff-lipped hostility— the "easy blend of politeness and cutting rudeness which only the British aristocracy can carry off" as a newspaper put it—with which the half-brothers and their seconds met. It was exciting to gaze at the lissom French wife Geoffrey had brought with him for the hearing, and good for the literary imagination to typecast Geoffrey as a figure from the stage, with his silver hair and his classic good looks— looks, incidentally, that were remarkably reminiscent of the man claimed not to be his father, the third Baron. In the end connoisseurs were left with the gem of the four-day hearing; the use of the rarest of legal phrases, *fecundatio ab extra,* which, Mary and Joseph would be pleased to hear, is regarded in English law as "a rare, but not impossible occurrence."

On 6 April, two months after the hearings, the Committee met again to announce its verdict. On the basis of the earlier ruling that illegitimacy could not be proved merely because one parent says so, the Committee said that "The petitioner, John Hugo Trenchard Russell, claiming to have succeeded to the Barony of Ampthill, has not made out his claim. . . ."

The House of Lords was being told, in effect, to deny John's claim and inform the Queen that the rightful holder of the barony was Geoffrey, the man who looked the spitting image of the third Baron anyway, and the one who had been challenged by the ambitious John. It seemed a pretty fair verdict.

The sad irony of the whole affair was that only the title was really at stake. Lands and fortunes were not on offer, and the legal fees involved in resolving the dispute were gigantic. A Labour MP tabled questions asking how much the hearing had cost the state, so incensed was he at this "field day for the lawyers." It was said to have cost about £20,000. It all seemed rather a large price to pay—and especially to the political parties who might have wanted him: Ampthill sits in the House of Lords from time to time, on the cross benches.

"If ever there was a family," Lord Simon of Glaisdale said in his Opinion on the case, "seemingly blessed by fortune, where the birth of a child was attended by an evil spirit bearing a baneful gift liable to frustrate all the blessings, it was the Ampthill Russells. Its curse was litigation."

For one member of the family there was, however, some small blessing. Christabel herself, the beautiful and determined virgin, who lived a life of the most extraordinary adventures until well into her seventies, died peacefully in County Galway a week before the hearing began. She was to be spared the final humiliations of the Ampthill curse, though at the price of never knowing the happy news that her cause was, eventually, to be vindicated.

FOUR

THE DUKES
Mightiest of Them All

The Aga Khan is held by followers to be a direct
descendant of God. An English Duke takes precedence.
> —Letter from College of Arms, quoted in
> *Housewife*

A fully equipped Duke costs as much to keep up
as two dreadnoughts. They are just as great a
terror, and they last longer.
> —David Lloyd-George, 1909, campaigning
> in Newcastle-upon-Tyne

Dukes Hotel, as befits its name, has an atmosphere of dignity and gracious living. Elegance
without ostentation is its keynote, together with
traditional and courteous service and tasteful
décor.
> —From an advertisement in *The Field*,
> 1976

PART ONE

For all the awe, affection, fear, myth and controversy that surround
the persons of the British Dukes, it is a little surprising to learn that
there are so few of the breed and, indeed, that few Dukes have ever
existed in the past. There are but twenty-five surviving today—not
including the Dukes of the Blood Royal, who account for a further
three, or the Queen's Consort, the Duke of Edinburgh. And fewer
than 500 have ever been permitted to use the title over the six-and-a-
half centuries during which it has existed (it was first created in 1337

by Edward III, who made his son Duke of Cornwall: the lad is better memorialized, however, as the Black Prince).

The Dukes are the only peers who do not have to suffer by being called "My Lord" and addressed as "Lord" this or that. A Duke is always a Duke—and in formal conversation both he and his Duchess are "Your Grace." Not everyone manages to remember this fine distinction: "Good morning, sir," said one child, on being introduced to the Duke of Sutherland at one Coronation. "No, boy!" hissed his embarrassed father, "Say 'Your Grace.' " "Beg pardon, father," rejoined the child, and looking the Duke full in the face, cried: "For what we are to receive, may the Lord make us truly thankful."

The Sovereign, too, regards the Dukes as being of sufficient rank and style to be worthy of a most special privilege—the application "Right trusty and right entirely beloved cousin," with the addition of the words "and counsellor" if, as is often the case, His Grace is a Member of the Privy Council. The precedence which a Duke and his offspring enjoy is very close to that taken by the Monarch herself —only the Consort, the Archbishops of Canterbury and York, the Prime Minister, the Lord President of the Council, the Lord Chancellor, the Lord Privy Seal, the Master of the Horse, Mr. Speaker, the senior members of the Royal Family and the resident Ambassadors and High Commissioners of foreign nations in London take higher placing than the Dukes. (The position in Scotland is similar. The Lord Chancellor, the Moderator of the General Assembly of the Church of Scotland, the Prime Minister, the Lord High Constable and the Hereditary Master of the Household are the only grandees who take precedence over Dukes north of the Border—and the Master of the Household, for now, is the Duke of Argyll, thus taking precedence over himself, as it were.) Their Graces are regarded as of higher rank than every Minister and Envoy, sons of Royal Dukes, every Bishop in the land and, of course, every other member of the peerage. Theirs is a position of stateliness unchallenged by any but the very grandest members of the Establishment; their children, too, whatever may be their courtesy title (and the Duke of Grafton's eldest son is a mere Earl, that of the Duke of Manchester a plain Viscount and, astonishingly, the eldest son of the Duke of Somerset is only a Lord), enjoy exalted status.* The eldest sons take the automatic rank of

* The older a dukedom or earldom, the more likely its second title is to be a lower one: it was a seventeenth-century custom to throw in a number of new lesser titles when creating an earldom or a dukedom.

Marquess, coming precedentially only just below full-blooded Marquesses of the United Kingdom; and younger children are styled as "Lord" or "Lady" whether they be ninety-five years or nine days old. Similarly mothers of Dukes, former wives of Dukes—who are legion, thanks to the predilection among members of the degree for traumatic endings to their marriages—and widows of Dukes are given special favours. A Duke's mother is the Dowager Duchess; a Duke's widow— if the Dowager Duchess is still living—is known as, say, Mary, Duchess of Southampton, and stays as such until she accedes to the Dowagership; and the former wife of a Duke takes the same style—Christian name, title—until she marries again. Margaret, Duchess of Argyll, centre of the celebrated divorce scandal of 1963 that included the submission, in court, of photographs of the genitalia of at least one well-known politician, is a case in point.

In his book *Amazing Grace*, the humourist E. S. Turner lists the various duties men had to perform to be awarded the title of Duke. Some of the present company had ancestors who, like Marlborough and Wellington, won great battles for their country; other men performed sterling service in political and public life; dukedoms were offered for "Fascinating a male Sovereign; fascinating a female Sovereign;* betraying a Sovereign (i.e., for services to Protestantism); for being the bastard of a Sovereign [four of these still exist, sporting the heraldic device for bastardy as proudly as any rampant lion]; for having ancestors who served the State well; for having an ancestor who was unfairly executed; for defeating, subduing or otherwise taming the Scots or the Irish; for supporting, or not opposing, parliamentary reform; for marrying a Duchess." The last on his list is the award of a dukedom for "amassing, or inheriting, or marrying into enormous landed wealth"—the Duke involved was Hugh Lupus Grosvenor who, thanks to marriage, inheritance and a well-developed business acumen, had, by 1874, amassed sufficient wealth to make even Queen Victoria appear impoverished by comparison. "My dear Westminster," the Premier, Gladstone, wrote to him (he was already the

* Mr. Turner may well be wrong in this one respect in that no fascinated female sovereign appears to have created a dukedom: Queen Mary Stuart only did so in conjunction with her husband William III, Queen Anne's dukedoms were political or military and Queen Mary Tudor created none at all. Perhaps Turner was thinking of Queen Victoria, though she never offered a dukedom to her gillie, John Brown, who is said to have fascinated her more than any other man.

Marquess of Westminster) on 17 February, "I have received authority from the Queen to place a dukedom at your disposal and I hope you may accept it. . . ." The Marquess did so, and thus wound up a series of ducal awards that, so far as the current twenty-five survivors are concerned, stretched back for four centuries.

There are not even likely to be twenty-five for very much longer. The Dukedom of Portland is tottering towards sudden extinction: there are no further heirs now that both the seventh Duke and his distant cousin, Major Sir Ferdinand Cavendish-Bentinck, who succeeded in 1977 at the age of eighty-nine, childless, are dead. His heir, his brother William Bentinck, the former British ambassador in Warsaw, had a son, but he died without children, too. The title Duke of Newcastle seems similarly destined soon to disappear: the present title-holder has only daughters, and his sole heir is a bachelor who is over sixty. And although he is still eligible at fifty, the tenth Duke of Atholl—one of the few Dukes to grace the House of Lords with any regularity, and one of the most easily identifiable, by his spectacularly large nose—seems bent on bachelordom; if he remains unmarried the title will in theory pass to one of a number of remote and elderly gentlemen, among whom are some distant relations apparently well settled in South Africa. That title may remain, but may leave the shores of the kingdom for some long time to come.

If the Atholl title left these shores for Africa, it would not find itself alone. Two Dukes—Manchester and Montrose—have farmed in Africa for decades, the latter having been a member of the rebellious Smith Government in Rhodesia. The Duke of Bedford, too, is a persistent expatriate: he lives in Paris at present, and flits from Charles de Gaulle airport to distant capitals—Peking, for instance. The Duke has made over Woburn, his stately home, to his son and heir: his dukedom is bound to return, unless his son flees the coop as well.

The remainder of those living in the British Isles are determinedly non-metropolitan. One, the Duke of Abercorn, lives in Northern Ireland, fairly well insulated from the miseries of the place. Three, Norfolk, Richmond and Newcastle, live on the south coast of England; one each in Cheshire (the new young Duke of Westminster, Gerald), Norfolk (Grafton), Gloucestershire (Beaufort), Wiltshire (Somerset), and Berkshire (Wellington); two (Marlborough and Leinster) in Oxfordshire. Vast stretches of countryside in the English Midlands are considered unsuitable for ducal habitation, and it is not until we come to the southern side of the Pennines that we find the Dukes of Devonshire and Rutland living in vast mansions in adjacent valleys in northern Derbyshire. "Our estates march together," says Devonshire, using the old term. The estates, he means, share a common border, running along a thousand-foot hillside up on the East Moor. The Dukedom of Portland used to be based nearby, across to the east in the Nottinghamshire flatlands around Worksop. Then as we go north another hundred miles of Duke-free land: the ugly excrescences (though from which many have made parts of their fortunes) of Sheffield and Manchester and Barnsley and Rotherham provide homes, so far as can be seen, for virtually no peers at all of any rank, no matter how humble. And we have to wait until the far north of England and the lovely old town of Alnwick before we come to the many-towered castle that houses the Duke of Northumberland.

After that they appear thick and fast: a ghetto of Dukes in the Scottish borders—Buccleuch, Roxburghe, Sutherland; another of the species, Hamilton, a few miles out of Edinburgh. Up in the Highlands Atholl and Argyll hold sway, and the Duke of Fife lives obscurely in the well-heeled region of Kincardineshire, near Aberdeen.

Not that their titles have a great deal to do with where they live. Discounting the Duke of Bedford, who owned, until recently, property in Bedford but now lives overseas, only five of the Dukes either live in, or have substantial properties in the places from which they are mistakenly supposed to come: the Duke of Atholl lives at Blair Atholl in Perthshire;* the Duke of Northumberland is one of the most important figures in that wild and lovely county; Roxburghe's Floors Castle is in his own county; Argyll's Inveraray Castle is similarly foursquare in Argyll. And the Duke of Westminster, whose father retired to the remote fastnesses of Northern Ireland, and who himself lives in Cheshire, centres his enormous landholdings in the city of the same name.

For the rest, it is as though the titles were invented merely to confuse. So difficult did it become for the Dukes of Devonshire to disclaim any connection with the English south-west from their vast lands in Derbyshire that someone was sent to look at the patent to see if a scrivener had spelled the northern county wrongly—but

* Blair Atholl is the modern capital of the former Pictish kingdom of Atholl, which later became a royal earldom and which comprises a huge district between Dunkeld and Deeside.

he had not. "Dux Devon," the Latin firmly states.* The Duke of
Norfolk has precious little land in Norfolk—by ducal standards, that
is—and rules the roost from Arundel Castle in Sussex. The Duke of
Richmond, fifty miles from London's Richmond and 200 from Rich-
mond, Yorkshire, has lands in Sussex, and the part of the Duke of
Rutland's estate that marches with Devonshire's is in Derbyshire,
though most of the rest is in Nottinghamshire. The Duke of Portland,
whose old family seat is 200 miles both from the Bill of Portland and
Portland Square in London (though he owns the latter), lives in
London. And as we have mentioned, the Duke of Sutherland does
not own a single square inch of soil in the county of the same name.
That all passed to the heir general, the journalist's wife who is now
the Countess. Such is the mobility of the highest-ranking nobles that
even the Dukeries, that part of Nottinghamshire once stiff with
strawberry-leaf–wearing grandees, rates little mention: with the seventh
Duke of Portland dead, and Welbeck unduked, not a one lives there
now—the Scottish borders have replaced the dull fields of Nottinghamshire as the best-loved watering-hole for the finest specimens of the
breed.

Discounting the Duke of Fife, a somewhat anomalous dukedom
created because of Royal marriage, the string of extant Graces, from
that of Norfolk to that of Westminster, encompass 391 years' worth
of the grandest style of living history. We tend to think of our Dukes
as paramount rarities, splendid in title and fortune, supremely arrogant
and self-confident, strutting their great estates with an easy grace, gently
pursuing the vague interests of the fabulously idle rich. How true
that picture still is today can only be answered by looking at the
individuals more closely.

PART TWO

"What shall we do about your driver?" asked the Duke of Devonshire.
It said something about the courtly assumptions of the highly titled

* The title awarded to the Cavendish family was originally written as "Comes
Devon" (Comes meaning earl) and then, in 1694, when it was upgraded to a
dukedom, "Dux Devon." Realizing that this might lead to some confusion,
since there was already an Earl of Devon, the suffix "-shire" was later added "by
mutual consent." As to why Devonshire was not named Derbyshire—since
nearly all the Cavendish lands were in that county—that has never been fully
explained.

few that His Grace should assume that visitors to Chatsworth's inner sanctum all came chauffeur-driven. Sadly, though, it was all a mistake: I was driving a left-hand-drive car and Henry, the butler, helped me out of what most people would rightly assume was the passenger side. The shadowy figure glimpsed in the assumed driving side was, in fact, my wife.

"Oh gosh, I am so terribly sorry. So rude. How delightful to see you, my dear." (Henry had quite recovered his composure and had raced around the back of the car to let the lady out.) "What a most pleasant surprise. You will come inside won't you? And do stay for luncheon." To Henry: "Tell them we'll be three for luncheon." And that was that. No argument. No embarrassment. Perfect recovery. Faultless grace.

Andrew Robert Buxton Cavendish, PC, MC, the eleventh Duke of Devonshire, is said to be a snappy dresser, and photographs taken of him scurrying earnestly about as a government minister in the 1960s suggest he was a stickler for sartorial exactitude. Not any longer, however. Pictures of him in the journals of the horse world—the world that fascinates him most these days—show him in carelessly worn tweed jackets, mufflers and baggy trousers, precisely the way he was dressed when we met. All the buttons were on the jacket, but it had somewhat ragged sleeves; the Viyella shirt was comfortable, but had seen better days. The red polka-dotted neckerchief and the brown pullover, the scuffed suede shoes and the pale-beige corduroys, tousled and unpressed though they might have been, displayed the Duke precisely as he would like to be displayed: comfortable and relaxed, faintly academic, faintly bucolic, cultured, equipped with sufficient taste to carry the whole ensemble off in any surroundings, and ever so slightly dotty. The corduroys, as it happened, provided an excuse for him to tell a story.

They looked old, and probably were. They might well have been the very trousers he wore in the last war: it was the wearing of corduroy that brought the dukedom to him, and not to his elder brother, a tragedy and farce wrapped up together. Brother William, two years his senior and a worthy Marquess of Hartington (the Devonshire first courtesy title), who had married Kathleen Kennedy (of the American Presidential family) and seemed set for stardom, was a distinguished Major in the Coldstream Guards during the war. It became the custom for officers in the Eighth Army to wear corduroy trousers; and it became the custom for German snipers to weed out

British servicemen who wore the cloth, assuming that one in cords, being an officer, was worth ten in serge, being members of the other ranks. On 10 September 1944, a sniper acting on this assumption shot the Marquess of Hartington dead, instantly shifting the prospect of entitlement to brother Andrew, then serving in the Coldstream in Italy as a Captain. Andrew was summoned by his Commanding Officer. The news came, he said, as a total surprise; up to that moment he had been preoccupied with his own financial problems. The Devonshires were tough primogeniturists, and as second son coming to the end of a personally diversionary war, the difficulties of arranging a suitable peacetime future for himself with no fortune but noble name had been beginning to loom unpleasantly on his horizon. William's death, though a personal tragedy, lifted the load: where once he had a bleak future, now it was assured—though probably doubly difficult.

Three years before, while still a mere second son, Captain Lord Andrew Cavendish had been married to one of the five astonishingly talented Mitford girls, the daughters of the violently conservative Lord Redesdale, who is so horrifyingly caricatured in *The Pursuit of Love* by perhaps the most literate of his brilliant daughters, Nancy. How this creaking old autocrat and his weakly eccentric wife managed to bring up the rebellious and hugely funny group of girls is another tale altogether: Nancy became an accomplished writer, Jessica a sage observer of Americana, Unity a friend of Hitler and his circle, and Diana the wife of Sir Oswald Mosley—the last two both determined members of the British Union of Fascists. The baby of the gang, sweetest of all in the photographs, was Deborah, "Debo," with her pale-blue eyes and a haunted beauty. While the pubescent girls prayed nightly for their "Mr. Right" to come along, Debo yearned out loud that hers would be "the Duke of Right."

When in 1941 he did eventually come he was a mere Lord Andrew by courtesy: but soon the ghastly accident in Belgium ensured that her wish came true. Debo is still enchantingly lovely, and the couple, Duke and Duchess, are clearly, in an aristocratic world where marriage and divorce are taken far less formally than in the social horizons below, deeply fond of each other.

On this particular day the Duchess was away shooting, and the house was quiet and peaceful. The Duke seemed almost lonely, a little bored. His life certainly had been a good deal more active in the past than it is today.

After succeeding in 1950—he heard about his father's death while on a trip to Australia—he had to abandon his hopes of pursuing a political career in the House of Commons, even though it would of necessity have had to have been a brief one since peers were then firmly prohibited from sitting in the Commons. So his two attempts to win Chesterfield for the Tories, which had failed, were in vain anyway. In the Lords he was considerably more active than most of his fellows: during the mid-1950s, when attendance was well below 200, the Duke was there often: his interests were mainly in the field of foreign affairs (it was, he sneered, and as a consequence won some publicity, the membership of a "wicked canaille" who had suggested that "Israel attacked Egypt at our suggestion" at the time of the Suez crisis; strong inside-track rhetoric for the time). For two years in the early 1960s he was a junior Commonwealth Minister, and was promoted by his uncle, the then Prime Minister, to be Minister of State at the Commonwealth Relations Office and a man responsible for the final dismemberment of Empire. He represented the Prime Minister at President Kennedy's funeral and then, once the Tories were out of office, retired to the signal boxes of the Establishment to keep his mind going and his energies employed. He became Chairman of the Royal Commonwealth Society, Chairman of the St. Stephen's Club, Executive Steward of the Jockey Club. A racing, shooting and political peer, with interests in the City of London and a social life that was simultaneously glittering and restrained, Devonshire was one of the brightest stars on the ennobled scene—very much a sixties man, with impeccability stamped through him like a piece of that peculiarly British confection known as Brighton rock. Or Eastbourne rock, more suitably, since, as we shall see in a later chapter, he owns most of the town.

"I find my racehorses and my castles much more interesting than the House of Lords," he said once in 1969, when he was campaigning in a mild sort of way for the abolition of the Upper Chamber. His withdrawal from active politics began in the 1970s. He resigned from the Royal Commonwealth Society after voting in favour of sending arms to South Africa in 1971, left the Chesterfield Conservative Party bereft of a Cavendish leader for the first time in centuries after resigning from local politics, sold illuminated manuscripts to meet his bills, sacked eleven of the four hundred or so workers on the Cavendish estates in 1975 and, in his most unhappy setback, was ignominiously hounded by Labour members in the House of Commons for having the temerity to try and develop a yaching marina on the Sussex coast. Dennis Skinner, the perpetually angry Labour Member for Bolsover, went so far as to refer to the Duke—who was listening, seething with annoyance, from the galleries above—as a "benevolent despot." A Tory member interjected, asking the Speaker if it was in order to refer to members of the "other place" in such terms; the Deputy Speaker suggested that no, it wasn't, prompting Mr. Skinner to say that he was quite prepared to withdraw the word "benevolent."

All things considered, the 1970s were not so successful a time for the Duke as the 1960s had been, and one could hardly blame the tortoise for withdrawing his head under the comfort of his stately carapace—the windows of which had been finished in gold leaf in restorations in 1970—and to try to overlook the unpleasantness of an England hurtling towards Socialism. In the 1960s it was convenient for one writer to note that Devonshire sat at the centre of a vastly complicated genealogical network that firmly linked the Britain of the day with the America of the day: by blood or by marriage the Duke could count as relations the then Prime Minister, the Secretary of War, the Governor of the Bank of England, the proprietors of *The Times*, *Daily Mail* and *Observer*, the British Ambassador to Washington, the President of the United States and Fred Astaire. Virtually all those protagonists, save for David Astor at the *Observer*, have lost their empires, or their lives, and the world the Duke can see, should he take one of his splendidly successful racehorses up on to the moors above Chatsworth, is one in which he would now have precious little influence. One suspects, too, he has little interest now, and prefers to cultivate his interests as a Duke, rather than anything else.

Apart from his immense landholdings in Derbyshire and Yorkshire, he owns a great deal of the seaside resort of Eastbourne; Barrow-in-Furness, the industrial city of the Lake District; and a few houses in Carlisle. Oddly enough a house in which I spent many years in that last town was until recently part of the Duke's estates: Cavendish Terrace, one of a hundred British streets named after him. His landholdings alone probably make him worth about £33 million and his urban rent roll, or the capital value of his entire mass of brickwork, would probably double that fortune. And yet at Chatsworth he doesn't give the appearance of ownership: rightly so, since in fact he pays rent for his quarters in the big house, and is a tenant of his estate's company. Not an unusual arrangement, and one that, ignominious though it may sound, helps meet the inevitably gigantic tax bill.

"But I am very much against the rich pleading poverty, you know. It is a habit some of the landowners have fallen into. I am a rich man, there's no doubt about it. But I could be richer. I could sell up and invest overseas; I could live overseas. The fact that I don't says something about my feeling for this place."

He sits in a study crammed with stud books and newly bought pictures and deep leather armchairs. A silver tray on one desk is littered with bottles: the inevitable gins and Rawlings tonic water, but some good whiskies (Famous Grouse the principal blend) and some excellent malts from Campbeltown and Speyside. There was soda water, but the bottled Malvern spring water was upstairs: he did not ring for Henry or one of the footmen to bring the water, but rushed upstairs, all flapping tweeds and perspiration, and returned five minutes later, triumphant, with a jug in his hands. Such staff as he has, receive, it appears, the most elegantly polite treatment. His secretary at Chatsworth is called Patience, and he speaks of her as gently as one of that name deserves.

There are all sorts of oddities in his house that he loves to point out. One door of the study, and several in libraries upstairs, are false sets of bookshelves, such that when closed the room is all books and windows, an unspoiled panorama of leather, gold and vistas of parkland. The trick of the old library masters was to indicate the location of the doorway by a series of urbane literary puns. Thus, the false books on the door have titles that ring oddly true, but only oddly: "*Dipsomania*, by Mustafa Swig"; "*The Open Kimono*, by Seymour Hair"; and a set of Johnsonian travels across the Western Isles with titles like "*Skye*, by McCleod." Not all are puns: some, like "*Homer's Craniology of the Pygmies*," are just plain silly.

It is in this cramped old study, surrounded by books by Rudyard Peddling and Hoo Flung Dung, by bottles of Grouse and lists of horses at his stud farms, and with great Brontë-esque views of Pennine hills sweeping away to the north, that the Duke likes to live. He writes: his book on Park Top, his best-loved and most successful racehorse, did well in the racing circles in which he was well known. He performs his functions as Chancellor of Manchester University— which consists principally of writing letters—and he worries about the future of Chatsworth, which loses £100,000 a year, even though it has been open to the public for two centuries and is one of the most famous of the nation's great houses.

"But my problems are really voluntary ones. I could duck them all if I wanted to. It is very unbecoming to complain. Our losses here are very substantial; the new taxes are making life very difficult for the big landowners. And yet I believe passionately that what I am doing here in Derbyshire is important for the people and for the county. I have a duty to see things are not changed too violently." Why, one wondered, did he take that duty so seriously, especially since there was a possibility that public disapprobation of the titled, privileged and wealthy minority might become too strong for comfort?

"Frankly, I like it. My family has been here for a long time [Chatsworth first sported a grand house for the Cavendishes in 1552; the present house, built under the personal supervision of an enthusiastic first Duke, is three centuries old]. I don't think I ought to take the step of changing the family habits of so great an age. In sum, I live here for quite selfish reasons. The duty is always there at the back of my mind, but what prevents me pushing off to the Bahamas or somewhere like that is that a man could hardly want for anything more pleasant than to be able to live in this perfectly lovely house in this wonderful park, in England. A man like me, anyway."

Besides, he did have responsibilities to people. The Chatsworth Estates looked after about 400 people including present employees, former employees, relations and old-age pensioners. It is not difficult to find stories of injustice and feudal cruelty on almost any large estate,* but Andrew Devonshire tries to take pride in the very low degree of criticism from his tenants, or from his employees, past and present. Patience was asked to run up a list of the number of employees as of January 1977, and came up with figures to show that 133 people were employed by the Duke in Derbyshire alone; 102 of these were married, and an additional 76 children were believed to belong to the various families. Of the employees, 86 had houses provided by the estates, free of rent (though the weekly wage was doctored to account for the provision of the housing, as one would expect). Of the people living on the estates 109 were counted as old-age pensioners, and of these, 90 were given houses—houses which, like Albert Hodkin's Brook Cottage in Beeley, cost about a pound a week in rent. In

* It is perhaps fair to remark that in all my travels across the landed estates of England and Scotland I did not come across one example of feudal cruelty. The press in Britain insists, though, that it occurs.

addition there were 111 farm tenants, who paid the Duke rent for buildings and land, and made what they could of the acreage for themselves. In Derbyshire alone there are three post offices, two pubs, the Cavendish Hotel, a mountaineering club, a pottery, a smithy, two schools and two shops all operating in cottages and houses owned by the Duke. It seemed, as he suggested, a considerable responsibility: "More than the average factory owner. And I think the people we house here are happier and more secure. It's a country life. They are taken care of by the Estates from the moment they are born until the day they die. They feel great affection for the land and the estates, and I don't in all honesty think that's an exaggeration.

"You know, I was on the BBC, the wireless, the other day, and I made a mistake. I told the interviewer I supposed I felt guilty having all this land and all this wealth and all these people working for me. Well, I thought about it coming home that night, and I don't think I ought to feel any guilt at all. I've done nothing wrong. I inherited a property, and I am doing my best with it. A great number of people benefit—and yet we are attacked nowadays to such an extent that I tell people that I feel guilty. Well, I don't. I should never have said any such thing. It was an accident of birth, that's all." And remembering Hartington, and the German sniper, an accident of death besides.

Luncheon was a marvel of simple felicity. A small round table in a long gold-and-white room, half shut off with a black lacquered screen to keep us warm. The room itself had a Rubens portrait of Philip II of Spain (a copy of the Titian), paintings by Cornelius Johnson, Giovane, Coello and Hans Eworth, as well as a vast portrait of the founder of the Grenadier Guards that, to the probable rage of some purists, had been cut in half by the Duke so the bottom six feet could swing away to reveal a hidden lift to the kitchens. There was something rather disturbing in seeing a pair of elegantly turned seventeenth-century boots and a sword swinging to and fro as the door opened and closed, but since "the servants would take about three minutes bringing the food upstairs until we put in the lift," it seemed eminently reasonable to halve the poor man. Since so many of the good general's contemporaries had been quartered, and in the flesh, not on canvas, it seemed an appropriate fate, anyway.

Henry the butler and a footman, who made not the slightest of sounds, stood behind the white, gold and red scrolled chairs, sliding them back under your knees so that, like Queen Victoria, there was absolutely no need at all to look behind to make sure you would not fall on the floor. You walked between chair and table and moved downwards to sit in precisely the position where you wanted to eat, and, magically, there was something below you to sit on. It took a little while, dining at various ennobled households, to win your self-confidence; but sitting without looking for the chair is regarded as a peculiarly British mark of assuredness: observers at operas tended to notice how lesser Queens glanced around to make sure the footmen were doing their job. But Queen Victoria always knew, and so do guests at Chatsworth.

The food was simple and unaffected. A plain vegetable soup, a game bird and fresh vegetables, pears from the estate orchard steeped in red wine and offered with thick cream. It was the little details that marked the table out from the normal groaning boards: pepper and salt holders, solid silver, were at each setting, giving the idea that the communal containers were very much an invention of middle-class expediency. The knives were incredibly sharp: their razor edges sliced chunks of the tinily muscled birds away as if they were fashioned from marzipan. Coffee was offered in a manner peculiar, it seemed, to the great houses: a footman handed a cup, a jug of cream and containers of white and brown sugar before any mention was made of coffee itself. You took the cream and poured it into the cup, and the coffee was poured from behind a few seconds later: it was easy to stumble over the unfamiliar procedure—though without a doubt many coffee drinkers will have engaged in that precise ritual all their lives, and find it unworthy of any remark at all.

The Blue Drawing Room, where the family relaxes each evening, would be almost chintzy in its cosiness, were it not for the splendid Reynolds and Canaletto, the Battoni and the Sargent on the light-blue silk wallpaper that gave the room its name. Only over the door is there a touch of modernity: half a dozen portraits by Lucien Freud, whom the present Duke regards as an artist worthy of his patronage and who, in consequence, is enjoying success that might not have come so easily. Artistic patronage seems less of a hobby of present peers than is artistic collection (or disposal, since so many paintings have to go on the market to settle death-duty bills; one of Devonshire's Poussins was sold in 1981 for nearly £2 million), but the Duke believes it should be another part of *noblesse oblige*, one to which he gladly subscribes.

He is a shy man, in the sense that he appears glad to have his opinions sought and diffident in the manner by which he offers them. One imagines he abhors loud and tasteless behaviour, but is not wholly intolerant of it. He is not as rigidly conservative as so many of his colleagues are supposed to be: he voted for the abolition of hanging; he doesn't hunt, though has no disapproval of those who do. His letters are models of urbanity: one recent brief note from him has phrases and words that exemplify studied gentility: "thank you so much," "charming," "quite enormously," "do be good enough," "delightful," "warm regards," "yours ever." He signs himself "Devonshire" until he gets to know you, then "Andrew Devonshire."

As we shall explore later, there is much to be said for and against the ownership of land and wealth on the scale of a man like the Duke of Devonshire. Many find his notions of feudalism* unpalatable, and his vast fortunes indefensible. Cynics will say that the tenants and workers are in fact unhappy, and that they are afraid to speak out for fear of being turfed out. All this may be true, though at first and second examination it does not appear to be so. What remains undeniable is that, if all peers and privileged nobility are bad, those behaving like the Duke of Devonshire are probably the least bad; and if they are good, then men like the inhabitant of present-day Chatsworth are quite certainly among the best.

In the realms of Cotswold Gloucestershire are the 52,000 acres of Badminton Estates, the Duke of Beaufort's principal landholding. Sir Henry Hugh Arthur Fitzroy Somerset, KG, PC, GCVO, the tenth Duke, is principally distinguished for his close friendship with the Royal Family, with all the concomitant advantages that brings, and the steadfast maintenance of his position as the Greatest Huntsman in England.

Arguments for and against foxhunting rage with extraordinary passion across the British Isles. It is arguable that more temper is wasted discussing the methods of controlling the island's fox population than in debating the rights of the elderly or the very poor: certainly people are angered more by hunting than by hereditary privilege. The Duke, the pre-eminent practitioner of the sport, is thus regarded as the arch-villain of the piece by those enrolled in the League Against Cruel Sports, and like bodies. The League certainly has done

* The true meaning of "feudalism" is a hereditary security of tenure with rights that are specifically coupled with duties, on both sides of the bargain. Strict feudalism was abolished in England by the Statute Quia Emptores in the thirteenth century.

its cause precious little good in recent years: its extreme methods and its attraction of hooligans who merely enjoy participating in the disruptive japes used to foil huntsmen have turned much public opinion, previously on the side of the fox, very much into no man's land.

For a man with two essentially domestic interests—the horse and his land—the Duke has been the recipient of a quite extraordinary number of other titles, and legions of colourful foreign orders. No doubt his membership of the Royal Family by virtue of his marriage to the late Queen Mary's niece (he was also for forty-two years a Great Officer of the Royal Household as Master of the Horse, with precedence over all other Dukes)* played some small part in his harvest of the European glitter. As for titles recognized on the British scene, this sole descendant of the Plantagenets (he can trace his line back to John of Gaunt, no less) is also the Marquess and Earl of Worcester, Lord Botetourt, Lord Herbert de Herbert and Baron Herbert of Raglan, Chepstow and Gower. He holds any number of local dignities: he has been Lord Lieutenant—the Monarch's representative—in Gloucestershire and Bristol since 1931; he holds the Royal Victorian Chain, a truly splendid gift from the Throne; he has been Lord High Steward of Bristol, Gloucester and Tewkesbury, Hereditary Keeper of Raglan Castle . . . the list goes on almost without end. So far as foreign orders are concerned he has that of Leopold, Faithful Service, House of Orange, St. Olav, Dannebrog, North Star, Menelik II and Christ, ensuring him free dinners at the embassies of Belgium, Holland, Norway, Denmark, Ethiopia and Portugal;† and he is one of the few Knight Grand Commanders of the Royal Victorian Order—an award handed out by the Queen to her personal favourites at Court. An immodest amount of international decoration, one might think, for a man with a record of essentially British, and bucolic, achievement.

The Duke's reputation rests on his ability as a huntsman, and his family's prowess in the field for the past several generations. His Bentley, as is well known, has the initials MFH 1—which prompted the owner of the car registered FOX 1 to write to the Duke via the

* The Master of the Horse has overall responsibilities for the Royal Household "out of doors," and so includes all transport on State Visits by foreign Heads of State.

† It is said that the Order of Kutusov, First Class, entitled the holder to free travel on the Moscow Underground Railway; the honours given to the Duke of Beaufort do not, literally, permit him to dine at foreign embassies.

columns of *The Times*, asking, jokingly, to be assured that there
would be no "unseemly incident" should the two vehicles meet. The
Duke, whose public sense of humour is a little limited, dismissed the
letter by pointing out that his Hunt went nowhere near the factory
that owned the car. The Hunt, while still massive and impressive—
rarely more so than in the days when Beaufort would ride at the head
of it on a frosty Cotswold morning—has been badly hurt by the
construction of the South Wales motorway; the construction of motor-
ways often places conservationists firmly on the same side as huntsmen like Beaufort, which perhaps makes for an uncomfortable
partnership.

The Duke is neither an ardent conservationist nor a man
generally happy to ally himself with those who dislike his chosen sport:
he is, in truth, something of a loner, a man who gains his support
from local ruddy-faced farmers and those from farther afield who
would be followers of the hunt. All of which is not to sneer at the
Duke or his kind: it is simply to note that he presents an advertisement for ducal attitudes which is at considerable variance from that
presented by, say, a man like the Duke of Devonshire. While Andrew
Devonshire is a lover of elegance and wit, art and intellect, politics
and responsibility; "Master" (for hunting) Beaufort would not disagree with a thumb-nail sketch of himself as an ebullient sportsman
with little time for the effete in whose company Devonshire would
feel quite happy. If Devonshire's friends would tend to be political
dandies, Beaufort's would be the horsey members of the county set.
Each man believes, no doubt, that his contribution to the British
scene is the right one; since public opinion is starting to matter now,
when the question of the hereditary nobility's survival is concerned,
it might not be too reckless to suppose that it could well be the
Devonshires of this land to whom the public at large might be more
kindly disposed.

The Duke of Beaufort, though, has the Queen. Her Majesty, a
faithful patron of the county set, is a regular visitor to Badminton at
the time of the famous Three-Day Event, held each April. And there
is no denying that the occasion is a stylish and remarkably beautiful
happening, held in the magnificent grounds of one of the country's
most elegant Palladian houses. While playing host to Her Majesty
the Duke is as punctilious as a Royal Servant, a model of monarchical
rectitude. In 1957 he was purple with rage when he found that the
Royal Standard which normally flies from the Badminton flagstaff

when the Queen is in residence was missing: a functionary had forgotten to send it down. A new standard was placed on the next down express, which stopped at the railway station that a former Duke had insisted be built by the Great Western Railway Company as part of the price for being allowed to bring iron horses, rather than real ones, across the land. The standard was fluttering from the staff by the time the crowds had gathered for the first day of the Event, and all was well. Should the mistake occur again the Duke may not be so lucky: Badminton station was closed down in 1968 by British Rail, who found the luxury provided for the Duke and his family by the taxpayer just a little hard to swallow. His Grace put up a mighty battle with the railway chiefs, but lost, to his lasting fury.

The Duke and Duchess, she a descendant of George III, a niece of the late Queen Mary, live alone at Badminton, except for the servants and a pet parrot called George. They have not had children, and the heir is therefore his close cousin, born in 1928. Since the Duke, though a fit man and the survivor of innumerable hunting accidents that would have put paid to lesser mortals, is now over eighty it must be presumed that the end of this extraordinarily lengthy ducal tenancy is in sight. For more than half a century this robust Nimrod has presided from the halls of Badminton: one cannot help but wonder whether his successor, the eleventh Duke of Beaufort, will fit more easily into an era and a society that is perhaps less tolerant of the nobility than it was when "Master" Beaufort assumed his robes and coronet in 1924.

One dull March day in 1971, the Conservative Member of Parliament for Edinburgh North, an indubitably Scottish-looking countryman known to his friends and foes alike as "Johnnie Dalkeith," was riding his hunter out on the low hills near Selkirk when suddenly his horse stumbled. "I remember pitching over and down on to the grass, and then the horse fell on top of me. There was a sharp cracking sound from behind me, and I could not feel my legs or my feet. I knew I had broken my back. There could be no doubt of it."

He lay there for fifteen minutes. "The moment I realized what I had done I tried to adjust mentally to what lay ahead. I thought to myself: your life is going to be totally changed—wheelchairs, walking sticks, no driving, no politics maybe; you'd better come to accept that pretty quickly. And after five minutes' thinking along those lines I decided there was not much else I could do but come to terms with the new facts. Then I lay back on the grass and had ten minutes of quiet blissful peace, before they found me and carried me off."

The idyll ended when other, more distraught members of the Hunt found the injured Dalkeith, lifted him on to a five-barred gate and carried him off to hospital, where he stayed for the next month— cheering himself up a bit by giving up smoking. The convalescence lasted through most of that summer, and by October the Member for Edinburgh North was being wheeled back up the Tory aisles in the House of Commons. "Splendid chap, splendid chap," murmured the Member of Fife Central and patted Dalkeith on the shoulder as he was rolled past.

It is not easy to decide which is more remarkable: the total sang-froid of the burly Dalkeith during those agonizing moments on the Selkirk turf; or the greeting from the Member from Fife Central. Perhaps the latter—since the Member concerned was the scourge of the nation's titled rich, Mr. Willie Hamilton, and "Johnnie Dalkeith" was more accurately known as the Earl of Dalkeith, heir to two of the grandest dukedoms in the nation, those of Buccleuch and Queensberry. But in fact Willie Hamilton, though he would have all Dukes burned at the stake, the blaze tindered by Monarchs and fuelled by a mixture of all the other ranks of peerage, would probably make an exception for the man who, in 1971, was Johnnie Dalkeith. Without a doubt he is an exceptional man, a member of one of Scotland's greatest and most reputable families.

The discomfort of appearing, chairbound, in the House of Commons, was only going to last for a further two years. In 1973, the eighth Duke of Buccleuch died, leaving Dalkeith to change his name and assume the ducal robes—and assume a responsibility for the greatest amount of land held by any individual in all Europe.* More than a quarter of a million acres of England and Scotland come under the direct control of the Buccleuchs, together with a clutch of some of the most beautiful architectural treasures in the land, and a collection of paintings and furniture to rival any collection on the face of the earth. The Duke of Buccleuch is the owner of the only Leonardo da Vinci painting in private hands, and presides over an empire which, by and large, is the only private suzerainty that has not been forced to make accommodation with the attitudes of this century.

---

* Experts say the latifundia of the Duchess of Alba are larger than the estates of the Duke of Buccleuch.

To enter the world of the Dukes of Buccleuch is to experience the ennobled life on a high plateau of privilege and excellence, far from the arguments and political manoeuvres that have torn so many lesser holdings assunder.

A century ago the fifth Duke had more houses than any other Briton: of the grander estates he owned Drumlanrig Castle, Dalkeith Palace, Bowhill, Eildon Hall, Branxholm Hall, Boughton House, Beaulieu Abbey, Dunchuel House, Cawston Hall, Ditton House, Montagu House in Whitehall and "a villa on the Thames near Richmond." The present Duke has only a few less than this impressive array: of the Scottish castles and halls, Dalkeith is loaned to a computer company and the others form part of the estates; the three grandest are still kept ready for the Duke and his entourage. In fact he stays at each of the three for four months in each year; from January to April he is at Bowhill, near Selkirk; for the summer he is at Boughton, in Northamptonshire; and for the autumn he is at the magnificent pink fantasy of Drumlanrig Castle, near Dumfries. A perfectly organized logistical machine transports the family from caravanserai to caravanserai with the minimum of fuss and bother: only the Leonardo travels with them. In the houses, incomparable collections of paintings, furniture and treasure remain to delight the Duke and Duchess—and members of the public who, in 1976, were first permitted access to the homes of this most private of men. That visitors are being allowed through the gates is one small sign that the plateau's edge is coming into view and that it may not be for long that the fortunes of this remarkable family will be able to survive unscathed: but, public or no, the world of this Duke is still quite unlike that of any other.

At Bowhill, probably the least attractive of the Buccleuch mansions, it had been snowing hard. The house squatted humourlessly on the hillside above the Ettrick Water, grey and Manderley-like against the white fields. On the winding, gravelled drive up to the front door a party of guns strolled by—businessmen from Edinburgh, down for a day's shooting in woods that have provided good sport since the earliest days of the realm. Indeed, it was somewhere deep in the Ettrick Forest that the name by which the Duke is principally known had its origins: a man named Scott, acting as a hunting ranger for the King of Scotland, seized a cornered buck by the antlers after it had turned on his master's hounds, and threw it over his shoulders into a deep ravine, a "cleuch." The ravine came to be known as the Buckcleuch, and Scott was awarded a regional appendage to his clan name—Scott of Buccleuch. The land around the Ettrick Water has remained with the Scotts ever since, and the first house was constructed on the site of the present Bowhill early in the eighteenth century. What glowers across the valley now, a house disliked more than a little by the present Duke and his son, the new Earl of Dalkeith, is a structure that dates from the beginning of the nineteenth century —a time when many asylums were constructed along very similar lines.

The first sign of the Duke's present infirmity comes at the front door of Bowhill. Two wooden runners, built to take the wheels of his electrically motorized chair, slope out on to the driveway so that the Duke can cruise around the gardens or take to his car. He likes to drive a curious eight-wheeled vehicle known as an "Argocat" when touring his estates. It is advertised as a "go-anywhere" car, ideal for foresters, keepers and stalkers; the Duke, like his father, is not a man to stand on ceremony and happily churns around the mud and bog of his lands in a vehicle that would normally suit only ducal employees. But he does drive a normal car—a hand-controlled Mini; his only concession to his injury is a red flag he keeps in the glove compartment. "If I break down I hang it out and someone is sure to stop and see what's the matter. Anyway, I'm fairly well known around here."

After the Polish butler—the old Duke's valet and chauffeur, kept on out of affection and, coincidentally, to reinforce the Duke's arguments about landownership (85 per cent of Polish land is still in private ownership, he likes to say, nodding to the butler for agreement)—ushers visitors into the library, there is a faint, distant humming and His Grace appears, expertly managing the electric wheelchair that has been his daytime home for the past ten years. He insists on steering his way through the labyrinthine house himself: the chair is just slim enough to pass through doors, but opening and closing them can be a nuisance. Up to the door, hold handle and turn, put chair into reverse, scoot back holding door, stop, release door, into forward gear, grab door handle on way through, pull door behind, close it and proceed. Other men might have legions of liveried flunkies to perform the task: it says something for the way the present Duke was reared that he does it all himself, insisting that he must.

He is an imposing figure still, tough and spartan, with a long sail of a nose and thinning sandy hair. He dresses smartly in Pringle pullovers and pressed twill slacks, eschewing any temptation to sink into a quite excusable chairbound untidiness. He insists, even though it must be dreadfully tiring, on showing a visitor everything in his house. The Leonardo, of course, first of all: *The Madonna and the Yarnwinder*, a tiny, exquisite beauty on a stand away on its own; splendid Reynolds portraits, including the quite priceless portrait of Elizabeth, Duchess of Montagu, which would be the last painting to go if a sudden decline in the family fortunes led to a wholesale disposal of the treasures; Gainsborough, Claude Lorrain; an intricate painting of Whitehall by Canaletto and several scenes of Venice by his contemporary, Guardi. He loves, he says, the treasures in his houses, lending them quite liberally to museums and art galleries across the world and delighting in his decision, taken comparatively recently, to allow people to walk through his properties.

If the art collection were not enough, the French furniture amassed at Bowhill and the two other houses is the envy of the world. Disputes arose early in 1977 with the news that Lord Rosebery was being forced to sell the entire estate and contents of his house, Mentmore, near Leighton Buzzard—contents that were said to include one of the finest collections of French furniture in Britain. One suspects that the laziness of journalists, easily able to travel to Mentmore and back in an afternoon from their offices in Fleet Street, had much to do with the sympathetic press treatment the Roseberys received for their case. The suggestion that the nation would "lose" a priceless hoard of fine furniture might have become somewhat less strident had anyone cared to point out that the Buccleuch collection, incomparably finer than not only Rosebery's, but also that in the Louvre, was likely to stay in Britain for generations to come. So the Louis XIV Boulle commode, the Louis XV kingwood writing tables, the ancient Boucher clocks, the Aubusson tapestry-covered chairs, the jardinières and the marquetry card tables, the Meissen (from Saxony) and the Cary globes—all will stay at Bowhill, thanks largely to the financial foresight of the Duke's father; when he died in 1973 the Government was deprived of £10 million in death duties.

In great houses it is invariably a single object that strikes the visitor as truly remarkable, rather than a mighty collection or a display of special charm. At Chatsworth many are struck by the witty *trompe-l'œil* violin, which appears to hang behind a door in one of the music rooms but is actually painted on it. At Bowhill one comes away haunted by memories of one of the most magnificent pieces of silver ever created. It is a great cistern—or wine cooler—standing foursquare on a plinth carved from a solid block of coal from one of the Duke's mines at Dalkeith; from handle to ornately carved handle (both in the shape of rearing horses) the brute measures nearly five feet; it has the arms of the Duke of Argyll carved inside on the base. It is solid silver, with a 1711 hallmark and fashioned by one Benjamin Pyne. And it weighs no less than 130 pounds—more than nine stone of exquisitely carved silver, once gracing the British Ambassador's residence in Madrid, and worth more than the elusive fortune earlier granted by King Charles I to the then Argyll in the form of what is still supposed by many fortune hunters to be in the treasure chest of a great galleon lost beneath the swirling water of the Western Isles. "I think before all those divers go down looking for the Argyll treasures," says the Duke, "they ought to come over to Bowhill."

The Duke, presiding from the very pinnacle of privilege, has taken a great deal of criticism from the press in the past, and dislikes giving interviews. He is thus little known outside the immediate policies of his great estates, and prefers to keep things that way. He takes those few meetings he has with outsiders very seriously indeed: he had prepared four pages of notes, in a neat and elegant hand, for our long-sought encounter. They are worth quoting in full, since they indicate the defensive attitudes struck by even the most confident of the nobility.

"There is a tendency abroad to think of the existence of the Dukes and Earls, with their large estates, as politically divisive and likely to lead to Communism. Yet the experience is in fact the reverse. It is in a community where there are more Dukes and Marquesses and Earls per square mile than anywhere that you find the fewest Socialists. You really have to look for them here in the Scottish borders. On the other hand in areas where there are no Dukes and aristocrats with estates are fewest—the central belt—the Socialists and Communists thrive.

"This theory is amplified by personal experience of political door-step campaigning over fourteen years and four elections—not in the lush pastures of the countryside but in a City that then contained some of Europe's worst slums. I think it was accepted that I was less suspect than many of seeking to feather my own nest: perhaps because it was already well enough feathered, but more important because it was clear that I fought Socialism by trying to eradicate the root causes of Socialism—deprivation, slums, lack of opportunity and the many sufferings contributing to discontent.

"There is a popular misconception that the aristocracy all live on huge estates devoting every minute to 'huntin', shootin' and fishin'.' Far from it—although sport is an important part of estate life, it is more normally a highly organized activity rented out to syndicates on a commercial basis.

"Because land is so limited and population so huge, landowning is a most serious business of making the best use of the land, and ensuring multiple use of it. Unlike any other business it has a very long-term nature: fertility, flocks and herds are a lifetime interest, crops of trees anything from forty to one hundred and forty years or more. Planting high-quality oak, ash or beech needs extremely long-term planning and continuity spanning several generations: this is crucial to success. Likewise estates with groups of farms are better placed than single owner-occupied farm units to tackle problems of multiple land use—that is to say, the harmonizing of the often conflicting interests of farming, forestry, conservation, landscape protection, public recreation and amenity and sport can all best be blended in one well-run and managed estate. I would go as far as to say that the comprehensive and balanced development of the countryside is only possible with the large estates like this.

"Perhaps I am the only Duke to have served incognito as an ordinary seaman on the lower deck of a destroyer on active service in wartime, to have been elected four times and to have escorted Ava Gardner to a ball."

(He did not actually mention those last facts in conversation.)

Talk was a total defence of the propriety of mighty landownership along much the same lines as outlined in his notes: Dukes keep out Socialists, are possessed of the long-term view essential to the best development of the British countryside and are, like Guinness (the family of which has, naturally, been ennobled too), Good For You. And it is a remarkable fact that, since Tolpuddle and the Luddites and the Captain Swing riots, there have been precious few disturbances in the rural fastnesses of Great Britain—the fastnesses of the Dukes and Marquesses, Earls and Viscounts, and the lowly Barons all. Landed nobility is essentially an immovable object, and yet the areas of the country well settled by peers—Wiltshire, Perthshire, the Scottish Borders and rural Oxfordshire—are regions without strong Socialist movements, despite the temptation that the resident squires and lairds have presented for so long.

Why does the International Socialist Movement not blockade Bow-

hill, pillage Drumlanrig or kidnap the Duchess? How, in so rapidly
changing a society, can a vastly wealthy Duke drive alone in the
Scottish countryside with perfect impunity, assured in the knowledge
that no one would want to waylay him with arguments, or worse,
about the evils of the system he supposedly represents? Is it that
the British are unusually tolerant of their Tsars? Are they ignorant of
their existence? Or do they know that, so far as the bucolic denizens
of Perthshire and Wiltshire, the Borders and Oxfordshire are concerned, the sound of protest would be quickly and effectively stilled?
And if the answer is the latter—why? Does the Duke of Devonshire
so satisfy his workers and his tenants that they will happily vote Tory
year after year to preserve that status quo—one in which they own no
land, pay fealty, know their standing, observe the niceties of feudalism,
touch their forelocks when necessary and, like Albert Hodkin, refer to
"His Grace" or "Her Grace" as naturally as they might say "Father"
or "Mum"? Why do the people admire the Duke of Buccleuch—why
tolerate him still, bearing in mind he can command a fortune at a
flick of his fingers that the inhabitants of five and a half villages* in
his ownership could not raise in a lifetime? The questions are disturbing, and go to the heart of the debate that smoulders beneath all
discussion over the question of the future of nobility, entitlement and
privilege. We will return to them again.

The Duke of Buccleuch is not a frequent attender at the House
of Lords—and he is not one of those who would be likely to be
tempted by the 1980 increase in allowances for those peers who have
to stay overnight in London, an attempt to persuade the farther-
flung members to attend more regularly. Not only is he an infrequent
attender: he actually believes the hereditary right to legislate is "indefensible." He does not wonder why the institution is attacked, and
cannot rise with particular sincerity to defend it. Having said that,
however, he pressed an article from that day's *Scotsman* into my hand
—an article that said, in passing:

"I feel quite happy with the way things are in the Lords. A blood
test tempered by nomination seems to me to produce a highly satisfactory mix. There is nothing to convince me that the ballot is any
more likely than birth to produce the right man for the job."

* They are all in Northamptonshire: Wheatley, Warkton, Grafton Under-
wood, Little Oakley, Newton and half of Gaddington. More than 200 houses
are run by this department of Buccleuch Estates Ltd., the company the present
Duke's father set up in 1923.

One felt he wanted to say that, but being a man who now steers adroitly away from those high waters of controversy he enjoyed as an MP, now felt he ought not to. An example, one suspects, of the delicate art of compromise which has helped the peerage maintain its role in Britain—if it's politically unwise to say so, then keep your mouth closed! "I hate making speeches now, from this sort of pedestal, anyway, I'm all for lobbying behind the scenes. It is far more effective, and it doesn't activate the opposition!" Not surprisingly the Duke is an active participant in the Twenty-Five Invisibles, and follows the meetings in London with extreme concern. His factor, the Honourable James Galbraith (son of an ennobled doctor-politician, Lord Strathclyde), is a prominent Invisible, steering the proceedings at 53 Davies Street with all the power that a quarter of a million acres, five and a half villages and innumerable farms can muster.

Landownership brings in its train all sorts of curious responsibilities and perks, of which the Duke of Buccleuch is a keen recipient: one is the entitlement to be paid the "Wroth Silver" by the twenty-eight parishes in the Hundred of Knightlow, in Warwickshire. The ceremony, performed every Martinmas Day for many centuries, involves the payment of but a few pennies to the Duke; but should anyone default—no one ever has, records say—then he has to pay a pound for every penny the Duke is short or, if that proves too onerous a task, provide the Duke with a white bull with red ears and a red nose. Bowhill is not, however, host to any peculiar herd of cattle—unlike Chillingham Castle, a few miles away over the Cheviots in Northumberland. There the seat of the Earls of Tankerville boasts the sole remaining herd of wild white cattle in the British Isles*—but not the Earl, sad to say. He lives in San Francisco.

The Duke, who married in 1953—breaking the precedent of generations of Buccleuchs by marrying completely outside the nobility, though into the distinguished Western Islands chieftainly family of McNeill—is well endowed with heirs: Richard, the Earl of Dalkeith, can expect to rise to the dukedom one day. When he does it will no doubt be a sobering thought that, as well as having to take charge of the grandest estates, the finest collections and the noblest houses in Europe, he will also assume a bewildering variety of titles. He will become Marquess of Dumfriesshire, Earl of Buccleuch, Dalkeith,

---

* The Duke of Hamilton is preserving an equivalent strain of Cadzow White cattle at Lennoxlove.

Drumlanrig and Sanquhar, Viscount of Nith, Torthorwald and Ross, Lord Scott of Buccleuch, Whitchester and Eskdale, Lord Douglas of Kinmont, Middlebie and Dornock, in Scotland; Earl of Doncaster and Baron Scott of Tindall, in England. (Sir Iain Moncrieff, as Albany Herald, had to recite this intimidating list from memory at the old Duke's funeral in 1973—a task he performed with nary a single slip.) He will also be entitled to add his supporters to one of the richest and most impressive coats of arms to be seen—and one that tells the significant details of the dukedom's origins. The coat of arms is quartered, with the arms of King Charles II in the upper left-hand setting. The Caroline arms are, of course, similar to the present Royal coat of arms, except for the inclusion of the French fleur-de-lis in two of the quarterings. But the Buccleuch quarter has a narrow white band running across it from upper right to lower left: it has been "debruised," as the heraldic jargon has it, "by a baton sinister argent": the historic representation that the offspring awarded the particular quarter was the "natural child" of Charles II—"children of the mist" of that libidinous monarch ending up the holders of no fewer than four of the dukedoms existing today. To sport a baton sinister over a Caroline coat of arms, as do the Dukes of St. Albans and Grafton, or a brodure company, like the Duke of Richmond, is regarded now as the highest of honours. "Grace by the Grace of such mothers," Swinburne wrote, "as brightened the bed of King Charles."

The supporters to the arms of the eighth Duke of Buccleuch were two women "richly attired in antique habits, vert, their under-robes azure, the uppermost argent, and upon their heads plumes of three ostrich feathers of the last." The present Duke's supporters have conducted some heraldic striptease, presumably with the Lord Lyon's approval, and now stand tantalizingly half-naked: "two female figures, habited from the waist downwards, in blue kirtles gathered up at the knees, the arms and bosoms uncovered, around the shoulders flowing mantles vert, suspended by the exterior hand." It is not, one gathers, that the present Duke is in any way an admirer of cheerful vulgarity— he decided against calling the outfit running his houses "Buccleuch Recreational Activities" because of the slightly rude acronym, and dropped his vague plans for forming a "National Union of Dukes and Earls" for much the same reason. But precisely why the supporters lost a few of their antique habits vert, and whether we will soon see more of their under-robes azure, or, heaven forfend, their blue kirtles gathered up unto the thighs is not yet known. Richard Dalkeith is a sensible young man, given to the cold-bath regimen of the English public school and unlikely to want to disrobe his ladies for any other than the very best of reasons—so we may all end up disappointed.

Finally, we should place matters in perspective by noting that the Dukes of Buccleuch have not always been the grandest in Europe. A Prince of the Austrian Esterhazys once met a Duke of Buccleuch in London, at Court, and was told by the Duke that there were a good five thousand sheep on the latter's estates. "How odd!" replied the Prince. "That is exactly the number of shepherds I have." Today the Esterhazys are bereft of their old influence;* the Buccleuchs are not. Still, one suspects they are doing their best to be careful: they all remember the fate that befell their ancestor, the first Duke of Monmouth (a dukedom to which the Buccleuchs are, in theory, entitled). He fell foul of the Monarch of the day and was executed—with a blunt axe. Three times the axeman tried, failing each time to sever the neck of the nobleman. Finally, to spare the agonies of the Duke, the executioner performed the attainment with a knife. Monmouth's saddle and spurs, his shirt and cap are still at Bowhill—the saddle on a life-size horse moulded from plastic. The Dukes of Buccleuch and Queensberry are not ones to forget their ancestry, and appear to be bent on sparing themselves from the creeping evils of Socialism in the manner that Monmouth so sadly failed to do in the time of James II.

PART THREE

The trial of Patricia Hearst, who was accused of co-operating with her terrorist captors in carrying out a bank robbery in California in 1974, was a costly affair. America's highest-priced lawyer took the brief in what was to become one of the most celebrated crimes and subsequent court cases of the century: the details are well known, and are not relevant to the British peerage, save for the single fact that the case cost the Hearst family a great deal of money. When they were meeting these bills they found it convenient to sell a few items of value they had accumulated over the years. One such was a set of china, made in England in the eighteenth century, and decorated

* The present Prince Esterhazy still has huge estates in the Austrian Burgenland, but, after his long imprisonment and ill-treatment by the Communists in Hungary, says he is alarmed to go to Forchestein lest he be kidnapped. He now lives in Switzerland, sadly.

with the crowned heart and the three white stars on blue of the great
Scots family of Douglas. They were willing to part with the set for
$8,000, and, for the fifteenth Duke of Hamilton, 6,000 miles away
in the great, grey Scottish castle of Lennoxlove, the sale came at a
most propitious moment. An agent who lives in New York and keeps
a weather eye on any British heirlooms up for sale in America saw the
Hearst sale and snapped up the china service: it arrived back at the
castle late in 1976, well in time for the Gathering of the Clans on 17
April, when all family treasures from Gretna Green to the far tip of
Dunnet Head were due to be on proud display.

The ducal house of Douglas Hamilton provides a family better
known for their romantic and occasionally bizarre history than for
even their great present-day distinctions such as the VC, the Cabinet
Ministership and the boxing championship that have come of late.
Consider, for instance, that there was in the family a young man
given the unfortunate name of Lord *Anne* Hamilton, in honour of
Queen Anne but to the fellow's presumed deep embarrassment; that
the family from whom the Hamiltons bought Lennoxlove had provided the original model for Britannia, and had named the house
after her—the Duchess of Richmond and Lennox; that there was a
Duke of Hamilton sufficiently eccentric to order a syenite sarcophagus
to be buried in and then order his servants to "double me up" when
they found, as he was dying, that he was too long for it (he had to
have his feet chopped off to get in); that a "majestic and modest"
(this from Horace Walpole) . . . Irish girl named Elizabeth Gunning
could so captivate one particularly debauched Hamilton that he
married her at midnight and set her on a road that eventually gave
her more peerage dignities than any uncrowned head on the face of
the Earth—all these facts are woven well into the legend of the Hamiltons, the premier Dukes of Scotland. It is something of an anticlimax,
then, to find the present Duke Angus Douglas-Hamilton to be an
extremely normal young man with a passionate interest in ancient
motorcycles and a beautiful wife who is being continually coached in
the art of riding a small Suzuki, but finds the complexities too subtle
and keeps falling off.

The Duke, though pleased with his agent's discovery of the Hearst
china, which left the Duke's family some generations ago, is not so
well off as he would like. The giant estates around the industrial city
of Hamilton do not provide the income necessary for maintaining the
castle and the other money-crunching interests of the family: the

castle was due to open in 1977, with tourists from Edinburgh lured
to see a supposed death mask of Mary, Queen of Scots (but which one
historian claims is a fake), some grand paintings and a museum of
Border history of some of the best-loved families in the lowlands. In
addition to opening the house, the Duke is having to sell off some of
his pictures—a Canaletto went late in 1976, causing some critical
comment, for it went abroad. Taxes dog the present Duke and his
estates company, Hamilton and Kinneal Estates Ltd.: High Parks was
gifted to the nation in 1978; Lennoxlove has been open to the public
on a regular basis since 1980—so far, this venture has been a success,
but if Lennoxlove ceases to attract fee-paying tourists then, quite
possibly, the wealth of the Hamiltons may soon evaporate.

It is perhaps a matter of regret then, that the dukedom has arrived
at its most critical stage when the holder of the title is a young man
who quite frankly admits he wishes he had been something else rather
than the administrator of a worrisome legacy. As Lord Clydesdale,
Angus Hamilton was a young blade at Eton and Oxford, and plunged
with great spirit into the grander sports of the 1950s and 1960s. He
rowed, stroking the Balliol boat at Torpids; and got a Fourth Class
degree in engineering—no mean distinction in itself. He raced cars at
Le Mans and the Nürburgring; he learned to fly, he became a test
pilot, joined the RAF; he is a skin-diver and a skilled motorcyclist—a
dashing, buccaneering, rich young man, eager still to use his energy
for the kind of activity he likes, rather than presiding over the
gradual decay of titledom.

His is a talented family. His brother, Lord James Douglas-Hamilton,
is MP for Edinburgh West. Another brother, Lord Hugh, is a distinguished historian and a bearded, bekilted member of the Scottish
National Party. Of brother James, an arch-Tory, Lord Hugh says: "I
regard his position with respect. I think he's doing his best according
to his lights." A cousin, Iain, is a noted zoologist, an expert on elephants and an adviser on the beasts to the Government of Tanzania.
And father, the last Duke, who died in 1973, was famous as a brilliant
boxer; the first man to fly over the summit of Mount Everest; and
the man chosen by a misguided Rudolf Hess to carry a plan for peace
to Winston Churchill and the British Government in 1941. In fact,
for no other single event are the Dukes of Hamilton better known than
the sad saga of Rudolf Hess, who parachuted on to the Duke's estates
with his offer of peace, was disbelieved and then locked up in the
Tower of London for the remainder of the conflict. Hess lived on,

alone and now in Spandau prison, long after the old Duke died: his navigation maps, which show his intended flight passing directly across the Western Isles, are lovingly kept at Lennoxlove, and are one of the major attractions to the tourists the Duke so badly needs to keep the trappings of nobility attendant upon him still.

Other Dukes live more obscurely. The Duke of Somerset manages to keep away from the public in a small country house in Wiltshire, where he listens to the music of men with the kind of names he knows: Count Basie and Duke Ellington. His private passion is jazz. The household still dress for dinner at Maiden Bradley, but the land that once enabled the Seymours—the Duke's family name—to be classified among the greatest landowners in the country, is virtually all gone. Somerset House, where records of births, marriages and deaths of Britons of rank high and low were maintained, has not been in the Duke's possession for generations. There are about 5,000 acres around Totnes, in Devon, which are now being sold off in little chunks to help pay for the ravages of inflation. Few people know the Duke exists. He rarely comes up to London, virtually never speaks at the House of Lords and—unthinkable for a ducal family only a single generation ago—the Duchess at home does the cooking.

The Duke of St. Albans, another descendant from the well-worn bed of Charles II (in St. Albans' case, by the best known of all courtesans, Nell Gwyn) lived until recently in similar obscurity in London: the only concession to grandeur is the name ST. ALBANS, in thick black letters, on the lintel over what until lately was his modest house in Cheyne Gardens in Chelsea. He has no land and, though he is Hereditary Grand Falconer of England, and Hereditary Registrar of the Court of Chancery, has no notable privileges attached to his title. He once lived in furnished rooms as a salesman (and did once live in St. Albans, though the family has no connection with the town, and it was either sentimentality or coincidence that led the then Charles Beauclerk there) and inherited the title in 1964 from a distant cousin. At the time he became Duke he worked for the films division of the Central Office of Information, at a salary far from lordly. He stayed on at his job for a full six months after acceding to the title, determined that no dukedom would obtrude on a career he clearly enjoyed. But his rise in the financial world was swift once the mantle of nobility was firmly upon him, and soon the information services were behind him.

Before long he was heading trusts and advertising companies aplenty, in numbers that would suggest to any cynic that he was worth a thousand times more to the City as a Duke than as a plain, untitled Mr. Beauclerk. The companies with which he associated were not always successful or of a calibre one would imagine Dukes being attracted to: one was closely investigated for improper share dealings. The family appears often in the gossip columns of the London press. The last time was when tax problems forced him to sell his little house in Cheyne Gardens, lintel and all.

The Duke is a genial and kindly man, more interested in his business and rebuilding the family fortunes that earlier Dukes had squandered. He refuses to take his seat in the House of Lords, and does not own a robe or a coronet. He had a splendid collection of pictures in his Chelsea home, but precious few heirlooms: he was amused when a poor American tourist arrived one night having been tricked into buying a holiday in New York that included a stay in the "castle" of the Duke of St. Albans. There is no castle, and is never likely to be one again. Like the Duke of Somerset, St. Albans is an inactive Duke; but unlike Somerset, he does not manage to dodge public scrutiny.

Belvoir Castle, the principal home of the Duke of Rutland (the other, Haddon Hall, is across the ridge from Chatsworth, and sits at the centre of lands that "march" with the Duke of Devonshire's), was once perhaps the most romantically noble of England's great houses. With huge turrets and spires and indeed a *"bel voir"* across the great Vale that bears its name, the castle was run with little thought as to expense or prudence. Until quite recently a watchman would pace the grounds, shouting the hour, and "All is well," to the consternation of sleeping guests; trumpeters in powdered periwigs and full livery would pace through the chill halls of the immense structure, blasting on their instruments when it was time for the inhabitants to rise, or dine, or leave for the morning constitutional. Musicians, who were never to be seen by guests, played from a chamber adjoining the dining-room; peacocks, which form the Rutland crest, strutted around the grounds by the score. To visit Belvoir in the early part of this century was to drift back into an elegant Regency fantasy with mediaeval overtones— and to see the castle today is to recall some of the magic of those times, even if only the peacocks are left, and a sad old Duke, who wears monogrammed slippers, and whose energies are now devoted almost entirely to stopping the National Coal Board from driving mines into his beloved Vale.

There is a striking irony in the battle for Belvoir Vale. The Duke of Rutland, who presides over a fortune built, to some extent at least on the winning of coal from northern mines, is now in fierce combat with the Government over its plans to dig mines in his lands. In this combat, his greatest allies are not the farmworkers of Leicestershire, but the white-collar commuters whose high incomes in jobs in the big local towns now enable them to live in the country. The National Coal Board has told the Duke that there are some 450 million tons of coal beneath his castle and his estates. He has told the Coal Board to go and look elsewhere. His position as Chairman of Leicestershire County Council, and his rank as a Duke, have given him enormous powers to win headlines in the local press and, at the time of writing, have turned his campaign into a *cause célèbre*. Hundreds of tons of lime, spread out in vast letters on one local hillside, proclaim "NO PIT"; yellow posters screech "Achtung—Minefield"; the Duke helps it all along by telling the local reporters that he will lie down in front of the first bulldozers that come to dig the first pit. "Oh, it's true we mined coal in the past," he told one reporter. "But we surface mined, and we did resurface and build no end of public buildings with the money." That the taxpayer, and the average Briton, will benefit from the winning of 450 million tons of coal from the Vale of Belvoir seems to have taken second place, and some hostile editorial writers wondered out loud how the Duke's predecessors would have acted had they found the reserves of coal before the Government geologists, and in days when it was legal for them to mine it themselves.

The Duke is a pessimist when it comes to discussion of his own kind's future. "I don't see Dukes like me in two hundred years' time," he said early in 1977. "What with capital transfer tax and inflation I don't see how we could go on in the same way. But I don't think you should pack up and get out before you have to." Charles Manners (the Duke's family name; "Bad" Manners, they used to say of a former Duke; "Salisbury's Manners" when another was Principal Private Secretary to the Prime Minister, Lord Salisbury) was probably right to predict extinction of the Dukes in two centuries' time. At the present rate of natural wastage there should be no hereditary peers at all by the year 2175: between four and five noble names disappear every year.

Rutland is one of the richest nobles in the country, and receives, as such, a considerable amount of incidental interest from the press. There was unconcealed glee when the County Council decided, in 1974, to provide the Duke with an official Daimler because it was considered "undignified" for His Grace to have to try to find a parking space for his own Rolls-Royce. His occasional brushes with the constabulary are reported with closer attention than are the mistakes of lesser men: his one-pound fine for failing to stop at a road sign, his speeding offences—all such peccadilloes are lovingly chronicled by both the regional and the national press.

Indeed, close scrutiny of the newspaper cuttings relating to Charles John Robert Manners says something about the constant fascination of the British with their titled nobility. The news is invariably in the form of snippets—rarely is there anything approaching a profile of the man, an analysis of his suitability, or otherwise, for his official position in the county hierarchy, no scrutiny of his riches or his successes or failures as landowner, employer, conservationist or accruer of wealth. The items are simply there, recording baldly the occasional notable doings of an otherwise not particularly notable man. His application for a building license for a hotel is rejected; his Bentley is stolen; he is convicted of speeding. In 1955 he sells the freehold of his house in the West End of London; he catches a couple cheating at whist at a public party up at Belvoir Castle; he wins an award of £1,000 in the Premium Bond lottery. His butler gets six years in prison for fraud; His Grace sells the Peacock Hotel; he makes a speech in which he says he will not "emulate the antics of Dukes like Bedford" and bring a zooful of lions and elks into his castle grounds. He gives two peacocks to a local school; 16,000 of his own turkeys die; he buys an hotel in Dovedale. He grumbles about the state of the nation; causes questions in the House after starting a training flight of the country's little force of atomic bombers; is forced to give up a token horseshoe to the Lord of the Manor of Oakham (the fee for any peer going into the county town of the now sadly defunct county of Rutland it seems); and is given the CBE.

All this and more—and it is much the same for every Duke, every Marquess, Viscount, Earl and Baron of whom the newspapers ever take note—and yet only in the extremely rare case is there any attempt at a public examination of this most privileged group of men and women, and how these privileges are used. There seems just to be a placid acceptance among most Britons that in every village there is a squire, and in every county a brace or so of the Quality, and in every region a man with close constitutional ties to the Monarch, and the wealth and social position with which to maintain them. No one seems to worry about asking why—why the Duke of Rutland is able to use influence to try to stop an industry from which his family once made money, why he merits attention, why he is different from a man with equivalent wealth but no title. It seems a little disturbing, as though the Dukes and their colleagues unwittingly manage to anaesthetize the common populace into a form of apathy, ensuring that the two far-distant edges of the spectrum of class remain precisely where they are.

The Duke of Richmond, found sweeping out the offices of a garage in the London suburb of Cricklewood; the Duke of Roxburghe, now married to the lissom and beautiful sister of the new young sixth Duke of Westminster; the diminutive Duke of Argyll bravely raising money to repair his magnificent home, Inveraray Castle, after a disastrous Bonfire Night fire in 1975; the Duke of Wellington, being induced by a New York antique firm into publicizing their exhibitions —all such events make good copy for the press. But as to why, for example, the Duke of Westminster has managed, despite taxation deliberately set to trap the very rich, to maintain a position as the wealthiest man in the realm—such matters are never discussed. Which is fine for the Duke of Westminster, of course.

The marriage between the fifth Duke's daughter and Guy Roxburghe, the tenth holder of that dukedom, who acceded in 1974 when a youth of only twenty, inextricably welded two of the greatest bank balances in the world. Westminster, owner of much of central London, of lands in Durham, Shropshire, Cheshire, Flintshire, Lincolnshire, Norfolk, Gloucestershire, Merioneth, Surrey, Westmoreland, Sutherland and Wester Ross, plus a good chunk of Ireland; of territory in British Columbia, Massachusetts and Hawaii, in San Francisco and Bronxville, in South Africa and in Australia. The owner of all this wedded his most beautiful daughter, Jane, to one of the most eligible young men in Britain—it was almost too good to be fair. Guy Roxburghe, a slim soldier with the Blues and Royals, a curiously pre-Raphaelite face and considerable charm, has as his seat the enchanting and ageless Floors Castle, set in an island of 80,000 acres in the Borders. He was left more than two million pounds by his father, a proud old soldier Duke, who once caused a mighty brouhaha by shooting a fox he thought was about to attack a grouse—the ultimate dilemma for a country sportsman. So terrible was the reaction to the shooting that he was forced to resign as Chairman of neighbour Buccleuch's Hunt Committee, and only his generosity as benefactor (a thousand pounds to his butler, a like sum to his valet, his blood-stock and a quarter of a million pounds to his widow) permitted him to regain, in death, the reputation he had lost in life.

Three Dukes, as we saw at the beginning of this chapter, live abroad. Bedford, one of the first to recognize the necessities of open-ing his house to the public simply to permit it to be maintained sufficiently well to keep it standing, now lives in Paris. He was only a tenant at Woburn Abbey anyway, his father and grandfather having engineered a powerful estates company and wily trustees who did all they could do to prevent the present Duke from setting foot in the Palace. Not only did he not see it until he was sixteen, but also he did not know he was the heir; no one had ever bothered to tell him and it was a servant who let the information slip. Family squabbles within the Russells, the Bedford family, have been of legendary length and degree: many successive Dukes refused to talk to one another, resulting in gigantic financial complications—such as the awesome claim for nearly eight million pounds from the deaths of two Dukes in 1940 and 1953 respectively. Woburn is all that remains of the Bedford estates; in such former jewels as London's Bedford Square, nothing remains belonging to the family. The last houses there went in 1970.

The Duke lives in Paris today simply because he wants his son, the Marquess of Tavistock, to get to know Woburn and the responsibilities of senior titledom early enough in his life. Bedford has uncomfortable memories of his own youth—disinheritance, a measly allowance, formal disapproval from above of his first marriage. That kind of thing—coupled with ruinously high rates of taxation, the public dis-approval of pomp, a certain stuffiness among Dukes and their un-bridled classiness—he believes could well be the end of all of them. So for him it is all lions and circuses, the burning down of derelict farms for public enjoyment, the permanent display of a room full of ten million pounds' worth of Canalettos, gimmicks, a reputation throughout the world for being an authority on tourism, for making stately homes pay and for bringing history up to date. Some of the crustier members of his rank disapprove. Some of the public think the whole Bedford machine too graceless. Most Londoners, for whom

Woburn is a country sideshow just a Cortina ride away from the television sets, admire the Duke, and what he has done.*

Bedford, back in his modest home on the quai d'Orléans, hopes young Tavistock will take happily to the responsibility thrust upon him by his father, and learn the lessons the eleventh Duke so cruelly omitted to teach the present incumbent. That way, he hopes, dukedoms will survive—perhaps their political powers will have been taken away; perhaps some of their influence will have been forcibly diminished. But at least, unlike the dreary grandees of neighbouring nations, they will manage to retain some of their old style, dash, grace and panache. Far better extant and stylish, Bedford says, than bent on power, but extinct.

The two others, Manchester and Montrose, are less flamboyant characters. Manchester, who left for Kenya in 1946, lived in a style that would be unthinkable in present-day Britain; he had a staff of 187 at his "farm" at Hoey's Bridge, twenty of whom were gardeners. When he first went to Africa he lived out in the bush: what he had when he died it is fair to say he built up himself, and he enjoyed the dividends of his labours, and the collective zeal of his forebears, in the sun. Most of his properties in England, Kimbolton Castle pre-eminent among them, are long since sold. "The only thing I miss about England is the shooting," he said once. He missed little else: the Holbeins ("I think there are seven, but I'm not sure") he brought with him, along with some Van Dycks, an Aubusson carpet and a library of several thousand volumes. Some of the paintings left behind in his rush to get away from the dank mists of the Atlantic, including gigantic works attributed to such masters as Tintoretto and Veronese, went for less than twenty guineas apiece. His first wife resolutely declined to call native Kenyans anything but "niggers"; her son, who had the title of Viscount Mandeville, and is the new Duke, lives in Kenya too. He belongs to a club that sounds rather less worthy than the Brooks's or White's or the Turf that follow most titled names: it is called the Muthaiga Club, and, from what one can gather about the future of the Manchesters, it will be the surrogate Boodle's for some generations to come.

The old Duke finally married an American woman from San Francisco; Lord Mandeville, the present Duke, married a girl from

* The original zoo at Woburn was no tourist gimmick, but the scientific collection of the late Duke, who had a profound and scholarly love for animals and birds.

South Africa. The last Duke of Manchester to marry an English woman was George, the sixth Duke, in 1822: there has been foreign blood, and a great deal of wanderlust, in the Mancunian veins ever since.

The other expatriate, the Duke of Montrose is Rhodesian, a one-time member of Ian Smith's illegal Government until he proved too racialist and reactionary for even the former white chiefs of Salisbury. In theory, the Duke might have been liable to prosecution for treason for his associations with the Smith regime, and until the Zimbabwean settlement of 1980 there were moves in Britain to have him formally stripped of his privileges as a Member of the House of Lords.* Declining lands in Scotland—he once owned 130,000 acres of the Montrose estates, now his son manages the remaining 10,000 from his home near Glasgow— forced him to flee to Africa (as he puts it) in 1931. He used to trot home to London on the BOAC jet every month or so until the 1960s to make a speech on the impending disasters in Central Africa. During the Rhodesian rebellion he stayed away from London—he might have been arrested for treason had he ever arrived at Heathrow. But now that Zimbabwe has been born he comes and goes as he pleases, and policemen do not give him a second glance. Some of the family are members of Moral Rearmament, lending to the Grahams (the Duke is Chief of the Grahams though never could attend a reunion supper or, as in 1977, a once-in-a-generation Gathering) a curiously evangelistic air that sits uncomfortably with the coronet. One sister, who stands six feet two, makes marmalade on the island of Arran.

The Duke once wrote that "It is common observation that the African child is a bright and promising little fellow up to the age of puberty, which he reaches in any case two years before the European. He then becomes hopelessly inadequate and disappointing and it is well known that this is due to his almost total obsession henceforth in matters of sex."

In 1976, when talks on Rhodesia's future were proceeding in the great capitals of the world, he wrote to me: "For forty-five years I have played a part in developing this land that has been called 'The Jewel of Africa,' from primitive barbarism to a sophisticated society. The development is not only of the land but of the African people too. For instance in 1931 many of them were still walking, even into

* The Duke of Montrose's father designed the first aircraft carrier for the Royal Navy, and the family claims great patriotism.

town, in nothing but a loincloth; today many are holding down good jobs or have considerable businesses of their own and are dressed as well as the white folk—better in many cases.

"Now it seems that to satisfy the political dogma of intellectuals who will never have to live with the results, the whole edifice is to be thrown to the ground. Believe me, this is what will happen if black government eventuates in no more than two years."

Remote, awesomely rich, irredeemably upper class, the Dukes live on like ancient oaks, bending slightly in the gales of reality, occasionally crashing to the ground in a spectacular shower of branches and twigs. Tales of their distance from the cruel world outside their palaces abound. The tenth Duke of Marlborough, father of the present one, once visited the home of one of his three daughters—a mansion considerably less grand than Blenheim, given to the first Duke by "a grateful nation" for his victories against Louis XIV. Before breakfast on the first day of the visit the daughter was surprised to hear the old Duke bellowing down the stairs that his toothbrush was "not working"—it was not foaming properly, and would she kindly arrange for him to have a new one? The puzzled daughter went to investigate, finding the cause immediately. Toothbrushes only foamed, she carefully explained to her father, if you applied toothpowder: the valet at Blenheim usually performed the task for His Grace each morning, but since no one was available at the daughter's house, the Duke had to be taught to do it himself. Doubtless he was grateful to get back to Woodstock and away from the horrors of middle-class life.

Another Duke, unidentified in the anecdote, presided over estates that were ravaged by financial mismanagement. Decay abounded; bank balances had plummeted; the tenants were in constant fear of collapse. The Duke himself accepted the situation complacently, uncaring and uninterested. The trustees ordered a full review of the situation: the Duke's finances would be relentlessly probed. For six months the wizards slaved, coming to the inevitable conclusion that severe cuts in expenditure had to be made. Someone must tell the Duke the bad news—how, a terrified staff wondered, would he react?

Eventually the agent was selected to carry the news to His Grace, and travelled down to the Castle. The Duke was slumbering in a deckchair out on the Capability Brown gardens. The agent woke him.

"Your Grace," he trembled, "I regret to have to tell you we are going to have to make some cuts in the expenditure of the estate."

"Oh yes," harrumphed the Duke, angry at having been woken, dismayed at the trivial nature of the intelligence. "Such as what, precisely?"

"Well," the timid man returned, "Our staff have calculated everything down to the last penny and we urge that, to start with at least" —he paused to draw breath—"one of the *two* Italian pastry chefs employed in the kitchens at the Castle will have to go."

The Duke went faintly purple, then darker as his face suffused with rage. His white moustaches twitched. He sat bolt upright, aghast. "What!" he boomed at his terrified subject. "What! Can't a fellow even enjoy a *biscuit* any more?"

The sixth Duke of Portland may well have been the subject of the tale:* it is perfectly true that when he was faced, in the 1930s, with an urgent request for some trimming of his expenditures, he could only come up with one proposal for economy. The supply of sealing wax in the guest bedrooms at Welbeck Abbey could, he conceded grandiloquently, be dispensed with. The consequence of the smallness of this concession was that the Portlands had to give up the Abbey, with its underground passages, wide enough for a coach and horses to be driven through, its massive subterranean ballroom and its underground riding school lit by five thousand jets of gas. The Army took over the place, and the then Duke moved into the much smaller Welbeck Woodhouse down the road. There could probably be sealing wax in the bedrooms there, since there are fewer than a score of them.

The last dukedom to crash to the earth in the agonies of extinction was Leeds. The family was one of the five which were clustered, by chance or by the suggestive strainings of the Industrial Revolution progressing in the Black Country nearby, in what are now known as the Dukeries. Newcastle, Portland, Kingston, Norfolk and Leeds, with great houses at Clumber Park, Welbeck Abbey (itself once a Newcastle seat), Thoresby Hall, Worksop Manor and Kiveton Park, lived in an unparalleled concentration of nobility and wealth within twenty miles of each other. Today Newcastle is in a little cottage in Hampshire (about the only Duke to suffer the indignity of living in a house identified with a wretched *number*) and Portland is tottering towards extinction. Kingston became obsolete in 1773, though his bogus and bigamous Duchess—found guilty by her peers after one of the most celebrated Lords trials in history—survived until 1788; the

---

* The biscuit story is also linked to the last Duke of Buckingham.

Duke of Norfolk's official seat is Arundel, in Sussex; and the curtain
fell in Leeds in 1964. The Ordnance Survey still calls the area The
Dukeries, though its appearance as a ducal housing estate, with park
marching with park and crenellated battlement peering over forests at
Tudor mansion and Grecian folly, is long gone.

The Duke of Leeds who was rightly associated with the sad extinction was the eleventh, and actually died on 26 July 1963 after a
wretched illness that involved the cutting off of both his legs. For a
few months a distant cousin, Sir Francis d'Arcy Godolphin Osborne,
assumed the mantle of Leeds at his house in Rome. But he was
seventy-nine when he acceded, and died soon after, half from the ex-
citement of it all. He left no sons, and thus the Leeds line chuffed
to its terminus.

The eleventh Duke left a daughter, Camilla, who was born in
1950. She married a relation of Lord Harris, a Kentish nobleman with
an exotic coat of arms that includes hedgehogs, bombs, the standard
of Tippoo Sahib, a tiger (the latter beast with a curious Persian
symbol on its brow, an arrow in its chest and a crown on its head),
a grenadier* soldier of the 73rd regiment, the flag of the French
Republic, a sepoy of the Madras establishment of the East India Company and a nice little sketch of the drawbridge and the gates of the
fortress of Seringapatam. He is a nephew of the actor Robert Harris,
and lives at Belmont Park, near Faversham, somewhat obscurely. Thus
was the name of Leeds buried, though the old Duke would probably
not mind that the last surviving holder of the remnants of his title
is bound up with bombs and hedgehogs and drawbridges. It all seemed
a rather proper burial casket for the last member of a rare species;
unhappily for the story, though, Lady Camilla Osborne and Mr. Harris
were divorced in 1976.

There have been 162 ducal titles created in history, leaving out those
of the Blood Royal. Many have been rogues and villains; some have
died on the block for their excesses, some have been killed by gout,
some have vanished in a stupor of scandal. Those few that remain are
some indication of the variety and ineradicable éclat that must have
been a characteristic of the Dukes who went before. None of those

---

* In the old days every infantry regiment had a grenadier company, who
originally threw grenades; they had nothing to do with the First Foot Guards
who were made into Grenadier Guards for defeating Napoleon's Grenadiers
of the Old Guard at Waterloo.

surviving holders of this grandest of British titles—the most noble men in the land, save for the Throne—can be classified as mundane. Some are dull; some pompous; some excessively stupid. Few take an active part in the running of the nation; most are content—or have been forced by financial circumstances—to spend much of their time maintaining their estates, which, in general, are still impressively large. But they are not a group that can easily be classified. They have disparate interests, responsibilities, values, valuations and political views. They are twenty-five individuals, almost as varied—as Harold Macmillan, himself a Duke's uncle, said—as a selection of Britons whose names began with the letter G. They are all related, though some by a fair distance, and by marriage, not blood; and they are all entitled to be called "Your Grace," and "Our right trusty and right entirely beloved cousin" by the Monarch. Aside from that they share little—either with each other or, bent on preserving what they still retain, with anyone else. Dukes are above all an isolated and dwindling society, still able to make the timbers of the realm tremble a little, but increasingly given to trembling themselves.

FIVE

THE MARQUESSES
The Noble Misfits

"I'm a very fit man. I walk my dog every day. I
don't have to wear spectacles. I still have my
own teeth. Why should I marry some dried-up
old bag?"
>—The Marquess of Huntly, January 1977,
>announcing his engagement, at sixty-
>eight, to a twenty-year-old nurse.

Perched somewhat uncomfortably between the ancient dignities of
the dukedoms and the earldoms, the marquessates seem the misfits
of the peerage rolls. The title of Marquess is a fairly recent invention:
the word comes from the Latin *marchio,* and was once applied on
the Continent to Counts who guarded the "marches"—the borders
with neighbouring countries. In Britain it became customary for
those who had territories along the frontier between England and
Wales, or between England and Scotland, to receive marquessary
honours, though, oddly, the principal Scottish peer on the English
border was the *Earl* of March and the principal English peer on
the Welsh border was given the very same title. The appellation
"Marquess," or "Marquis" has never been a particularly well-received
honour: the second ever to be dubbed with the title, a worthy named
John Beaufort, actually pleaded with King Richard to give him something else instead: "Marquis of Dorset is a strange name in this
realm," he said.

Of the thirty-seven who survive today only one, the Marquess of
Cholmondeley (pronounced "Chumley," of course), lives near the
Welsh Marches (in a castle at Malpas, in Cheshire), and one other,

Lothian, lives in the Scottish borders, near Jedburgh. The remainder
are scattered by the four winds to all corners of the kingdom, and
beyond. One lives in America, another in Canada, a third—the most
senior, as it happens—the Marquess of Winchester, lives in Zimbabwe.
There is one on the Isle of Man, a scattering in Ireland and five in
Scotland. The bulk of the holders of this second-degree peerage live
in the south of England: three in London, two in Kent, two in
Wiltshire, one in Sussex, others in East Anglia and the Midlands; a
brace, Normanby and Zetland, make the English north their home.
One lives in Wales—the Marquess of Anglesey, whose stately home,
Plas Newydd, is one of the finest in the principality. He has the
distinction of being the senior peer to live in the land of the Ordovices
and the Silures: there are no Dukes at all in Wales, only one Earl,
a scattering of Viscounts and perhaps a dozen Barons—precious few,
bearing in mind there are several hundred of the last rank. Peers still
own plenty of land in Wales, of course, but for some reason they
find Scotland more congenial as a rural retreat, probably because of
the distribution there of the red grouse, the trout and the stag, which
means so much to so many of them.

Marquesses are evidently lesser men than Dukes, but scarcely
grander than the Earls they precede in the official rolls of the land:
indeed, very many of the Earls are infinitely wealthier and more
formidable than the holders of the marquessates. And probably the
grandest Marquesses of all are those like Hamilton, whose title is
only there by courtesy, but who one day will succeed to the dukedom—in his case, of Abercorn—currently held by his father. The
Marquesses who are lords-in-waiting for higher things can rank as
potentially splendid: those who have the rank by right are neither as
meritorious as the Earls like Eden and Kitchener and Mountbatten,
nor as innately impressive as Dukes like Westminster and Devonshire. Theirs is almost a title to embarrassment, a falling between two
gilded stools, provoking comments like that directed to present-day
drivers of the Bentley motor car. If you're so rich, why not have a
Rolls-Royce: if you're so grand, why aren't you a Duke?

There has not been a Marquess created since 1936, when the Earl
of Willingdon retired after five years as Viceroy of India, to be given
a marquessate for his services. Subsequent Viceroys either had the
degree already (as did Linlithgow, who was Viceroy from 1936 to
1943) or were promoted to an earldom (like Wavell and Mountbatten, both of whom flew in to calm the troubled subcontinent as

mere Viscounts, but who departed through the sandstone Gateway of India in Bombay as exalted Earls, advanced one degree of the peerage for their pains in the heat and the dust).

The Marquess of Reading, whose title originated in 1926, was a Viceroy too; the Marquess of Milford Haven, a prince who had married into the British Royal Family and became a British subject, was given his marquessate when he changed his name from Battenberg to Mountbatten, from something signifying foe to something redolent of friendship. The Marquess of Cambridge, who was the result of the union of the Duke of Teck and the granddaughter of George III, was similarly raised to a British marquessate on the assumption of the surname Cambridge. The Marquess of Linlithgow had been an Earl, became a Court favourite of Queen Victoria's and was given his title on completion of his tour as first Governor General of Australia. The twentieth-century Marquesses, in short, display the variety of service required for the degree: either service to the greater colonies in the farther reaches of the Empire, or the penetration of the more private reaches of the Royal Family. Nowadays there are no colonies of any grandeur left to administer (one would presumably not merit a marquessate for looking after the natives of Belize or the British Virgin Islands), and those who marry into the Royal Line become Dukes (like Edinburgh, who chanced upon the heir to the Throne) or Earls (like Snowdon, who was married to her younger sister). There would seem little chance of any future marquessates being handed around, even if the political inhibition towards the creation of hereditary peerages lapses.

There is, by the way, no Marquess of Lorn, nor has there ever been. (Though the son and heir apparent of the Duke of Argyll is the Marquess of Lorne, spelled with the additional vowel.) The phrase is cockney slang, of an arcane variety, and means an erection. The Marquess of Granby does exist, as the courtesy title of the eldest son of the Duke of Rutland; but it is also one of the most popular public-house names in England, drawing its use from the popular eighteenth-century soldier of that name. The fact that he was bald has since rendered him an eponymous hero in barbers' shops, as well.

For some reason unknown to the demographers of the peerage—and there are some, industriously riffling through the birth, marriage and death records of every ennobled Briton who ever was, and producing volumes of scholarship on the relative length of life of Dukes compared to dustmen (considerably greater)—Marquesses have an unusually high divorce rate. All the peerage suffers from, or enjoys, a higher rate than the rest of the British population—a combination, perhaps, of the informally arranged marriages that still go on at the top of the social scale in class-conscious countries, and the great wealth many peers can command with which to pay alimony to discarded spouses. That their riches and their status make them doubly attractive to fortune-hunting females also has more than a little to do with the statistic, one suspects. But why Marquesses should be significantly more liable to divorce than the other four ranks of ennoblement, no one knows. They are, though: of the Marquesses who have married, only nineteen have married but once. Thirteen have married twice (though one was, for a brief while, a widower; the others are recorded in the reference books as having had their "m. diss."), and four have married three times. There are said to be some forty Duchesses for the twenty-five Dukes; there are some fifty-six women in Britain entitled to be called Marchioness—the female form of an already fairly feminine-sounding title.

One of the most hallowed names in British Conservative politics is that of Salisbury. Three times Prime Minister, the third Marquess of Salisbury was the last peer to enjoy the Premiership, but quite suitably took the kingdom into only the very outset of the twentieth century, during which he and his kind were to become increasingly regarded, politically, as whales stranded on the beach and thrashing hugely, but uselessly, against the relentless pressures of a more egalitarian form of democracy. That is not to say that the Cecils—the family name of the Salisburys, and one of the most talented families in recent history, rivalled only, perhaps, by the Russells—did not make an impact on the twentieth century: they did, and still do. But the impact is lessening by the hour, and while the famous fourth Marquess, James, was a Tory elder statesman almost from his coming of age in 1882, and led the Conservatives in the Lords during the 1920s and 1930s; and while the fifth Marquess, "Bobbety," bravely championed the Empire and all that British imperialism had stood for in the quarter-century of his reign—despite all that distinction and all that energy, the political Cecils are now almost washed up, finally out of synchronization with the mainstream of their beloved party and their beloved country. The fifth Marquess might have seemed more at home in the capital city of Rhodesia, which took its name from the marquessate, than at Hatfield House, the great Jacobean mansion north of London from where successive Salisburys imprinted their stamp on the conduct of British foreign policy.

Bobbety, one of the four children of the fourth Marquess, was born into a theatre of privilege and talent rare even in its day. His brother went on to become Professor of English Literature at Oxford; one sister became a Lady of the Bedchamber to Queen Elizabeth the Queen Mother, and married Lord Harlech; the other, grander still, though younger, was Mistress of the Robes to the Queen, and married the tenth Duke of Devonshire. The Marquess, spokesman in the House of Lords for his own entrenchedly Establishment kind, fought all his life for the retention of the standards and views he had known as a child; politically he never grew up: he failed to recognize the strainings of social democracy, set his heart on the maintenance of British supremacy in Africa, ignored the call of Europe and the siren song of the Welfare State. He was anachronism personified.

It was this Lord Salisbury who, in 1968, had led rebellious Tory peers into an abortive fight to defeat the Order agreeing to the imposition of United Nations sanctions against the illegal regime in Rhodesia. With other diehard Tories like Lord Coleraine and Lord Grimston, Salisbury huffed and puffed his angry way into the division lobbies, actually defeating the Order and reversing the Labour Government's majority in the Commons. But it was a slight victory, and a Pyrrhic one at that: for when the Government reintroduced the Order and had it passed, despite fresh grumblings from the noble Bobbety, the first signs of new reform measures designed to curb the power of the Lords came too. The reforms were later defeated on technicalities, but it can be safely said that it was the intemperate actions of Lord Salisbury that did much to bring about the present climate—one so unfriendly to the House of Lords that it now no longer seems unrealistic to predict its demise within the next decade or two. If the House does go, it will have been the fifth Marquess of Salisbury who, among others, took it close to the precipice, and, unwittingly, gave it a shove towards the edge.

His son, the sixth Marquess, Robert Edward Peter Gascoyne-Cecil, is altogether a more placid being. When he succeeded to the marquessate on the death of Bobbety in 1972 there were groans in the Tory press that, so obscure had been Lord Cranborne (the courtesy title he wore) during his time as MP for Bournemouth West, and so quiet had he been when out of politics, that he might actually demur at taking his seat in the Upper House. "The first time there has been no Cecil in either house for four hundred years!" the columnists forecast, in dread. But then, fortified perhaps by a £1 million will and the inclusion of Hatfield House and two London theatres (Wyndham's and the New) in the estate that came to him, the new Marquess did grasp the challenge and proffered his hand to the Lord Chancellor and bowed before the Woolsack. Once in the House he succeeded as President of the Monday Club for a while, and opened the debate on Rhodesia in the Lords in 1976.

Little else has been heard since, save for an announcement that Hatfield House would open to serve Elizabethan-style dinners for wealthy visiting Americans. The new Lord Salisbury was, like his fellows, having to turn showman to survive. From three times Premier to purveyor of comely serving wenches to the aristocracy of Texas in three-quarters of a century!

In the *London Gazette,* the official newspaper of the realm, announcements concerning changes at Court come at the head of the front page, well before the irritatingly complex notices concerning the running of the country. One day early in 1977 there was a brief note, datelined "Buckingham Palace," and reading to the effect that "Her Majesty the Queen has been graciously pleased to accept the resignation of the Earl of Rocksavage as a Page of Honour with effect immediately; the retirement is necessitated by the Earl's age, which has reached the point at which retirement is stipulated." What the notice did not say was that David George Philip Cholmondeley, the Earl, and son of the Marquess of Cholmondeley, was sixteen years old. Early retirement is one of the disadvantages of employment in some of the byways of a monarchical system.

The Marquess of Cholmondeley is one of many peers whose life is inextricably entwined with the workings of the monarchy—he is one of a number of the most highly titled who have sprung up, like glittering convolvulus plants, to cosset and enclose the Throne, to help ensure its survival and its exclusivity. Cholmondeley is one of the so-called Great Officers of State who, together with the peers in the Royal Household, form the inner sanctum of the Establishment, the core, if you like, of the realm. The Great Officers are the Earl Marshal, the Lord Chancellor, Lord President of the Council, Lord Privy Seal, Lord Great Chamberlain and the Lord High Steward— the last appointed only at coronations. (There is also a Lord Steward of the Household and a Lord Chamberlain of the Household but these, *in sensu stricto*, are not Great Officers of State. They are just rather nice to have around.) There are Hereditary Grand Falconers (the Duke of St. Albans; he is permitted to drive carriages along Birdcage Walk as his sole privilege for this defunct office). There are Hereditary Chief Butlers (Lord Mowbray, who would pour the wine at the coronation banquets, if there were such things these days), Hereditary Keepers of Dunstaffnage Castle (the Duke of Argyll), and so on.* Marquessates and ceremony go well together, it seems: the Marchioness of Abergavenny is a Lady of the Bedchamber; the Marquess of Exeter is the Hereditary Grand Almoner of England; the Marquess of Abergavenny is Her Majesty's Representative at Ascot; and the father of the now retired Earl of Rocksavage, the sixty-two-year-old sixth Marquess of Cholmondeley, is Joint Hereditary Great Chamberlain of England. The job is not entirely a sinecure.

Since 1133, when King Henry I appointed a man named Aubrey de Vere to run the Palace of Westminster for him, the site of Britain's Parliament has been administered just as though it was a Royal palace—which, in theory at least, it is. That is, until 1964, when Harold Wilson, in the days before he too became overawed by the trappings of inherited privilege, decided to try and "nationalize" the Palace of Westminster and wrest control from the Monarch. It proved a complicated task, not least because of the complicated history surrounding the person of the administrator, the Lord Great Chamberlain.

It had started out quite simply in the twelfth century. Aubrey de Vere's heirs became the Earls of Oxford, and the Chamberlainship with which Henry had endowed Aubrey passed neatly from father to son for generations—missing a beat from time to time because of the inclinations of the day for Earls to take part in treasonable activity—and looked all set for eternity. But, as we have seen, titles do occasionally become extinct, and when the fifteenth Earl of Oxford died without a son the succession deteriorated into an ugly shambles. All sorts of noblemen took the task on until 1625, when matters became royally complex, and the Monarch passed the job to a man named Robert Bertie, Lord Willoughby de Eresby. Still further

---

* The various hereditary officers—Falconer, Butler, Almoner, Keeper of Dunstaffnage, and so on—are not paid. Nor, for example, are the Archers of the Queen's Body Guard for Scotland, who turn out for numerous ceremonial duties, quite free.

confusion lay ahead, with four groups of claimants to the task by
1779; two years later, in a decision that shocked the staid *Complete
Peerage,* the office was divided equally between two sisters of the
fourth Duke of Ancaster. Six centuries after Aubrey de Vere, it said,
the office was "split up between two ladies who were not his heirs
and were not even entitled to the de Vere arms." If that wasn't
complicated enough, great problems arose when someone had to be
chosen to officiate at the Coronation of Edward VII, by which time
the "senior" descendants of the two ladies had become the Earl of
Ancaster and the Marquess of Cholmondeley. Who was to be Chamberlain for the new King? The Crown argued among itself for weeks:
a House of Lords Committee got in on the act, but the ruling they
produced was so difficult to follow that they might as well not have
bothered. Following the death of Alberic Willoughby de Eresby in
1870, unmarried, it was decided that the Willoughby half-share
should be divided between the Willoughby and Carrington families,
the Monarch of the day having as always the final word as to who
should act as Lord Great Chamberlain. The Earl of Ancaster last
had the job when George VI died in 1952; the fifth Marquess of
Cholmondeley took Elizabeth II's offered posting in 1953 and stayed
with her until he felt it prudent to retire, at the age of eighty-three,
in 1966. His son took over the onerous duties in 1966, adding the
title of Lord Great Chamberlain to a bewildering set of dignities
that include the Earldom of Rocksavage—which he lends out to his
only son—the Earldom of Cholmondeley, the Viscounty of Malpas
and the Baronies of Newborough, Newburgh and, once again, of
Cholmondeley. With the peerages he also has 10,000 acres of land
in Cheshire and another 8,000 in Norfolk—but for the prosecution
of his Palace duties, the landownership is scarcely relevant.

One would imagine that, since aristocratic scuffling has broken out
at least once every century since Henry I handed out the job, the
post of Lord Great Chamberlain is either highly rewarding, inordi-
nately stimulating or endowed with some great and ancient privilege
peculiar to no other mortal. It is indeed the last: at the Coronation of
Queen Elizabeth in 1953 the fifth Marquess of Cholmondeley found
himself carrying all manner of trinketry and womanly accessories for
the new Queen to wear—gloves, a coif, swords, Royal robes and
crown. When the Monarch is a King this sixth great officer of the
Crown actually dresses and undresses the man on Coronation Day,
acting like a particularly costly valet and footman rolled into one.

With a Queen, Mistresses of the Robes manage the more private tasks, but there is a lot of fetching and carrying for the Marquess to do besides.

In addition to this pleasantly servile role that the Chamberlain has to fulfill every two generations or so, he also had overall responsibility—and this is where Mr. Wilson comes in—for the Palace of Westminster. Until 1964, when Charles (now Lord) Pannell managed as Minister of Works to gain control of the House of Commons from the Cholmondeleys and the Ancasters, the Chamberlain could, for example, forbid Members of Parliament from entering the precincts between Friday and Monday. Marcia Williams, as she was in the days before she was ennobled as Lady Falkender, was once physically prevented from visiting Mr. Wilson's room in the Commons when he was Leader of the Opposition—the kind of high-handedness that Labour politicians understandably found obnoxious and sent Mr. Pannell to eradicate.

After a protracted but decorous struggle with Palace officials, the Marquess of Cholmondeley was eventually forced to relinquish half of his hold on the Palace. A red carpet begins where the Lords Lobby leads off the echoing and noisy Central Hall of the Palace: from that carpet, clear through to the Victoria Tower, the Palace is still firmly within the bailiwick of the Lord Great Chamberlain. He has the House of Peers itself, the four main Courts—Royal, Chancellor's, Judge's and Peers; he has the Royal Gallery and the Robing Room, the Peers' Libraries and the inner courts and half of the River Terrace. The remainder, from the Commons to the Clock Tower, is the responsibility of the House of Commons and, ultimately, of the people. The fixtures and fittings of half the Palace still come under jurisdiction of the Monarch through the Ancasters and Cholmondeleys: elsewhere the Monarch's writ has now ceased to run. The degree to which nepotism remains a feature of the House of Lords— and it is, mercifully, on the wane—depends entirely on the wishes of the Chamberlain of the time. From what one can see the conduct of the present sixth Marquess has been exemplary and the Lords, at an annual cost of some four million pounds, runs itself tolerably well.

The Marquessate of Cholmondeley is a fairly ancient peerage, redolent of much of the mystery of national majesty; the Marquessate of Queensberry, though more than a century older, draws its associations from the sport of boxing, the fall of Oscar Wilde and latterly from a curious little demi-scandal that first drew public attention after an event in a country lane outside the village of Chipping Norton, in Oxfordshire, in 1965. The great-grandfather of the present-day peer, who drew up the rules that form the basis of modern fisticuffs, and the sorry tale of Oscar Wilde's exposure are both well known. The outcome of the present Marquess's tutorial activities in the Cotswold lanes is, in its own way, scarcely less fascinating.

His Lordship is, by way of introduction, a talented master of ceramics—Professor of the science, no less, at the Royal College of Art in London. He likes to drop his title for his students, and be called merely Professor Queensberry. He is adept at judo, rides motorcycles and has a sound commercial head on his shoulders. He says he inherited his artistic side from his mother; but from his father, the eleventh Marquess, who was a stockbroker and "a fair philistine over things visual" according to his son, he inherited the genes that go with profit making. So he runs two emporia called the Reject China Shops in Beauchamp Place, a ritzy little street in Knightsbridge; and he once owned two stalls in the magnificent old Covered Market in Oxford. In 1977 he launched a new line of wine-glasses for the common man, though they were called "The Connoisseur Range," and the makers made jolly sure everyone knew that a real Scottish Marquess had a hand in making them: there seemed no stopping the commercial instincts of this very ambitious young man, nor his contribution to what is regarded as good British design.

Lord Queensberry lives on the fringes of the avant-garde, largely by virtue of his calling. In 1961, when he was just thirty-three, he was to be seen on the marches organized by the Campaign for Nuclear Disarmament—but his radical tendencies in youth must have mellowed a little, since he does not care to take the Labour Party Whip in the House of Lords. He fostered an eighteen-month-old Nigerian child once, called Bimbo. He went to the Lords to talk about the problems of homosexuality during the second reading of the Earl of Arran's famous Bill in May 1965; and sent his daughters to Holland Park Comprehensive School. So far as credentials were concerned, the Marquess was impeccably endowed with what passed in London for radical chic, and was much loved for it.

In 1965 near Chipping Norton he was giving driving lessons to a young lady named Miss Alexandra Mary Clare Wyndham Sich. It seems as though the then Marchioness of Queensberry, who had been

Anne Jones before she married her first husband, took a rather dim view of her husband giving driving lessons to pretty young ladies, and the ennobled pair split up in 1966. Two years later they were divorced, the grounds being adultery with the aforenamed Miss Sich, who, inexplicably at first reading, had by then changed her name to Douglas, which is also the Queensberry family name. What, one wondered, was the purpose of the young lady going to all the trouble of changing her name to that of her husband before the probably inevitable marriage that the approaching divorce would free them for? An answer came a year later. In 1967, while Miss Douglas was still, technically, Miss Sich, she had a child by Lord Queensberry—a child, moreover, who was a little boy.

That, students of the subtleties of these matters will discern, pro-duced problems of a most vexing nature. By his first wife the Marquess had had two daughters, Emma and Alice. He was, at the time of his divorce, technically without a male heir of his body—though the marquessate could pass to his brother, Lord Gawain Douglas, nineteen years his junior and at the time unmarried and thus without heir.

Yet the appearance on the scene in 1969 of a child named Sholto Francis Guy Douglas posed a dilemma—for Sholto was an heir, all right, but the offspring of an adulterous relationship and, at least at that time, an illegitimate child. Peerage law, in Scotland as well as in England, provided that heirs could only be children who were the legitimate offspring, which Sholto most certainly was not. "Although young Sholto is the son of a Marquess he can only be plain Mr. Sholto Douglas when he grows up," intoned one authority, rather spoiling the announcement of the wedding between His Lordship and the young Alexandra, made the same day. "Had he been born in conventional circumstances he would be Viscount Drumlanrig. The law about hereditary peerages is very clear and very strict in this point."

So the Marquess, being a Scottish peer (his titles date from 1682 and include an Earldom of Queensberry and a Lordship Douglas of Hawick and Tibbers), applied to the arbiter of these matters, the Court of the Lord Lyon King of Arms in Edinburgh. Lyon in those days was a much respected, if slightly eccentric man by the name of Innes; but he had a tiny voice like a mouse, and when, as he usually did, he answered the telephone by squeaking into it "Lyon!" most callers just collapsed in a heap, it sounded so very peculiar. The Lord Lyon was not a man to be hurried by Queensberry's demands, and neither were his assistants, men with archaic titles like Rothesay, Albany and Marchmont Heralds, Unicorn, Carrick, Ormond and Falkland Pursuivants. They accepted His Lordship's plea for a formal declaration of the legitimacy of Sholto Douglas, and left the Marquess and the new young Marchioness to sweat it out.

Then the new Lady Queensberry became pregnant, causing further complicated speculation: if the child is a boy—and thus an undoubted Viscount Drumlanrig—what would Sholto's position be when he grew up? How would the precision of primogeniture be applied? Would the Viscount inherit the title and Mr. Sholto Douglas the money? Would the two boys swap names at the coming of age of the older? Would one have to be sent off to join the French Foreign Legion? Happily the Marchioness provided the waiting world with a girl, Kate Cordelia Sasha, and all was well. Precautions to prevent a recurrence appear to have been stringently observed from that moment on.

Finally in 1973, after no less than three and a half years of the most recondite deliberation, the Lord Lyon announced his verdict. The Scottish Legitimation Act enabled the eventual union of the Marquess and his new bride to bring Sholto into that category of the human offspring legally regarded as being "a lawful heir"—and since there was no doubt he was the child of the two purported parents, he was therefore "an heir male whatsoever" (the Scottish peerage law gives the marquessate the characteristic destination to *heredibus masculia quibuscunque,* quite different from the English destination for the same rank, which makes reference to "heirs male of the body lawfully begotten") and entitled to succeed to the Queensberry title.

(It should be noted at this point that only some Scottish earldoms and lordships guarantee that a female can inherit in default of a male heir, and only English Barons whose creation was authorized by a writ, rather than by Letters Patent. Merely because a title is Scottish does not mean it can pass through the female line: marquessates cannot—or more precisely, the marquessate of Queensberry cannot. Only males can take that title.)

There was much relief and celebration in the Queensberry home in the immediate aftermath of the ruling. Amusingly, the sober authority of *Burke's Peerage* tried to overlook Sholto's existence altogether: the last edition, printed in 1970, indicates the marriage between the Marquess and Miss Sich, but only the presence of two articles of "issue" resulting from the first marriage. The 1976 edition of *Debrett's* is frank about it, but—and this is what makes *Debrett's* such a treasure trove of familial oddities—it merely notes coldly the dates involved. The Son Living is "Sholto Francis Guy, born 1 June 1967 (by second wife)." Marriage to second wife, if the eye happens to wander through seven lines of rubric about "crowned and winged hearts and six cross crosslets fitchée," took place in 1969. The anomaly—sadly it is missing from the 1980 edition of *Debrett's*—hides a fascinating tale.

There are, surprisingly, rogues among the peerage. Three present members of the House of Lords have spent some of their time in prison—slightly more than the national average—for, variously, the offences of fraud, sexual assault and robbery. It was a Marquess who was involved in the robbery—and what an event that was, to stir the hearts of the masses in the sultry heat of that last summer before World War II!

The suave villains who robbed a jewellery shop in London's Burlington Arcade became known as "The Mayfair Gang": for his part in the heist, in which diamonds and silver were taken across on the night packet for disposal in Paris, a gay young blade who has since become a Marquess got three years' penal servitude, and was released in 1941 when he was just twenty-six.

At about that time Victor Hervey (the name is pronounced "Harvey," like the sherry-importing family from Bristol, the Hervey seat, and title, too, though they are unrelated) was in all kinds of hot water, constantly in the yellow-press gossip columns. Before his father was made Marquess of Bristol, a title to which he succeeded much later, in 1960, he was involved in attempted arms running to Spain— which served to make the young heir one of the darlings of the penny-paper readership between the wars. He was declared a bankrupt for a while, with liabilities of £123,000 and assets of what he had in his trouser pockets on the day of his hearing—eight shillings and twopence.

The Marquess, now over sixty, and settled in the Monaco sun, used to live at Ickworth House, near the town of Bury St. Edmunds, in the Suffolk of which he owns some 16,000 of the very best acres. He installed a book-vending machine in the mansion, dispensing detective novels to patrons too bored with the sights.

He is certainly a man in favour of autocracy. His membership of the Grand Council of the Monarchist League permits him to mingle with many members of Eastern Europe's Royal Houses, the Zogs and the Lekas and the Margaritas of the Bulgarians. He likes to wear a number of gaudy, and rather meaningless, chunks of European metalwork that date from the halcyon days of the Balkan Kings and Queens. At the christening of his daughter Victoria, born in 1976 to his third Marchioness, he wore four silver-gilt stars and a sword: among the godparents of the new Lady Victoria were King Simeon and Queen Margarita of the Bulgarians, Queen Susan of the Albanians and Mary, Princess of Pless. The sword, handed by the British Marquess to the Bulgarian King and thence to the two Queens, was used to cut the cake. Photographs of the event show the young nanny standing three paces to the left of His Lordship, while photographers snap away at the ennobled pair: "The nanny who kept to her station," one paper sneered.

One oddity about Lord Bristol is that his title gives him the advowsons of some thirty local parishes. This practice, whereby rural squires can exercise patronage in the appointment of vicars to the local church parishes, is ancient and revered: it was created in days when peers enjoyed the kind of freedoms that rarely placed them in conflict with the law. No one has seen fit to deprive the marquessate, even temporarily, of its rightful links with the Established Church. So, Lord Bristol, when he takes time off from entertaining Ruritanian Kings and Queens, from dealing in properties and holidays in sun-dappled islands in the tropics (Dominica, the Bahamas, Cyprus among them), and from running his stud, can appoint no fewer than thirty men to livings in his churches—a record, it is believed, for the greatest number of livings within the purview of one man.

The only Marquess to make his permanent home in Wales is Lord Anglesey, one of the peers most closely connected with the world of serious artistic endeavour and conservation, and as such a well-respected and admired noble. The marquessate was awarded in 1815 to the then Earl of Uxbridge after the battle of Waterloo, and after one of the most celebratedly reserved exchanges of any battlefield. After his brilliant handling of the cavalry in the field that June day, Uxbridge was riding off to camp with the Duke of Wellington, to whom he had been second in command, when a stray round of grapeshot smashed his right leg into pulp. He is renowned as having said to the Duke: "By God, sir, I've lost my leg!" and Wellington, taking a spyglass from his eye, looked across at his wounded colleague

and retorted: "By God, sir, so you have!" and calmly resumed his
scrutiny of the retreating Napoleonic forces. Uxbridge had the ruins
of his leg taken off and was back in London three weeks later, a
delighted Prince Regent making him Marquess on 4 July. This best-
loved of all Marquesses of the day had the world's first articulated
wooden leg provided for him—an "Anglesey leg"—of a type still to
be found on sale in medical stores in Edwardian times.

The home of the Angleseys since the creation of the title, and the
home of the Paget family for four centuries before that, has been the
magnificent "New Place" or Plas Newydd on the heights above the
Menai Straits, on the island from which they took their title. It is
one of the grandest houses—certainly in one of the most spectacular
sites—in Britain: the windows on the East Front command a sweeping view across the strait to the Caernarvonshire shores and the high
peaks of Snowdonia. From the Welsh mainland the low, white
façade of the house stands out as, along with the famous Tubular
Bridge, one of the two great sights of an island otherwise little distinguished for visitors. But it has been a costly house to maintain—
indeed it was not until the sixth Marquess spent his fortune on both
the inside and outside of the mansion in the 1930s that Plas Newydd
was properly used by the Angleseys as their principal home. The sixth
Marquess was the chief patron of the artist Rex Whistler, who was
commissioned to cover the walls of one specially reserved room with
huge works of *trompe-l'œil* that stand as the finest memorial to his
brief life. Thousands come to Plas Newydd each year to pay homage
to Whistler, and only incidentally to the descendants of old "One-
Leg" of Waterloo.

The present, seventh Marquess, born in 1922, maintains the standards of patronage and sober responsibility that have marked nearly all
the members of the Paget family—except for the fifth Marquess, who
spent money wildly. It is said he kept braziers alight in his forests
during the winter nights just in case he should wish to warm himself
while taking his walk: and that when one of the fires burnt him,
he threw a bejewelled coat worth some £3,000 onto the coals.
Scarcely surprisingly, the Marquess went bankrupt in his own estate,
though Plas Newydd, thanks to a careful separation of his personal
and his more obviously endowable wealth, was spared.

His successor is, fittingly, a steadfast member of all kinds of
British bodies that have as their end the protection of the finer
buildings of the nation: he is a member, among other offices, of the

Royal Fine Arts Commission, the Historic Buildings Council for Wales and the Welsh National Opera; while the Marchioness has been Chairman of the National Federation of Women's Institutes and the Welsh Arts Council. He has an abiding interest in church buildings of the nation: he is a member of, among other offices, the Friends of Friendless Churches. He writes books—his biography of "One-Leg" was well received, and his history of the cavalry regiments with which his family has long been associated was published in two volumes in 1973 and 1975.

In 1976 he gave the house and 160 acres of surrounding lands, together with a mile and a half of the beautiful coastline, alive with Mediterranean trees and shrubs, to the National Trust—fulfilling the conditions by which the Trust accepts such buildings by providing a cash endowment that will enable the Trust to keep the house open without digging into its own, not substantial, coffers. The Marquess and Marchioness live in a wing of Plas Newydd, but their connection with it will be the last: before long Plas Newydd will become just another museum, with a caretaker drawn perhaps from a family that has no connection with this assembly of some of the most talented of Britons. All the Marquess has retained for himself is the famous Anglesey Column—but it is hardly possible for his heirs to live inside a sixteen-foot-thick limestone pole.

One pleasant little custom in which the Marquesses have engaged for the last 50 years has been their mode of letting the neighbours know the time of the arrival, and the sex, of all their ennobled offspring. Each time a boy has been born heir to the marquessate, ten cannon shots boom out across the Menai Strait: each time a girl has arrived, five shots. Answering shots are fired from the Caernarvonshire shore. There is an heir, Lord Uxbridge; he has a younger brother, Lord Rupert Paget, and three sisters. Since the present Marquess has been at Plas Newydd, the cannons reserved for the announcement of a birth have fired thirty-five times from each side of the mile-wide water.

One of the means of spotting the territorial influences of the landed families in Britain is to look at the street names in the bigger cities. So in London there is Grosvenor Square, belonging to the Grosvenors, Dukes of Westminster, and Bedford Square, belonging once to the Duke of Bedford; and Cadogan Square, and so on. Cavendish Terrace, in Carlisle, indicates part of the northern realms of the Dukes of Devonshire; Bute Street, Bute Terrace, Dumfries Lane, Dumfries Palace and Bute East Dock in Cardiff, capital of Wales, indicate the influence of a peer whose home and principal lands are 200 miles to the north, the Marquess of Bute.

Lord Bute—who holds as one of his subsidiary titles Baron Cardiff of Cardiff Castle—is one of the larger landowners in Britain. His father used to own St. Kilda, the group of islands out in the Atlantic to the west of the Hebrides, but bequeathed them to the National Trust. He still owns Great Cumbrae, an island in the Firth of Clyde, plus a good deal of land on the Isle of Bute, the long island that stretches southwards off the western Scottish coast. There have been attacks on his landownership, mostly in the nationalist-minded press north of the Border. But his friends insist he is one of the kindest and ablest of men, cut to the quick by the criticism of the "give us back our land" style. To whom, his friends ask, should he return it? The Isle of Bute never belonged to anyone other than the Marquess and his ancestors, they say. (Bute is, incidentally, a Roman Catholic— and thus is also perhaps, the major Catholic landowner in the country.) He is totally uninterested in the House of Lords, and devotes as much of his time as possible to a welter of committees and to the National Trust for Scotland. He, like Lord Bristol, is a patron of a number of livings—nine, compared with Bristol's thirty. But since he is a Roman Catholic he is in the frustrating position of being "unable to present" to those livings in the Church of England, which is, after all, of the Protestant persuasion.

The Marquess of Huntly raised a few eyebrows early in 1977. Huntly, whose title was created in 1599, bringing him the distinction of being the Premier Marquess of Scotland and the moniker (perhaps unfortunately apt in view of his escapades) "Cock o' the North," became engaged to a twenty-year-old nurse in January of that year. He had been divorced by his wife (who, keeping the ranks nicely closed, had been the daughter of Viscount Kemsley) some dozen years before, when he was a mere fifty-six. Now, at sixty-eight, he planned to marry again, making the celebrated remark that appears as the epigraph to this chapter. "I'm Cock o' the North," yelled the head- lines, over a picture of a beaming, portly man with a wickedly curling set of moustaches.

Huntly was, in fact, no stranger to controversy. When he inherited

the title in 1937, he was found by newspaper reporters working as a
car salesman in Farnham, Surrey. The eleventh Marquess had died
without a son, and the title passed to a somewhat surprised great-
nephew. There was virtually nothing to inherit, save the title: a little
land in Aberdeenshire, but absolutely no estate of significance, no
fortune, and a castle, Aboyne, that was fast falling into ruin. A year
after he inherited there was an inconvenient claim to a peripheral
Huntly dignity known as the Lordship of Gordon, from a man named
Sir Alexander Seton. He suggested that as a Papal Bull had declared
that a divorce that took place in the Gordon family (of which Huntly
is the clan chief) in the fifteenth century was invalid, so he, Sir
Alexander, should inherit the Scots Lordship. The Committee for
Privileges at the House of Lords admitted that the claim was a
serious one, but after a long deliberation—followed by the press
of the day, though hardly as assiduously as the Ampthill baby case
of 1976—decided against in any way diminishing the honours due
to the former Farnham motor-car salesman.

The Marquess—a singer and, later, the adopted parent of a pipe
band, no less—is an admitted "backwoodsman." Like his colleague
Bute, he is a Tory of the Old School; he—Huntly—thinks that
Harold Wilson "should be suspended from the end of a long pole."
He has left the running of the Aberdeenshire estates to his son, Lord
Aboyne, and takes his ease now in a wing of a seventeenth-century
house near Guildford. When pressed to answer whether or not he
felt it appropriate for the Cock o' the North to marry a twenty-year-
old girl while he was well towards his fourscore years and ten, he
performed a trick for watching reporters: he bent over and touched
his toes, just to show how fit he was.

The estates of Bute are considerable; those of Huntly are insig-
nificant; and there is plenty of evidence among other Marquesses that
reduction of their landholdings is proceeding apace. They have not
managed to insulate themselves as nicely from the ravages of the
present century as have the Dukes. We see holders of old titles like
the Marquess of Normanby successively sell piece after piece of his
once sprawling estates—a few miles of Sussex coastline between
Bognor Regis and Littlehampton going for £3 million (it was bought
by the Post Office Superannuation Fund), the great Ingleby Green-
how Estate near Whitby up for auction, other portions of the Yorkshire
lands allowed to melt away. Normanby is still able to pay for the

services of a butler at his Mulgrave Castle, however, and to send his
sons to Eton and to rear five daughters besides. But the days when
the Normanby lands were a force to be reckoned with are over.

Likewise, Lord Linlithgow, owner of the greatest Adam mansion
in Scotland, Hopetoun House, has had to go on a selling spree:
books, paintings, a house in Sussex, all have had to go, either to pay
taxes or to offset losses incurred by his somewhat less than successful
business ventures. This Marquess, who spent more than two years
in Colditz Castle during World War II (and won the Military Cross),
is another who has to put up with the public poking among his
possessions—Rubenses, Van Dycks, Canalettos among them—and
wandering through his deer park, as part of the price of survival.

Generally then, the story of the Marquesses is more notably a story
of decline than is that of the present-day Dukes. There seem to be
more tragedies—the Marquess of Lansdowne, for example, had to
endure the shooting deaths of both his wife and daughter at the
famous Meikleour House, in Perthshire, considerable sales of furniture, and separation from his next wife. The Marquess of Northamp-
ton, who died in 1978, owned a large part of Islington, in north
London, is still listed in the record books as having paid out more
for a breach of promise suit (£50,000, to an actress named Daisy
Markham to whom he decided not to plight his troth) than any other
Briton. At the age of ninety the Marquess was forced to quit the
family seat at Castle Ashby, because of rising costs. He, too, joined
the queue of those wanting to dispose of land, or paintings or other
assets, and the son who succeeded him is having even greater difficulty in maintaining the Castle estates.

And there is a slight trace of the mercantile man among those of
the second senior rank. The Marquess of Zetland, a landowner in
Yorkshire—5,000 acres near Aske, another 9,000 on the coast near
Cleveland, and further tracts near Newburgh, in Fife—was owner
of a printing firm that, to his horror, he found had the contract for
producing the radical journal *Black Dwarf*; his son, Lord David
Dundas, wrote a television jingle for a company selling jeans. The
Marquess himself didn't seem too worried when an alderman in the
Yorkshire town of Richmond refused to stand for the entry of Zetland
into the Council Chamber. "The days of tugging forelocks are over,"
he said—a fairly bold statement, considering it was made in 1964.

The Mayor of Richmond threatened to take legal action against the rude alderman, but nothing came of it. Suffice to say no alderman would have refused to stand for a Duke in 1964: it says something for the marginally less exalted image of the Marquesses that this kind of rebellion is allowed to surface before one of their rank.

There are thirty-seven marquessates today—twenty-nine of them being eligible to a seat in the House of Lords and a thirtieth, the Marquess of Milford Haven, expected to assume his seat when he comes of age in 1982. The remaining Marquesses—Sligo, Waterford, Ely, Ormonde, Headfort, Donegall, Downshire and Coyningham—are Irish titles that will be dealt with in a separate chapter. Observant followers will realize that the addition of the thirty able to sit in the Lords, together with the eight Irishmen, exceed the stated total by one. This is because the clerks of the House of Lords recognize the Duke of Abercorn by his United Kingdom marquessate, the title by which he is able to take his seat. We classify him as a Duke, though, and so, typically, does the membership of the House: whenever the Marquess of Abercorn appears—which is infrequently—he is referred to as His Grace, not His Lordship. It is that kind of mismatched appellation that makes for confusion, and no wonder.

By the end of this century there will be many fewer of this degree: at present three of the marquessates are to be regarded as "at risk" in that the holders are rapidly approaching, or have reached, the term of their fecundity, with no heir on the horizon. The Marquessate of Cambridge, first offered in 1917 to the son and heir of the late Duke of Teck by the latter's marriage into the British Royal Family, is expected to disappear within the decade. The title of Marquess of Willingdon, given to the Indian Viceroy in 1936, became extinct recently, despite the best efforts of the heirless last Marquess to keep the title visible and active. He would travel up to the House of Lords each week—a journey of sixty miles that must have been onerous for him. He was over eighty when he died, still in harness. The Marquess of Ormonde, also born in the nineteenth century and the holder of the seventh in succession of an Irish dignity handed out in 1825 to a former Lord Lieutenant of Ireland, lives in the United States: when he dies the marquessate dies. He has only daughters (Lady Constance Butler, now, to egalitarian-minded Americans, simply Mrs. Henry Soukup, of Hinsdale, Illinois; and Lady Violet Butler, now just Mrs.

Donald Robb of Chicago), and only males in the distant family can
inherit just the earldoms of Ormonde and Ossory—such is the
brutality and complexity of the law.

And the Marquessate of Dufferin and Ava—that, too, is wanting
of an heir. This, among the most glamorous of British titles, could
go to the wall, except that the holder is still a youngster, and has
been married only since 1964. The young Sheridan Frederick Terence
Hamilton-Temple-Blackwood, with family connections to the Guin-
nesses, a seat in County Down and houses in London and Kent,
has been a perpetual darling of the gossip columnists and the social
butterflies. He inherited when he was seven, after his father was
killed in action in Burma. When he was twelve he sold Clandeboye,
the lovely Irish house, to his estates company for £120,000 "to
maintain his station in life," as the trustees said at the time. And how
he maintained that status! Joan Aly Khan, Billy Wallace, the Earl
of Dalkeith, Lady Daphne Cadogan and a myriad other luminaries
of the 1950s café society came to his nineteenth birthday party. The
fireworks at one of the three massive coming-of-age balls two years
later were said to be "just like Woomera rocket range." The young
Marquess spent a "considerable sum" redecorating his room at Christ
Church, when he went up to Oxford in 1960. And when this "debs'
delight" of a young man finally did get married, it was to a precise
equivalent in breeding and station—a cousin, of course, in the selfsame Guinness family, named Serena Belinda, but known then and
ever since as Lindy, a painter of note and, like Duffy himself, loved
by all in the brief world of glitter and gaiety.

The marriage was at Westminster Abbey, and was perhaps the
grandest non-Royal wedding of the 1960s. "Everyone was there,"
everyone said the next day—including no fewer than 100 people who
could call themselves Guinness (but not very many, one imagines,
who actually drink the stuff). Lindy and Duffy still flit into the lime-
light from time to time: as yet, though, there is no heir—and such
males in the outer circles of relations are in remainder only to the
Irish barony. Even the heir to that title, a remote and elderly Baronet,
Sir Francis Elliot Temple Blackwood, is childless—and he, like the
Ormondes, lives far away, in California.

Lindy and Duffy, Clandeboye and the Aly Khan—they somehow
sit conspicuously alone in the diminishing world of the British

Marquesses. The title still has its mighty figures—Anglesey, Salisbury, Cholmondeley, Bute—but even some of these show signs of decline now. Their position has always been somewhat anomalous: the little group, more weatherbeaten than their immediate seniors, show signs of reluctance to participate fully in a system in which they can be seen to be holders of such "strange names in the realm."

SIX

THE BELTED EARLS

I cannot conceive why you want to talk to me.
My opinions are crazy; I loathe politicians; and I
can't think where this country is going to!
　　　　　—The Earl of Carlisle, 1976

Gamekeeper/Bailiff required in Mid Staffordshire.
Single-handed duties to include game-rearing on
a small scale, management of duck lighting,
supervision of syndicate fishing pools, care and
training of gun dogs, control of vermin and tres-
pass. Applicants should be energetic, adaptable
and country bred.
　　　　　—Advertisement placed in *The Field*, 1977,
　　　　　by the Earl of Lichfield

Just after the war came, I became a second lieutenant. Then I had a nervous breakdown—collapsed. I've always hated obedience. Having done
exactly what I wanted since I grew up, I found
being under orders intolerable.
　　　　　—The Earl of Longford, quoted by Susan
　　　　　Barnes in *Behind the Image*

The Earls, backbone of the British peerage system, have been with
us for longer than any other rank. Indeed, the peer with the most
ancient title of all is accorded the rank of an Earl—a Scottish
countess, Lady Sutherland, whose family won its coronet back in
1235 or thereabouts. (Naturally, the Sutherland claim has its chal-
lengers. The Earldom of Arundel was created in 1138, and, while
it is normally held by the Duke of Norfolk it can, in certain rare
circumstances be separated from the ducal array of titles and stand

on its own. And there is the oldest peerage of all, the Earldom of Mar, which is held by a lady living in a small house at Number 10, Cranberry Drive, Stourport-on-Severn in Worcestershire. Lady Mar's title is "lost in the mists of antiquity" and is claimed to have been going strong under the guise of being a "mormaer"—a local dynast that later evolved into an Earl—as long ago as 1114. But the Countess of Mar is given actual precedence as holding a title created in 1404, so, in terms of setting table, Lady Sutherland, with her title going back all the way to 1235, is the senior.)*

The word "earl" derives from the Norse word "jarl," and it was introduced to England during that gloomy period in the eleventh century when Britons were under the harsh and costly subjection of the brutal Danes. But there is also an Old English word, "eorl," which was supposed to signify a nobleman as distinct from a "ceorl," from which we get our modern word "churl," and which means a lowly peasant. The *Oxford Dictionary* further defines that last word as "a rustic, boor, a rude, low-bred fellow." Sad to say, events of the latter months of 1974 which lifted the veil for a few brief moments and exposed the inner working of aristocracy for all to see, have convinced many that the definition is perhaps more suitable for Earls than churls—some of them at least. The third most senior of the five ranks of the British peerage has, thanks to the activities of one Richard John Bingham, seventh Earl of Lucan, been weighed in the balance of public esteem, and found badly wanting.

Richard Bingham has been missing since 7 November 1974. For most of 1975 a caravan of British policemen and attendant reporters hunted the errant nobleman from the Sussex coast to Patagonia. So many supposed "sightings" of the tall, stern, heavily moustachioed, thirty-nine-year-old Englishman flooded in to Scotland Yard—from South America, Swaziland, Portugal, Mozambique, Germany, the United States, and a dozen other nations besides—that there was a brief craze for wearing T-shirts printed with "I am not Lord Lucan." The saga is still not over. Scotland Yard, which wants the man for murdering his children's nanny and for attempting to murder his wife, maintains an open file, though dust is beginning to accumulate. Items of the wreckage strewn in the wake of his sudden flight still

* The holders of Scotland's two *oldest* earldoms—Mar and Sutherland—are not senior in precedence. These are the Earls of Crawford and Erroll.

pop up. "Lucanalia for auction," one headline read, giving the world a new eponym to slide between Hansom and Macadam, and doubtless giving the reluctant peer reason, if he is still alive, for a vicarious sense of triumph.

Lord Lucan is not the only titled Briton to disappear into thin air, as one would imagine. On 5 October 1971 Sir Peregrine Henniker Heaton vanished after spending the morning peacefully at home: three years later his son discovered his skeleton in the lumber room of his house. He had crept away to die in peace. An even more mysterious case occurred in 1943 when Lt.-Col. Sir Bruce Colin Campbell of Ardnamurchan vanished without trace from a boarding-house in West Kensington. He had only just succeeded to the baronetcy after the death of his father in a prison camp in Sumatra. A note was found telling his mother he was going away. All his bills were paid, his estate in perfect order. There were some reports he was suffering from sleeping sickness, picked up while he managed a tin mine in Burma; he may, some think, have been lost in the heavy London bombing of the time, and be buried somewhere in a pauper's grave. Other reports say he had been married in Burma, having a son and two daughters. But there is no firm evidence of either possibility—though clearly if there is a son somewhere in some steamy jungle, and the Baronet is dead, he would be the rightful heir. *Debrett's* merely records Sir Bruce as the title-holder with the note: "No information concerning this Baronet has been received since 1943." (Sir Bruce came from a family of great military distinction. Of the fifty Campbells of Cawdor, to which Ardnamurchan belongs, who have lived in this century, three have won Victoria Crosses, fifteen have won the Distinguished Service Order.)

The case of "Lucky" Lucan was altogether more sensational, not least because a particularly unpleasant murder was involved, but also because for a short while it shed some light on a corner of British society generally only romanticized about, rarely accurately reported. The picture which emerged was of a tight-knit group of moneyed men and women, their views of the ultra-right, their bigotry deep-rooted and intense, their intelligence severely limited and their attitudes and behaviour as decadent as thirties' Berlin and as repugnant as seventies' Uganda, and all engaged in a giddy, boisterous, quite irresponsible dance around the seedy gambling clubland of after-midnight London. The exposure shocked Britain even more than the murder itself. That such people could exist and thumb their collective noses at the rest of the nation came as a dull blow at the head of the body politic: a further symptom, many said, of the steady decline of Britain as a nation still worthy of respect or pleasant in which to live.

The actual crime that precipitated Lucan's disappearance was shocking enough. Just before 9 P.M. on Thursday 7 November, Lord Lucan arrived at his terraced house at 46 Lower Belgrave Street, the quietly smart quarter of the Duke of Westminster's vast estates. Inside the house, as well he knew, would be his estranged wife and the children. Absent from the house, so he suspected, would be Sandra Rivett, the young daughter of a factory worker from Coulsdon who, four weeks before, had been hired as nanny to the children. She was the eighth nanny in the past eighteen months, but, unlike her predecessors, seemed happy, and liked Veronica Lucan. Her day off, as Lord Lucan knew, was Thursday: that evening, if all was as normal, the only woman in the house should have been the thirty-seven-year-old Countess. But on this particular Thursday Sandra Rivett had a cold, and decided to stay in too. It was to be for her a fatal decision.

When Lucan arrived he was carrying all the equipment he needed to rid himself of the wife he despised and hated. He had a United States Post Office mail sack; and he had a length of lead piping wrapped in sticky tape. He let himself into the darkened house, removed the light bulb from the basement socket and waited for the woman—his wife, as he thought—to make her way downstairs for the cup of tea she habitually made in time for the BBC nine o'clock news. He heard the footsteps, saw the form of a woman, and lashed out with his lead pipe with quite extraordinary ferocity. Once, twice, three times and more he brought the blackjack down on the woman's skull. Tea tray, cups, jugs went flying down the stairs. The woman pitched forward. Blood splattered everywhere over the walls and ceiling. Pieces of bone fragment were smashed over the stairwell. When he was satisfied she was quite dead, "Lucky" Lucan crammed the body into the mailbag—a difficult task, considering the bag was only four feet deep, and the dead woman, whom Lucan probably still assumed was his wife, was a good foot and a half longer.

Then, however, he heard his wife—not dead, but yelling down the stairs for her nanny. "Sandra! Sandra!" she shouted, racing down the stairs into the dark.

"And what happened then?" asked the Coroner at the inquest the following June.

"Somebody rushed out and hit me on the head," Lady Lucan replied.

"Was there more than one blow?"

"About four."

"Did you hear anybody speak at that time?"

"No, not then. But later I screamed and the person said 'Shut up!' "

"Did you recognize the voice?"

"Yes."

"Who was it?"

"My husband."

Lady Lucan went on to tell of the violent struggle that ensued— Lucan thrusting two gloved fingers down her throat, she grabbing hold of his testicles and squeezing. Lucan stopping, running out of adrenalin, apologizing, letting his wife go and lie down in the bedroom. And then the terrified Countess fleeing from the house, running to the nearby Plumbers' Arms, bursting into the bar, covered with blood and screaming: "I've just got away from being murdered. He's murdered my nanny. He's in the house." And finally, collapsing.

Frances Bingham, the ten-year-old daughter, gave evidence at the subsequent inquest, displaying all the innocent impartiality towards the parents that a child is instinctively bound to utter. She had heard a scream after her mother had left the room at 9 P.M., but thought the cat had scratched her, nothing more. "But at about 9:05 P.M. when the news was on the television, Daddy and Mummy appeared in the room. Mummy had blood over her face and was crying." She went to bed, only to hear her father calling for her mother. She got up and "saw Daddy coming from the bedroom on the floor below. He went downstairs. That was the last I saw of him. He never came to the top of the house, either to look for Mummy or to say good-night to me." The house with the three children, a blaring television and the bloody body of Sandra Rivett lying at the foot of the stairs, was left that way until the police arrived shortly after, to begin a hunt that has never brought anything to light of value, save for the horrifying exposure of the group who had been Lord Lucan's friends. They were people who, in the words of one of their chief chroniclers, the *Daily Mail* columnist Nigel Dempster, were "An embattled race . . . the curtain, they know, is halfway down on them but they don't know when the final drop is coming so they've occupied the high ground. They think the scum are baying for their blood so they form clubs to keep the scum out, secure in the knowledge that they can behave boisterously and badly."

Lord Lucan's friends were, by contemporary standards, an extraordinary group. Many of them gambled heavily, usually at the Clermont Club in Berkeley Square—an elegant retreat for the richer and more dissolute of London's upper class.* Some of the gang with whom the seventh Earl associated had strong feelings about the racial and genetic superiority of the English upper classes: Lucan would talk openly about foreigners and "niggers" in derogatory terms; he believed passionately, or affected to believe, that "Wogs begin at Calais," and had an abiding dislike of everyone foreign, everyone not of his class. An article about Lucan published two years after the disappearance noted the stinging arrogance of some of the clique in a remark made by one of the Clermont members when John Aspinall, its owner, sold the club to Hugh Hefner and any Playboy was permitted entry. "They're hideous," one of the Lucan-like complained bitterly. "They don't gamble, they're noisy and they're skint. They just take up space and are unpleasant people to sit with."

Interest in the missing Earl had begun to flag a year later: the last evidence was his car, parked near the harbour at Newhaven, on the Channel coast; in the boot was a piece of tape-wrapped lead pipe, with blood of the same groups as those of Sandra Rivett and Lady Lucan staining one end. But by this time most Britons had come to the conclusion that it was the Lucan Set who were the truly "unpleasant people to sit with." The police, whom the moneyed men with their braying laughs would treat with contempt and open scorn, felt uncomfortable and, in truth, behaved with less ease and efficiency than had they been investigating a more routine crime, involving common criminals. The press, too, found it could get nowhere: a velvet curtain of silence had draped the witnesses, a Mafia-like code of imperturbable reticence stood betwen them and the possible truth. A *Daily Express* reporter, well used to the byways of villainy, commented: "To try to talk to this tightly knit circle of friends is like finding a traitor in Colditz. They shrink from interview . . . for fear of breaking that masonic bond which links that certain breed of men

---

* The Clermont Club did not exist by gambling alone. It was principally a "beautiful building in which to dine" in the words of a former member, and the gamblers "did their thing upstairs, without bothering the rest of us."

whose 'stud book' lines mostly lead back to the same stables—privileged prep schools, Eton, Oxford, the Household Brigade. The honour code binds their silence." But, one might have mentioned to the reporters, other criminal fraternities—nay, most other fraternities, criminal or not—have honour codes of silence. Why was this particular code to be singled out as being especially unpalatable?

The reason is to be found, one imagines, from one's inborn expectations of the English upper classes. One has for long recognized their style of living as being grand, out of touch with reality, unimaginably different from that of the masses; yet at the same time one expected of them qualities that were essentially British: honesty, reliability, decorum, taste, style, a lack of ostentation and a deeply felt loyalty to principle, rather than merely to person. One recalls the Tranby Croft gambling scandal, and the calm way the guilty party accepted his cashiering, his ostracism by his friends; one remembers the Profumo case, Harold Macmillan's shame at being lied to, and Profumo's long but successful climb back to acceptability. But this, the Clermont life and the Clermont people, this was something darker and less forgivable. There was a singular absence of dedication to any particular set of values; there seemed only a vitriolic hatred of those not of their kind and a determination to preserve their own way of life at all costs, to protect their privacy and their entrenched, neo-Fascist views from the light of public inspection. That was something neither the *Express* nor the heavy-footed policemen of Scotland Yard could take, and it has left a sour taste in the mouths of all who came into even the faintest contact with the affair.

And where is the seventh Earl? Is he alive, exiled in France, or South Africa, or Switzerland? Or is he dead, drowned in the Sussex Ouse, the river that runs between Seaford and Newhaven, where his car was found the day after the murder? The bones of a man who had gone missing in 1965 were found in the Ouse during the hunt for Lucan nine years later—possibly more noble skeletal remains will be found in 1983, held for all the intervening years by the thick mud of that sluggish stream.

He disappeared owing £62,000: at Christie's salerooms in 1977, £5,000 worth of his furniture was sold to help pay the bills. His coronet and robes have gone under the hammer too. In the autumn of 1981, having been absent for the legally prescribed seven years, he was declared extinct; his fourteen-year-old son George stood ready to apply for the elevation of his title from that of the courtesy appellation Baron Bingham, to that of the Irish Earldom of Lucan, of Castlebar, created in 1795. Few doubt that young George will make his application: for although many believe Lucan to be alive still, protected by his friends and financed by his cronies, there is confident assurance he will remain undiscovered. The sense of solidarity among the upper classes in which Lucan moved seems thick enough to cut.

And Lady Lucan? She lives on near Number 46, sadder but a little wiser in the wake of this ugly affair. She has given a number of interviews. In 1979 she criticized the actress chosen to portray her in a TV play: "I have a more delicate face than her, more gamin and fey and childlike. I was a model and have very good bones." At another time she said: "You may think that the night that Sandra Rivett was murdered was the worst night of my life. But, in a way, the horror of the years before, when my husband—aided by those closest to him—tried to have me declared insane, was cumulatively much worse." It was not an affair out of which many emerged with their dignity intact.

And some people lost a lot more than mere dignity. Dominic Elwes, a sad failure of a specimen who, in spite of more intelligence and wit than the entire membership of the Clermont gathered together, had somehow inveigled his way into Lucan's coven, was suspected of having given photographs of the Lucan Set at play to a Sunday newspaper—and so hounded was he by the thugs and bullies of the group that, despite his innocence, he killed himself with an overdose of barbiturates. "When one of their class, like Dominic Elwes," wrote Nigel Dempster, "seems to have been talking to the enemy—which is you and me—he is last seen heading down the hill into the enemy camp like a prairie dog, holding a white flag in his teeth." Elwes wrote a farewell note cursing those who, he felt, had driven him to an early grave: all he had tried to do was to present an honest picture of Lucan to the more responsible members of the press who were fascinated by the revelations the murder brought in its wake. "I hope they are happy now," he wrote. And at a service held later in 1975 for him, a service attended by many distinguished figures from the more distinguished edges of the stage on which Elwes briefly danced, there was further ugliness: John Aspinall, giving his version of a eulogy, was punched on the nose for his pains. He slumped back into his car as the assailant, a distant cousin of the dead Dominic's, walked off. "I'm used to dealing with animals," he said. Kenneth Tynan, hearing of the incident, quoted Belloc. Elwes, his friend, had been memorialized that day "to the sound of the English county families baying for broken glass."

And then there was Sandra Rivett—almost a byproduct of the *scandale,* her death seems now as irrelevant as did Officer Tippett's to the assassination in Dallas eleven years before. Perhaps she was about the only normal creature in the whole sad death-dance. Her husband had left her a few weeks before she happened on Veronica Lucan: all she had was her black cat which, so much did she apparently like the Lucan children and the Countess, she returned to Surrey one day to get and bring to Belgravia. Her death was a grisly mistake, but one which became swiftly eclipsed as the curtain was lifted on the world she briefly entered. Her role in this is similar to that of Stephen Ward, the osteopath caught up in the depraved and similarly arrogant world of the Cliveden Set. To that group, Ward was "m' doctor" in the same way other Sets would have had "m' butler" or "m' groom." Mrs. Rivett was "m' nanny," and it was characteristic of the callous attitudes of the Set which she so tragically encountered that one member remarked, according to the police, that it was a shame she had had to die "because nannies are so hard to come by nowadays." "Of course," one of Lucan's pals said later, "out of politeness, one says it's very hard on the nanny, although I don't of course feel a personal sense of loss."*

Neither did anyone else, apparently. She was buried six weeks after the killing, with suggestions still rampant that it had been a jealous boyfriend, rather than a belted Irish Earl, who had smashed her skull. Her parents and the police sent flowers. No one else sent anything. She left this world to the sound of the British upper classes merely moaning that girls of her sort were so hard to come by.

There are 173 non-Irish Earls and Countesses dotted around the country and the world. Mercifully for the breed few are of the same strain as Richard John Bingham: most are incomparably pleasanter men and women, rendering to the society benefits that are almost enough to offset the monstrous debt incurred by Lucan and his mindless cronies. Their geographical distribution, unlike the patterns displayed by the

* A critic says he has never heard the phrase "m' doctor" or "m' nanny," and the author must confess he has not, either. But the attitude, suggesting at least part-ownership of some who perform service, is common among the wealthier in Britain, as in other countries too.

Dukes and the Marquesses, illustrates the distribution of the most select regions of the nation. Central and West London account for twenty-six of their number; the chalk hills around Salisbury are home to a cluster of four (Pembroke and Montgomery, Rothes, Radnor and Chichester); Gloucestershire and the Wye Valley are inhabited by a string from the Earl of Suffolk and Berkshire in the south, to the Countess of Mar, who worked as a telephone saleswoman from her house in Cranberry Drive, Stourport-on-Severn. For some reason Earls favour the biting winds and salt marshes of East Anglia: Lords Albemarle, Stradbroke, Cranbrook, Cairns and Leicester tuck themselves away on huge farms and sombre granges in Suffolk and Norfolk, using Liverpool Street as their terminus for their clubs and the House rather than the more fashionable railway palaces of Paddington and King's Cross. Scotland too provides ample nesting territory for those entitled to be called "Our right trusty and right well-beloved cousin" and who are distinguished from Marquesses, in briefer formal form, by the appellation "Right Honourable" instead of "Most Honourable." A clutch nestle on the southern banks of the Firth of Forth, from Queensferry to Haddington—the Earls of Rosebery, Lauderdale, Dunmore, Haddington, Wemyss and Balfour; others rule from great houses on the salmon rivers from Tayside to Speyside. The northernmost is the Countess of Sutherland, up at Brora; the westernmost (aside from those who live in Ireland) is Granville James Leveson-Gower, the fifth Earl Granville, who has a house at Callernish, on the Outer Hebridean island of North Uist. Two—the Earl of Jersey and the Earl of Middleton—live in the Channel Islands; one, the Earl of Northesk, lives at Ballamodwa on the Isle of Man. One lives in America, another in Australia, and the Earl of St. Germans makes his home not at the village of his name in Cornwall but, perhaps more appropriately, in a distant canton of Switzerland.

The merciless decrepitude that hangs about the peers like green moss makes it likely that at least five of the titles will vanish in the next decade or so. One, the Earldom of Stamford, quietly lapsed into extinction in 1976 when the seventy-nine-year-old tenth Earl died at his house in a Manchester suburb. Roger Stamford had lived with his mother until she died, aged ninety-three, in 1959; he never had any children, and no cousins, brothers or nephews appeared on the scene to claim the title. It had been in existence as an English peerage since 1628; the Barony of Groby, which the old man also counted among his dignities, was created in 1603 and that, too, died with him.

Auberon Waugh was about the sole recorder of his passing: "It is my normal practice after I have met an hereditary peer for the first time to colour in his coat of arms in my *Peerage*. Now Roger Stamford's shield will remain for ever uncoloured, his tufted unicorns unguled." (A nice epigram, but sadly a little less than accurate. The Stamford coat of arms displays, as supporters, "two unicorns ermine, armed, unguled, tufted and maned or"; had Waugh permitted himself the pedantry he normally adores he should have written "his unguled, tufted unicorns unermined, their manes unorred.")*

Another earldom at imminent risk of extinction is Ancaster, which has especial significance, since that title and the Marquessate of Cholmondeley share between them the Hereditary Great Chamberlain's office. Unless James Ancaster can summon up an heir at the age of seventy, it is tempting to suppose the Cholmondeley's will inherit the office for life and for ever—or at least until their line has died out, which, according to the statistics of the matter, it should do between now and the end of the twenty-second century. Research shows, however, the matter is infinitely more complicated, and the Cholmondeleys will not have the good fortune, at least for the time being. There is a lesser heir to the Earl of Ancaster, the Barony of Willoughby de Eresby; and although the heir presumptive to that title is a woman—and one with two sisters, moreover—and although no Great Office of State can be held by a woman, there is every possibility the titleholder could name a deputy to take over the Ancaster share of the Great Office. In addition to that safeguard, the House of Lords says that the descendants of the extinct Marquessate of Lincolnshire can share the office as well.

In addition to Ancaster's imminent demise, the Earldom of Middleton recently became extinct, and the Earldoms of Fingall and Ypres look like grinding to an inglorious end in the coming years (the Earl of Ypres is banned from sitting in the Lords because of his bankruptcy). The Earldom of Breadalbane, held now by a man with a mother called Armorer, Countess of Breadalbane, and a history of having played the pipe in a number of pubs to earn money, looks like becoming, if not extinct, then at least dormant. No one has any idea if there are any Breadalbane cousins to inherit the title; the

* The Greys—the family name of the Lords Stamford—had been peers in the male line since the thirteenth century and the very beginnings of Parliament. For a brief, and all too sad, moment one of them, Lady Jane Grey, was Sovereign.

Earl has neither sons nor daughters. *Debrett's* is vague to the point of fascination: among those in remainder to the earldom are the "descendants if any" of a variety of long-lost cousins of the present Earl. Men like "Colin Campbell, Surgeon, 39th Regiment, eldest son of Captain Robert Campbell, great-great-uncle of the Sixth Earl, who died in Guadaloupe in 1794," or like "Duncan Campbell, youngest son of Robert Campbell of Glenfalloch . . . bookbinder to the Queen."

The guardians of the peerage rolls will not admit to an extinction if they can possibly avoid it: in the case of the mysterious Breadalbane family they will hold on for perhaps a generation after the present Earl is dead before they will admit defeat and declare the title gone to the grave with him. There is always the faint hope that some shaggy figure will crawl up from the Malayan jungle in twenty years' time and claim that a soggy mess of papers he found in a strong-box at the bottom of a tin mine there proves beyond all reasonable doubt that he is the holder of an earldom. Since the title was created in 1677 there is considerable attachment of history in keeping it going: the fortune and lands that once went with the Breadalbanes have long since vanished, the present titleholder lives in Hampstead, in London. His wife—they are now divorced—was named Coralie.

The Earls of Birkenhead, Lovelace and Woolton are all young and single and as yet have no heirs, either children or brothers. Lord Sondes, holder of another title with a shaky future, was first married for less than a year and now has married again, this time to Princess Sissy of Salm. Technically their titles, none of which is especially old, are at risk: but there is little likelihood, one suspects, of their remaining heirless for much longer. Thus only four of the titles will definitely vanish, and one will go into cold storage. For the other 168, their dignities can be expected, for the time being, to go marching steadily on. Even that of the execrable Lord Lucan.

"I gather there was something—how shall we say—something . . . peculiar about the Lucan marriage. You get to hear things at the House and from your friends, and all I can say is that the attitude of Lord Lucan towards life . . . was not exactly normal and the way you and I would look at things." The twelfth Earl of Kintore, a gruff and kindly former engineer who lives in a vast house fifteen miles from Aberdeen, takes a dim view of the Lucan affair, and the behaviour it exposed. He took the view that holding a peerage conferred certain privileges on the holder, and that to behave as Lucan did—and as two neighbour peers, one an Earl and one a Baron, had done in the recent past—"was simply not on."

"I take the view very strongly that a peerage does not confer any special rights or status on the holder unless or until he earns them. The title was given as a reward for special service, and unless you happen to be lucky enough to be a peer of first creation you find yourself saddled with a title you did nothing to earn. Look at me: there have been eleven Earls before me, all the way down from the Earls who were Earls Marischal of Scotland. To win my spurs I've got to work bloody hard to try and match their achievements. It's the only way. You have to spend your whole life trying to live up to the reward you've been given, your whole life earning your position."

Only once or twice in my long progress through the various degrees of nobility did the tenants of a hereditary title offer such views. Most, like Buccleuch and Devonshire, accepted their vast riches as the responsibility they had inherited: the title was, if anything, of lesser import. Some, men of Viscount or Baron status, looked upon their peerage as a means of getting a better deal from a preferentially shuffled deck—though not always for purely selfish reasons, of course. The Earl of Kintore, who succeeded to his title in 1974 after his mother died at the age of 101, has political views as astringently right-wing as most of his fellows: but he is possessed of an abiding sense of responsibility to his title.

"I've never pretended to be anything I'm not. I am sure I am the only member of the House of Lords ever to have dug a tunnel under the Thames, in highly compressed air, while wearing an Old Etonian tie. Mind you, the tie was holding up my trousers at the time—I wouldn't have gone down with it around my neck, it was too hot. But I do make a point of using my life sensibly, earning my keep, doing my bit. Without it no one will respect your title, no one will listen to you, and you can't blame them."

Lord Kintore and his wife Delia live on the top floor of the crumbling Keith Hall, which sits in several thousand acres of neat parkland by the village of Inverurie. Ringing the doorbell can be a frustrating experience: you know His Lordship is there, but it must be three full minutes after you first pressed the bellpush at the huge oak door, and still nothing has happened. Did he hear? Is the bell working? Should I ring again? Five minutes elapse and then the door creaks open. "Sorry I was so long. It's a hell of a climb. Glad to see you at last."

At the top of some sixty steps that wind up through landings and curtains and past dust-covered furniture and the faint smells of other people's cooking and the distant yells of children, is the long, very confusing, multi-corridored, multi-leveled apartment in which the old Earl and Countess spend their days. There is all manner of memorabilia: letters from Charles II hung up in the bathroom, a telegram from the Queen to the late Countess on her centenary ("and one from Barbara Castle too, the bloody woman. She had the nerve to send a telegram to my mother after doing everything she could to make living conditions terrible for people like her. So my mother gave a sort of Harvey Smith to her and popped off just after the party, stone dead. She was disgusted."), and a note from the whipper-in of a Hunt asking a former member of the Keith family to go and vote in the House of Commons—the origin, it is said, of the term "Whip" being used for the marshals of party faithful in the legislative assembly.

"I'm not a great one for class, you know," he said, as we settled down, rather out of breath. We were in a small, book-lined sitting-room at the very top of the house, the bright light from the snowy parklands below flooding in through the windows, giving everything a fresh, newly painted look.

"The only real difference between you and me is that I know my background very well. I've got a better filing system than you. For all you know you might be mixed up with the Marquess of Winchester: it happens, you know." From time to time he was delightfully vague about his relationships. "Do I know the Duke of Montrose? Yes, he's a second cousin, I think. John Logie Baird—I'm not quite sure where he fits in, but he must be mixed up with us somewhere. Lord Burton, up the road a way—I'm not sure if we're related, I'd have to look it up." The filing system was there in the library: volume after volume of Scottish and English peerage lore, vast rulings from the Lord Lyon, copies of articles of genealogy and papers on the Clan Keith, of which Kintore is the Chief. "I know that Europe is littered with Keiths. One of my antecedents was a Prussian soldier, with the result that there are at least twenty members of the Clan Keith in Sweden today. There are scores of illegitimate Keiths, or descendants, all over the place. It's quite a clan to be with."

Lord Kintore is an engineer—an Etonian who, rather than take the usual well-traveled path to Christ Church, Sandhurst or the Royal Agricultural College at Cirencester, to learn politics, soldiering or how to manage a country estate, chose to go to the School of Mines, where he learned tunnelling and mine engineering. He became a Royal Marine engineer, had a "pretty boring sort of war" in Iceland, the Orkneys and "just into Germany, right at the end" before settling into an occupation that took him from mine to mine from Kincardine-shire to the Rand. He became a Viscount in 1941, owing to some complicated formula of remainder, but declined to take his seat in the House of Lords until "I felt I had something to talk about."

He is a classically responsible member of the House—he attends three days a month, speaks only on subjects about which he lays claim to special knowledge, and has little regard for the Whips. "The House allows you to preserve some independence of thought. If you ever do happen to get a three-line whip, which is very rare, all they want is to ensure your attendance. They don't seem to mind too much about your vote. And if they do, well, you can always tell them to go and do the other thing."

Kintore travels down from Aberdeen Station once a month—usually on a Sunday-night sleeper, in which he travels First Class. "Well, if every little town-hall clerk can travel First on his expenses I see no reason why I should travel Second when I'm on House of Lords business."

When he arrives he goes to his club, the Beefsteak, in Leicester Square. "It's a pleasant little club. The only qualifications for mem-bership are that you've either got to be a peer who has learned to read and write, or a journalist who has learned table manners. We have all sorts there—there's an RC priest, heaps of authors, cartoonists, all sorts. All that is required of you is that you can talk. They have you over a barrel, you see. In the dining-room there is just one long table and lots of waiters called Charles ["Is that their real name?" "Oh no—they're just called Charles, just as one said 'Boy!' at school. Heaven only knows what their real names are"], and they can sit you just where they like. So I get to meet a different set of people every time, and I like it. It broadens my outlook."

After breakfast he makes his way around to the English Speaking Union, where he takes luncheon after a swim in the pool—the only London pool of which he knows that allows mixed bathing. He some-times takes his wife, so that she can catch up on her shopping. After a congenial Monday in London and the first convivial dinner of his short stay, he sets out for the House of Lords on Tuesday afternoon. "I go, and I sit, very occasionally I say something—if it is a debate on engineering, or forestry, or water, or devolution, or some thing to which I think I can contribute, then I'll tell the Clerks I intend to say something. I usually stay and listen in any case. I certainly wouldn't bother to go down if there wasn't any pay. The allowance is a great incentive. In fact the whole things is really an excuse to get down to London, which I like, once a month. I get my railway fare paid for, and the price of accommodation at the Beefsteak is not too high—though mind you, it shouldn't be, they put you up in those horrible little hospital beds, and the rooms are a bit shabby."

Politically he is quintessentially *Homo backwoodensis*. "My own view is that there is a considerable excess of democracy between elections here. I agree entirely in a democratic system of elections, but once the chaps are in I think the rest of the country should leave them to get on with running things. The media, the unions—they're forever poking their noses in and subjecting the Government to all sorts of inquiries that slow things down terribly. The unions have enormous blackmail powers which should be curbed—mind you, I think we're doing quite well. But the country is too far gone in the grip of Socialists like Michael Foot and Tony Benn. All they want is Communism, although not by name, and they're doing their best to create a climate in which it comes about. By attacking us, for example, they are just trying to foster a climate of envy in which we are seen as somehow different from the rest of the people. And some of our people don't help. Some are badly behaved, some do let their estates down, some do become dissolute, or have affairs with call girls and things. So that doesn't help. But so long as there are a few of us who feel that the House of Lords is a worthwhile institution and who feel that their peerages are a reward that they have got to pay back over their lifetime by doing something worthwhile, then maybe we will survive in public esteem, and that's what matters, isn't it?"

Lord Kintore said there was not "a single country in the world that has benefited from Socialism," and reacted with dismay when he was told that Sweden had managed to win the accolade as the nation with the highest of all standards of living under precisely such a system; he felt that Zimbabwe was not ready for majority rule for many a long year yet, and that no other African country had achieved any sort of success under black rule. Kenya? "Just wait a few years—

it'll be a shambles." Tanzania? "That's a Communist country now, so we don't know."

The views of this kindly old man, polite, slightly shabby, implacably British, traditional, buried in history and charmed by simple pleasures, are shared, it should be said in fairness, by millions. He thinks Britain is in a continuing and accelerating decline, which he attributes to the malign influence of the Left; the workers have too much power, blacks are unprepared to rule in Africa, Dr. Vorster and Mr. Smith had the right idea; why do things have to change so? The Lucan Set held similar views, of course, but there is a difference in the volume of protest, the form in which the protests are made, the tenor of the argument, the degree of tolerance. Lucan and his friends are loud, given to baying their dislike for the *hoi polloi* in flashy shopfront bars, are bitter and angry, bigoted and blinkered. Neither group is privy to much in the way of facts—for both, the objection to such spectres as "Socialism" is largely one of emotion, rather than informed thought; but Kintore is, at least, prepared to listen, to take his taxicab to the House of Lords and sit quietly in the wings, listening to his country diminish all around him, making the odd contribution to the debate where he can.

While the Lucans of this world do the peerage and their class a monstrous disservice, the Kintores continue to project an image that is part caricature, part legend, part truth. The British country gentleman, reticent, responsible, mindful of the sensibilities of those around him but perpetually dismayed with the decline he sees. And yet which example is more responsible for the decline, which of the pair will hasten on the evolution of true egalitarianism? Kintore has no doubts: "Some of my colleagues behave rather badly. They give men like Benn and Foot excellent ammunition for their attacks. I'm not saying I'm at all perfect—I'm getting on now, and I don't do all I could. A lot of people would say I was washed up and finished. But I can look back and feel fairly proud of what I've done. I feel I have at least tried to live up to what is expected of me. I don't think Lucan did."

"The thing about Frank Longford is that he's a very *peculiar* man," said a man who knows him well. "He's much more peculiar than most people we know." Few would question the observation. Lord Longford looks peculiar and he acts in a peculiar fashion and, by the standards of his peers, is quite extraordinary. He seeks for the satisfaction of his personal crusades—for downtrodden prisoners, against pornography, for homosexual law reform, for more tolerant attitudes towards drug addiction—with such frenzied zeal that he is in constant danger of being thought an ass, a showman—even a charlatan. "Frank Longford is one of the most foolish men in England," wrote one book reviewer, only to be politely slapped down a few days later by a charming letter from the noble Earl who, though he may be many other things, is most certainly not a fool, but is pleasantly tolerant towards those who think he is.

The appearance of the man often serves to confirm the impression that the seventh Earl of Longford is a very strange individual. He dresses more shoddily than even the most studied eccentric would need to: his suits are terribly crushed, when he bothers to wear a suit; at home he strides round in an ancient pair of riding-trousers, patched and frayed, with a torn polo-neck jersey round his thin, slightly stooped shoulders. His hair is invariably wild, his glasses, which are round and very close to his eyes, seem filmy with grime; he has baddish teeth and occasionally dribbles from the edges of his mouth.

Unattractive he may be, but Einstein and Schweitzer probably looked much the same in their day. And the fact remains that Frank Longford is one of the most decent, most sensible, most courageous and intelligent men in England. He is not well liked: his views are thought too patrician, too condescending, his interests dismayingly prurient, his dialectic impure. He consistently champions the very nastiest members of British society—criminals who have wrought the vilest of crimes and who have been sent to rot in prison for decades as a consequence. He takes too great an interest in matters that British people traditionally affect discomfort about discussing. And yet he often appears just the still small voice we feel perhaps we should be listening to, even though we might not like to admit it.

He was born in 1905, the second son of the fifth Earl; he went to Eton and Oxford (where he took a distinguished First), was converted to Socialism, to Roman Catholicism, became a don and fairly rapidly wrote one of the finest histories of Ireland ever to have appeared. He married Elizabeth Harman, an astonishingly handsome woman still, and together they produced a crop of children who, one feels, may one day parallel the Mitford girls for dazzle and celebrity. (Thomas Pakenham, who does not use the courtesy title of Lord Silchester, lives on the old estate in County Westmeath; Patrick is a lawyer;

Michael is a diplomat of coming distinction. Antonia, a splendid author of historical biography, married first Hugh Fraser, the distinguished and suitably aristocratic Conservative MP, then left him for Harold Pinter; Rachel writes; Judith graduated from Somerville; a fourth daughter was killed in a motor accident when she was twenty-three.) Elizabeth Longford is a distinguished biographer, too—certainly more happily received by the critics than her husband: he writes splendidly about ideas but when it comes to writing about human beings, President Kennedy, for example, about whom he wrote in 1976, he gets massacred by the literary pundits.

Paul Johnson, the former editor of the *New Statesman* and a shrewd observer of the British upper classes, says that without a doubt "The Pakenhams *are* the most remarkable family in England today. People say it's all publicity. It's not."

Frank Longford has managed to combine a sparkling political career with a series of personally directed campaigns for the world's less fortunate creatures, and at the same time participate in rearing this quite remarkable family. After his Eton and Oxford careers were sideswiped by World War II—his nervous breakdown culminated in his serving with "Dad's Army," the Home Guard, in Oxford itself—he became personal assistant to Sir William Beveridge, architect of the Welfare State, the mechanician of post-war Labour reforms. And by the end of the war, when Attlee's Government was put firmly into power, his political career began to take off: he first came to public notice as a man of unusual passion and compassion when he was set the task of administering the British Zone of occupied Germany. Contemporaries recall how shocked and distressed he was by the condition of the downtrodden, defeated, humiliated Germans; he worked in a manner best described as saintly to help relieve their suffering. Not surprisingly, he came in for more than his fair share of abuse, even though he was careful to reserve his compassion for those he considered "good" Germans—the majority, but assuredly not the Germans who had records of being unduly vicious in their prosecution of the war.

Labour was not in government for long; by 1951 Longford was back in opposition: during all the "thirteen years of Tory misrule" he was left almost in the wilderness. He did run the National Bank, accruing valuable and unforgotten experience in fiscal mysteries; he also wrote two books: *Causes of Crime* and *The Idea of Punishment.* His keen interest in helping the unfortunates had moved across the

North Sea from Germany: British prisoners formed the basis of his last crusade and the one for which, when he dies, he will best be remembered.

In 1964 he became Leader of the House of Lords—a position which, for an Earl of only three years' experience (though he had been created a Baron in 1945 when, without a parliamentary seat, Attlee gave him tasks to do that required attendance in the legislalature), was not bad going. He presided over his party's fortunes in the Upper House for three and a half years, betimes winning himself the reputation of "a respected and upright figure" and eventually participating in the Government's attempt to have the House of Lords savagely restructured. That move failed and it was not much later, in a row over cuts in the Government's education budget, that Frank Longford eventually resigned. Harold Wilson did not shed many tears over the parting: Frank Longford, looking back with slight traces of the nearest thing to bitterness an ardent Christian can recognize, believes he must have seemed an awful bore to the thrusting, energetic Cabinet of the day. He did tend to go *on* lecturing people on morality and Christianity; he admits now he must have seemed a bit tedious.

Today he is a publisher, Chairman of Sidgwick & Jackson, though he is careful to see that his own books are not in his house list: Weidenfeld publishes Longford, on De Valera and John Kennedy and Jesus Christ. He has written two autobiographies already, more than enough for a man of only seventy-five, but too little for a life that has been quite remarkable in its variety and complexity, and still shows no signs of entering a sedate phase.

Perhaps the most celebrated venture in which Lord Longford participated was his chairmanship of the Inquiry into Pornography. He became a constant fixture on the front pages of the more sensational newspapers, watching avidly the most bizarre sexual extravaganzas in both Soho and the Scandinavian capitals. The book that resulted was, thanks to its colourful prose style and its photographs, an instant commercial success: Longford has since been hard pressed to live down his later title, "Lord Porn."

His championing of the less fortunate of prisoners goes on—men and women involved in the most horrific crimes (notably Myra Hindley of the Moors Murders) merit his special attention. He is constantly to be heard lecturing against the evils of long-term imprisonment, even for the perpetrators of the most heinous deeds: it does no good,

he says, and tries to prove his case by telling the press he has managed to convert Myra Hindley to Roman Catholicism and is
persuading Brady to read Tolstoy. He visits them—as well as many
other, less celebrated prisoners; perhaps they may have been flattered
by the unusual attentions of the Earl at first, but by all accounts both
they, and the prison staff, are convinced that all Frank Longford is
trying to do is to help.

The first time I met him was in Northern Ireland: I gave him a
lift to the airport for his plane back to London, and he, in return, gave
me one of the best stories (the details of a conversation he had recently
had with a commanding general in the Army there) I had been able
to write for a long time. He further returned the compliment by quoting me at the opening of a Lords debate on Ireland's "Bloody Sunday."
When I saw him again recently it was first at his sparsely furnished
rooms at the Bloomsbury office of his publishing firm. He was not
talking publishing, but speaking softly into a telephone, about Myra
Hindley and her prison ordeal. "If you'll forgive me for saying so . . .
I don't feel I'd better argue with you . . . I hope you'll give careful
consideration to the points I've raised, even if you disagree . . . ?"
Never did he raise his voice; the telephone was placed back on its
cradle with careful grace. He was angry at being turned down, but
retained serenity that spoke either of some deep faith, or of yoga. He
talks of the need for "good manners" and "a sense of responsibility";
he, like Kintore, politely deplores the behaviour of some of his
ennobled colleagues. "I seem to remember Wayland Young [Lord
Kennet] doing some research on divorce rates among peers: he
found that Dukes were thirty per cent higher than ordinary people.
That must say something, and it doesn't sound too healthy to me."

On the wireless he once took the lectern to defend—though not in
a particularly impassioned way—the system of civil honours, a system
in which he stands, for hereditary reasons, close to the very top and
in which, for reasons of merit (he was given a Knighthood of the
Garter in 1971 for his services to youth and to prisoners), he stands
at the very summit. He believes there is too much snobbery in present-
day Britain (though he rather lovingly remembers the peer who
once exploded: "Snobs, snobs—where would I be without snobs?")
but does not believe the awarding of Orders of the British Empire,
or knighthoods, has much to do with it. Of hereditary peerages there
is, he concedes, some room for believing their involvement in the
system of snobbery, and he is quite glad that none has been created

since 1965. But the idea that ambulance drivers may see one of their number collect an MBE from the Queen after fifty years of loyal service—"it helps people with thankless tasks like that to know, as a body, they are recognized as being worthy of note, and of the concern of the nation as a whole. I would not much want to end that system." He is not, however, an ardent supporter of the monarchy: "The hereditary peers help prop up the Monarch and protect her (or him) from the toils of ordinary life: to that extent they should be abolished, and their supporting role in the House of Lords taken from them."

He admits there are certain advantages to being a peer, advantages he has been quick to exploit, albeit for the welfare of his chosen minorities, rather than for himself. "Being a member of the House of Lords is, for a chap like me, a bit of an ambiguous advantage. I think I would have been of more use in the Commons, and in fact I did try several times to give up my title. But Gaitskell, and later Wilson, preferred that I stay as I was. I think I would have sickened pretty quickly of the political infighting and the trivia of the Commons—but one misses some of the cut and thrust here in the Lords. I have mixed feelings about it.

"But there are other benefits. A Lord can throw his weight around a lot more than a man who doesn't have a title. When I started taking an active interest in what was going on in Northern Ireland I found I could easily get into places that others, even MPs, had some difficulty with. There was no trouble about getting into the internment camps, say, although times have changed. I went back recently [in 1976] and the police fobbed me off with a visit to the Crumlin Road prison in the middle of Belfast, and wouldn't let me go to the Maze, the old Long Kesh. Maybe the pull is not what it was. Then the Dukes have this right of access to the Monarch—I suppose that can be useful. More than anything it's the ability to get things done and have things done for you when you're a peer. People still do take notice when they ask who's talking and I say 'Lord Longford.' Is that because they've heard of me, or is it because I'm a Lord? I rather suspect it's because of my title rather than my name."

He thinks there should, perhaps, be a "Peer of the Year" competition organized by some newspaper, to try and bring out the talented aristocrats and raise the general level of public approval of those in the House of Lords. "They tend to be rather retiring, shy of publicity and thus not as well received as they might be. Look at what we've got—there are literary and artistic peers of considerable distinction, like Lord Methuen, Lord Esher, Lord Lytton, Lord Milford. There are fellows of enormous intellectual capacity—Hailsham, Rothschild, Halsbury. And there are some very dubious ones—perhaps there should be a wooden spoon given to the one who performs worst of all. The poorest landowner, the rudest man—the Duke of [he mentions a name] might have won that award at one time."

When Frank Longford added the New Horizon Centre, for drug addicts, to his New Bridge—for prisoners—many suspected he was just another of what Americans like to call "bleeding hearts." But as one of the staff said, admiringly, after Longford had set the Centre up and handed it over to professionals for their full-time management: "Being a peer and all that—and so good—we thought he would be resented by the addicts. Surprisingly he's not. They look on him as a father figure. He isn't much like the usual do-gooder. Unlike a vicar or a probation officer, he has no axe to grind."

Lord Longford and Elizabeth Longford represent the flowering majesty of the peerage in action. Theirs is a combination of inherited behaviour, ability and attitudes and tastes which, sculpted by a deep sense of responsibility and influenced by their Christianity, have produced a family of which the class system can be rightly proud. Longford would not have been accorded the acclaim, nor in all probability had the chance to strive for it, had he been untitled and bent on forging his mission from the basement, rather than the drawing-room. Rightly used, the benefits of nobility can reach to impressive heights, and Frank Longford, seventh Earl and first Baron, is a proven exception to the currently popular rule that ennoblement is, at its best, a Bad Thing.

When I first met the Earl of Seafield he had just finished doing the football pools. "You never know when you'll be lucky," he remarked drily, though he added that he always put an X in the box marked "No Publicity." "I doubt if it would do my image a lot of good to be found winning big on the football pools!"

Lord Seafield needs all the luck he can get. A very private man in his middle forties, he currently presides over an empire that dwindles by the day, like a puddle of water in the heat of the sun. At the turn of the century the Earls of Seafield were reckoned the third or fourth biggest landowners in Scotland: 400 square miles of the best sporting land in the Grampian Hills, and the better agricultural land on their northern fringes, belonged to the Seafield Estates. The present Earl's mother, Nina, Countess of Seafield, had to watch while, thousand-acre plot by thousand-acre plot, the landholdings were dismantled to pay the bills. And now the present Earl is having to sell again: land, bit by bit; whole estates, like the Ord Estate in Banffshire; and, in 1976, the remaining contents of Cullen House, a grand, turreted granite mansion on the southern shores of the Moray Firth. The sale, which, after death duties and other taxes had been paid, brought in only about £17,000 to prop up the sagging Seafield finances, was widely criticized by the nearby newspapers of Inverness and Aberdeen.* It raised tempers locally in the way that the sale of Mentmore Towers, near London, raised tempers nationally in 1977. One imagines that had Cullen been a few dozen miles up the motorway from Fleet Street, arguments about its sale would have been similarly on everybody's lips.

Nowadays the Seafield Estates run to about 90,000 acres—60,000 on Speyside, now crawling with skiers in winter and fishermen in the late summer; and 30,000 in the Moray Firth area. Some 50,000 of those acres are held in trust for the heir, Viscount Reidhaven, and his younger brother, the Hon. Alexander Ogilvie-Grant, who was born in 1966; under the direct control of the Earl are a mere 30,000 acres, one house (Old Cullen) and 140 farms. The heading "Seafield, Earl of" in the Aberdeen area telephone directory is a good three inches long, replete with numbers for Fishing Beat Number Three, Estates Office, Factor, Shooting Lodge, and on and on. There is more than a hint of Victorian Scots grandeur about the addresses and the obvious accessories of landownership as they are listed in the telephone book: reading the sad story of the attenuation of the Seafield fortunes, and meeting the Earl himself, dispel the illusion.

He sat at a desk that was littered with income-tax tables and the finished copies of the football pools. He is a rangy, nervous man with an air of self-conscious loneliness about him. His wife and children were away in London, he explained. Cullen House, half a mile away down the park, stands empty and forbidding in the January gloom; the Lodge, into which he moved in 1977, is neat and com-

---

* Lest this be regarded as wholesale criticism of Lord Seafield it ought to be pointed out that he only had to sell the contents of Cullen House to pay the enormous taxes levied upon him—some critics would suggest they, not the noble Lord, were to blame for a regrettable situation.

fortable, but utterly silent. The Earl went off to make his own tea, returned with a tray which he placed beside the day's copies of the *Daily Telegraph* and the *Daily Express*. There was an *Adelphi Paper*, the journal of the Institute for Strategic Studies, on the coffee table. He is not a soldier—never has been—"but I like to keep up with the global picture of the Soviet build-up. The British have a habit of being complacent—not me, though."

He blames the country's ills on taxation, which he regards almost as criminal. "The Socialist dogma that is rife in this country is doing everything it can to knock out people like me. There is no incentive for anyone in this country to do anything any more. I've thought about going abroad—if I sold up I'd be a rich man, and I could live in great style. But frankly there are only two real bastions of capitalism left I could go to—America and Canada. And I have thought about it a lot.

"But even then the tax man makes it so difficult. I'd have to change my residence permanently—I couldn't go on coming back to see the children or anything like that. You've got to show the Revenue you've really chucked this country.

"And they're gaining on us all the time. Look at France, and how well Mr. Mitterand did. Communism—it's creeping all over Europe and by the time it gets here we'll be quite content to let it in. It masquerades in all sorts of disguises in Europe. It's blatant imperialism in Africa."

And so his Lordship went on and on. He had recently joined the Institute for the Study of Conflict, a brazenly conservative organization. He is being careful not to damage his credibility by aligning himself with "extreme right-wing bodies," but he has pledged himself to do all he can to combat the Red Menace, as he actually calls it, in Britain. "Look at Scottish devolution—the Communists would love it if Scotland and England broke up. They know that unity is strength, and that disunity is something they can happily exploit. I can't understand why the people in London and Edinburgh don't recognize that instantly. Am I alone up here?"

There were 900 guests at his coming-of-age party in 1960; the entire village came to his wedding a few months later. Now, the faith and loyalty which Scotsmen show towards the Laird seem in his case to have evaporated a little. There is a marked lack of enthusiasm for the beautiful young Egyptian girl Seafield married after his divorce in 1971, but there is a generous sadness over the fading fortunes of what were once the most prestigious sporting domains north of the Border. The Earl shuns all publicity, rarely emerging to defend himself before his grumbling critics. He sits alone in his house by the shell of Cullen, avidly reading of the latest Soviet strategies for the domination of the Indian Ocean, penning occasional angry letters to the *Daily Telegraph* in an attempt to wake the nation up, scanning his great volumes of Tax Tables in the hope of finding the much-needed loophole, and all the while placing crosses against the footballing fortunes of Manchester City and Bristol Rovers and Hamilton Academicals, looking for his long-lost luck.

Perhaps more than any other rank of the peerage the Earls have provided us with a fund of anecdotes. The Dukes were mighty and remote; the Barons multifarious and all too common; Marquesses and Viscounts were of a station too complicated to explain. Earls, though: nice and simple, good and plenty, rich, landed, well known, ideal for the spinner of yarns and for the reader of the same. Take the Earl of Carnarvon—"Porchey," he was called, because of his courtesy title of Lord Porchester—who wrote his autobiography in 1976, entitled, oddly, *No Regrets*. How much larger than life is this account of his closing hours with the Army in India?

"On a raised and canopied dais the Viceroy, Lord Reading, and his guests, including Lord Inchcape, Chairman of the P. & O. Line, were enjoying the thrills of a close-run game. It was almost 4:30 P.M., the scores were level and we were playing the very last chukka. In the remaining few seconds, a brief opportunity occurred and, with a push rather than a stroke, I managed to hit the ball towards the goal. It caught the wicker of the goalpost then, more by luck than good management, trickled over the line.

"Our team, hot and thirsty, were presented to the Viceroy, Fielden was receiving the cup and each of us a commemorative trophy. It was just after I had shaken hands with His Excellency that a member of the Viceroy's bodyguard stepped forward. He was a handsome Sikh, dressed in white and wearing the scarlet Viceregal sash. He came across to where I was standing and, saluting, said, 'Sahib, a priority telegram from Egypt.' He handed it to me, saluted again and retreated.

"Turning to the Viceroy, I asked permission to open the cable. 'Certainly, I hope it's not bad news about your father.'

"I tore the envelope open and read the following: 'FROM SIR JOHN MAXWELL CINC EGYPT TO SIR CHARLES MUNRO CINC INDIA URGENT

PLEASE EXPEDITE AN IMMEDIATE PASSAGE FOR LORD PORCHESTER TO CAIRO WHERE HIS FATHER IS VERY SERIOUSLY ILL.' Typed beneath the message, which had been redirected from my regimental HQ were the words: 'Three months' compassionate leave granted.'

"Lord Reading murmured, 'I'm so sorry,' and Lord Inchcape, standing at his side, immediately made a helpful suggestion: 'The *Narkunda* sails tomorrow and will be calling at Suez. I know she is full to the gunwales but I shall instruct her Captain to have an officer's cabin made available. I shall also tell him to make maximum speed, the expenses of which,' he murmured as an aside, 'I shall naturally defray, in order that you can get to your father's bedside as soon as is humanly possible.'

"Then it was the turn of Lord Reading. 'I also have a suggestion.' He turned to one of his ADCs. 'I've an idea we ought to put Porchester on my train and send him down to Bombay tonight. He will then have sufficient time in the morning without any fear of missing the sailing.' The ADC agreed, but added: 'Perhaps I could suggest that instead we couple your personal coach to the Punjab Express. It'll reach Bombay by seven in the morning.' 'Excellent,' said the Viceroy.

"We reached Aden in record time, having averaged nearly twenty-three knots. The Chairman of P. & O. had arranged for the Arab coolies to be double-banked so that we coaled in eight hours instead of about twenty-four. There again, Lord Inchcape defrayed this considerable expense, which was most generous of him. At Suez, a launch came alongside with Sir John Maxwell's ADC and soon we were streaking across the harbour to the railway sidings at which stood Sir John's private train. . . . "

As it happened, Porchester was very nearly too late. His father, the fifth Earl, the man who had discovered, along with Howard Carter, the secrets of the Tomb of Tutankhamun, died soon after his arrival, and the sixth Earl raced home to England to repair the family finances and consolidate his position in a society he had left behind for soldiering in the Empire. His trip back to Cairo that day in 1923 was a model of the smooth workings of privilege and of how the Establishment can act to help one of its own rank and class. Civilian rank, that is. Doubtless the coolies would not be double-banked for an officer of similar military rank to Porchey, but lacking the rank donated by the fortunes of birth.

A brief note about Lord Carnarvon's nickname, Porchey. It became customary at the turn of this century to give heirs to some of the more celebrated peerages monikers that derived from their courtesy titles. Thus Bardie was Lord Tullibardine, heir to the Dukedom of Atholl; Weymie was Lord Weymouth, heir to the Marquessate of Bath; and Eddie was Lord Ednam, who would one day inherit the Earldom of Dudley.

The Earl of Derby, the "uncrowned King of Lancashire," is still one of the greatest landowners in northern England—though he, too, has suffered a savage slump from the days of his family's Prime Ministership and the institution of the horse race that still bears his name. He now sports "the largest herd of elephants to roam free outside Africa" at his grand house in a Liverpool suburban park. He claims to have lost £130,000 in one night's gambling at the Clermont Club. There are no children, but no shortage of heirs in close branches of the family. There seems little likelihood that the family will recapture its former glories, at least for some time to come.

The Earl of Suffolk—one of the ubiquitous Howards, and thus entitled to wear the "Flodden augmentation" on his coat of arms*— has, despite his youth (he was born in 1935 and succeeded to his title when he was only six), suffered a less than idyllic life. His daughter Lucinda died in a nursery fire when she was eighteen months old; the Earl, who affected long hair in the 1960s, was beaten up by police during disturbances in Paris; he divorced his wife and she, having been declared a bankrupt, worked for a while selling dresses (the next Countess, Nita Fuglesang, is a photographer). He used to be a regular on the London nightclub circuit and gained some fame as a bob-sleigh champion; his grandmother, an American heiress brought into the family by the shrewd nineteenth Earl, had nine cars, a helicopter and two planes when she died in 1968. She maintained a permanent suite at the Ritz Hotel. The twenty-first Earl, by contrast, lives in a cottage down the road from his official seat, a decaying Jacobean mansion outside Malmesbury, in Wiltshire. He has had to sell 3,000 of his 10,000 acres and, to protect his fishing, took the interesting step of building a horizontal barbed wire fence out into the pool.

Earl Nelson, descendant of the Admiral's sister and bearer of one of his Christian names, Horatio, had never been on a ship until the

---

* The late Earl gave his life in battle, winning a posthumous George Cross.

crew of HMS *Hampshire* decided to offer him their hospitality. The family had previously suffered at the hands of the Government: as a gift to thank Nelson's successors for the victory at Trafalgar, Pitt's Government awarded them a state pension of £5,000 a year; Attlee took it away in 1950, and the house, Trafalgar, is now just a pleasant memory to the present Earl. The State had given £90,000 for the purchase of the house: with the pension summarily removed, and without compensation, neither the sixth Earl nor the present holder of the title, the eighth, could possibly keep the mansion going. It was sold to a near neighbour, the Earl of Radnor. So the present peer is a retired publican, the Countess a part-time barmaid, and they live in middle-class comfort in a suburb of Swansea.*

Lord Radnor, who has managed to keep his house as well as Trafalgar in Wiltshire is an autocrat of the old school; he refuses to open Longford Castle since, according to one recent holder of the title, "I am told you can even smell the people who come round." He thus keeps the doors closed on one of the nation's most fabulous art collections—though he did let the public see his portrait of Juan de Pareja, by Velázquez, before it was sold for £2,310,000 by Christie's, to be hung, to the horror of the British art world, in New York's Metropolitan Museum of Art. In addition to his houses and collections in Wiltshire, Jacob Radnor owns a good deal of high-valued land in Holborn and a lot of the seaside town of Folkestone. His son and heir is Lord Folkestone, one of six children by his Lordship's two marriages.

The late seventh Earl of Mansfield lamented the then burgeoning crime rate in the country, and was on record as wanting the stocks, the pillory and the treadmill brought back into general use to curb the excesses of the criminal classes. His son, the present Lord Mansfield, holder of a minor post in Mrs. Thatcher's Tory Government, came to prominence briefly when prosecuting Jayne Mansfield (no relation—at the time he was known by his courtesy title of Viscount Stormont) for having allowed her two small dogs to be imported, without licenses, into Great Britain. Lord Stormont displayed his ability to exercise droll courtroom humour when he told the assembled that he intended referring to "the small, rat-like creatures," not by

* The great Admiral Nelson's actual present-day descendant (via Emma Hamilton's daughter Horatia) is another military hero—Marshal of the Royal Air Force Sir William Dickson.

Miss Mansfield's chosen names, Momsicle and Popsicle, but by the simpler modes of "Dog One and Dog Two."

The Earl of Buckinghamshire was plucked from the obscurity of a town-council garden where he worked pulling weeds to the status and dignity of a "Right trusty and right well beloved cousin" of the Queen; and the Earl of Albemarle, on the rare occasions he was, in his later years, able to come to the House of Lords constantly complained about noise—lorries, planes, motor cars. Earl Attlee, son of the former Prime Minister (most Prime Ministers were offered earldoms when they retired; Eden was the last to accept the honour, taking the title Earl of Avon; Harold Macmillan was offered an earldom, but turned it down), was, until recently, a public relations official with British Rail, and has written short stories for *Mayfair*, the "girlie" magazine. Similarly the Earl of Pembroke, who has a staggeringly beautiful house and art collection, Wilton House, near Salisbury (Rembrandt, Tintoretto, Raphael, Reynolds, Lely, Van Dyck, Watteau, Brueghel . . . the list of artists would fill a page; it is one of the oldest and most comprehensive collections in the country), has made a soft-core pornographic film.

Ah, one can hear them saying—keeping elephant herds, selling their Velasquez paintings, writing salacious books, working in council gardens, letting their Jacobean mansions fall to pieces—how are the mighty fallen! And to a large extent they would be right; there are, it appears, a considerable number of Earls whose habits, or whose fortunes, or whose sense of responsibility, have atrophied in recent years. There are some impressive figures left in the field, of course, giving strength to the rank; but whereas once it might have been said that the Dukes provided the peerage with its glitter and its swagger, while the Earls provided the backbone and solid standing of true nobility, I suspect that that honoured position has now been withdrawn from them, and largely through their own failings. It must now fall to the Barons to offer, by virtue of their vast numbers, the needed strength to the institution of peerage: the Earls have become bowed by some nobly arthritic condition, and, it must be said, are no longer what they were.

SEVEN

THE VISCOUNTS
Vulgarly Mercantile and, in truth, rather suspect

The notion that Viscounts are of somewhat dubious origins and of
a distinctly inferior status has proved, for the Viscounts, irritatingly
indelible. It is not as though they are by any means socially lacking:
beneath the 110 men (excluding the Irish peers) who count the rank
of Viscount as their proudest possession, are a bewildering variety
of lesser pillars of the Establishment. The eldest sons of Earls lie just
below them, as do the younger sons of Marquesses, the Bishops of
London, Durham and Winchester and all the other Diocesan and

Suffragan Bishops in order of the seniority of their consecration; then there are the various Secretaries of State—Education, Defence, Transport and so on—and the innumerable peers of the lowest rank of all, the Barons. For Thackeray to sneer at a European Viscount by suggesting he was merely the offspring of a penniless general, and for the doggerel writer to quail at the dignified sublimity of a Scottish ducal mansion are quite unnecessary: the status of a Viscount is far from worthy of disdain, ignored and unpopular though it may be.

Strangely, the title has never been welcomed by popularizers of the cliché, or the time-honoured circumlocution of the rhyming slang of London. You may well be invited to "dine with Duke Humphrey" —to eat alone; you may, if you act in an unduly servile manner, be contemptuously called "The Marquess of Marrowbones." In cards, the ace of diamonds has since the early nineteenth century been known as "The Earl of Cork" because, in the legend of the Anglo-Irish, "he was the poorest nobleman in the country." And if you were stout and jolly and happened to live in Edwardian London, it might have been remarked of you that you were "quite the Baron George." But no phrase has, at least to the knowledge of the compilers of modern lexicons, been invented to display the word "Viscount." It sits there in the *Oxford English Dictionary*, squashed between "viscose" and "viscous," with its only alternative meaning the obscure, and local, description of a particular size of Welsh slate. Viscounts rarely form the centrepieces of popular songs or stories: in peerage terms they have come to be figures, if not of actual contempt, then not to be taken quite seriously.

They are, though, a recently revived branch of high nobility. While only nine Earls have been created since World War II, the late King and the present Queen have seen fit to make thirty-six Viscounts: of the present total membership of the company, more than a hundred have been created during this century. The most senior English Viscount can trace his title back to only 1550, three centuries younger than the senior Barons and Earls and sixty years younger than the Duke of Norfolk's title. (It must be conceded that the senior Marquess is the holder of a title that goes back to only 1551; only six of that rank, though, have been launched during the twentieth century.)

The term means, literally, a deputy Earl—a "vice" Count. John Selden, the principal historiographer of titledom, writes in his mighty *Titles of Honour* that "when the great Dukes and Counts in the ancient times gained to themselves large dominion . . . which was afterwards transmitted to their heirs, divers of them placed in certain towns and divisions of their counties, such governors and delegates under them," who, they directed, should also allow their dignities to descend to their heirs. Viscounts had become hereditary nobles in mainland Europe by the tenth century, and the term was first given to English sheriffs in the aftermath of the Norman conquest—but for some reason the dignity never caught on, and withered to almost immediate extinction. Then in 1440 Henry VI made John, Lord Beaumont, Viscount Beaumont, setting a style that was to proceed, in fits and starts, for the next 524 years. Viscount Beaumont has long since vanished into the yellowing volumes of *The Complete Peerage*: the oldest of the viscounties existing today is held by a young film director, Jenico Douglas Dudley Preston, the seventeenth holder of a title, Viscount Gormanston of Ireland, given by Edward IV in 1478. The oldest strictly English viscounty is held by Robert Milo Leicester Devereux, a keen yachtsman who lives in Oxfordshire under a title that dates back to 1550, that of Viscount Hereford.

Viscounts are not addressed as "Entirely beloved" by the Monarch, only as "Well beloved," though they do retain the appellations "Right trusty" and "Cousin"—styles which would be taken away from them if ever they were found guilty of treasonable activities, as some few of all the peerage ranks have been, even in recent years. They wear perhaps the most garish of all the coronets of rank: no strawberry leaves for these men, sad to say, but a ring of sixteen silver-gilt balls raised on sixteen points above a silver-gilt circlet. The whole thing looks like a still photograph of the moment of impact of a raindrop on a water surface, and the coronets look particularly odd when they sit over the extraordinary coats of arms some of the Viscounts have chosen to sport. Viscount Massereene and Ferrard, one of the most conservative of all members of the House of Lords, has his coronet adorned with a mermaid brushing her hair, and below this, among other things, six bulls' heads as well as a couple of stags as supporters. Viscount Eccles has two devices that look like ice-cream cones, but which turn out to be torches (symbolizing his tenure at the Ministry of Education, where he was Tory Minister for a total of six years), as well as wolves, ships and black wings. It seems a rule of thumb that the more modern a peerage title, the more complicated and bizarre the coat of arms. Lord Gormanston has merely three silver crescents on a black background, a couple of foxes and a lion, while Lord Hereford has three discs, known in the trade as torteaux, a talbot (which *Chambers'*

Dictionary describes as a broad-mouthed, large-eared hound, usually white, now extinct) and a reindeer. The two most recent Viscounts, Muirshiel and Dilhorne, have, respectively, a lion, an anchor, a sailing ship and two birds called muirfowl; and a magnificent quartered shield replete with crosses, eagles, griffins, a Saracen's head, another talbot, an eagle, a winged horse, a hand, a thistle, a couple of portcullises and two armoured helmets—the whole mess above the motto "The eagle does not catch flies." The holder of the title, Viscount Dilhorne, is the former Sir Reginald Manningham-Buller, a Third-Class honours graduate from Magdalen College, Oxford, who went on to become a Conservative MP, Attorney General and Lord Chancellor; and was nicknamed by the more radical elements of society, whom he heartily detested, Reginald Bullying-Manner.

It is down in the company of the Viscounts that one first espies the rewards for mercantilism so reluctantly released into the peerage by an Establishment that had long thought trade a rather vulgar occupation for a true gentleman. So while our Dukes and our Marquesses move from country house to country house, disporting themselves in the most seemly way, and with little knowledge of, or interest in, the vulgar world of commerce; and while Earls are generally of Old English or Scots county stock, or distinguished heroes, or ex-Prime Ministers put out to grass, among the Viscounts we see the grudging national votes of thanks for ingenuity, risk, brains, fortitude and money. Captains of the fundamental industries were ennobled in the degree, giving us today makers of toffee (Viscount Mackintosh of Halifax), ships (Viscount Runciman of Doxford), beer (Viscount Younger of Leckie), soap (Viscount Leverhulme) and of newspapers (Viscounts Rothermere, Kemsley, Astor and Camrose). Those who drove their ships across the oceans of the world were given viscounties —Viscount Furness for one, founder of Furness Withy, one of the giants of pre-World War I English trading. The man who gave Britain the railway bookstall, W. H. Smith, became Viscount Hambleden; great soldiers and great wartime politicians like Alanbrooke and Allenby, Head and De L'Isle became advanced to this degree. Field-Marshals from World War I—Kitchener, Haig, Ypres—received earldoms for their troubles in foreign fields, but for reasons best known only to Downing Street and Buckingham Palace, Field-Marshals from the second conflict were rewarded only with viscounties. Some of those military leaders went on to receive promotion for other duties—Alexander of Tunis was elevated from his humble viscounty into the ranks

of earlhood for his tour as Governor General of Canada; Viscount
Mountbatten of Burma became Earl Mountbatten of Burma two years
later, following his Viceregal triumph in India.

But what of Viscount Montgomery of Alamein—why did he never
rise to the exalted levels of his colleagues from the Great War? Was
it that his political views were too extreme, were his habits too flamboyant, his military successes too controversial? There has always been
a faint air of disappointed surprise about Montgomery's title—though
Monty, His Noble Lordship, never displayed any bitterness during
the thirty years he lived, from 1946 to 1976, as holder of the degree.

Only three Earls—Huntingdon, Listowel and Buckinghamshire—
and only two Viscounts—Addison and Samuel—take the Labour
Party's whip in the House of Lords. No peer of the rank of Marquess
or Duke has any time in the House for any party other than the
Conservatives. Step down a little nearer to the levels of the common
man, though, and the ranks begin to break. In the Earls, there is only
little sign; among the Viscounts, though, there are two Labour Party
men and *five* Liberals. But it is only a small sign. The fact that the
Conservative Party has, since the war, bestowed viscounties in huge
numbers on its most favoured failures—failures, that is, to be re-elected
for Parliament—or its most faithful followers, has ensured that this
degree of the peerage is very nearly as true blue as its seniors. Had the
Tories kept their creations less blatantly political, as has been done
with other degrees in recent years, then the Viscounts would, perhaps,
have displayed more of the open-mindedness that tends to go with
soldiering and trading and building ships. As it is, forty-four Viscounts
accept the Tory whip, and fifty-two prefer to make a pretence of
independence of thought by declining any whip—though in House of
Lords parlance, "Independent" almost invariably means "Tory," giving
the Viscounts a ratio of Tories to other parties of about fourteen to
one.

Viscounts live, as one would expect of a largely newfangled group
of Tories, in the Home Counties. A map of their distribution shows
two semicircles on the western—or hilly—side of London, the one
about thirty miles distant, the other thirty miles out again. Twenty-
one Viscounts live in London; in the first ring, stretching from
Gravesend, via Basingstoke and north, live another thirty, among
them the Viscounts Monckton of Brenchley, Marchwood, Hambleden
and Wimborne. The second ring includes a lone noble, Viscount
Allenby near Ashford in Kent, and ends in Wiltshire, with Lord Long,

and up in Worcestershire, with Lord Monsell. The long finger of Devon and Cornwall sports six Viscounts—Viscount Falmouth is farthest away from the metropolis, near the town of his name; Lords Simon and Chaplin also live in Devon, near Plymouth. There is only one close to the Welsh Marches—Viscount Portman; none, repeating the pattern of previous ranks, lives permanently in Wales. Farther north, a clutch of four live in Geordie country, near the Tyne and the Wear—Viscounts Ridley (he is Chairman of Northumberland County Council, and a principal figure in policy-making for the rural north-east), Runciman of Doxford (close to his shipyards at Sunderland), Devonport and Allendale, the last a landowner with large estates let for the grouse shooting on the beautiful moors of County Durham.

There are no Viscounts in the Scottish Border country, perhaps because the lands between the Cheviot and the Lammermuir Hills are traditionally held by families who have lived in the region for generations and who collected their titles centuries ago—Buccleuch and Roxburghe and Linlithgow being good examples of the type. The next Viscounts are to be found near the cities of Glasgow (Muirshiel, a former Secretary of State for Scotland) and Edinburgh (Melville—a one-time MP for Edinburgh and First Lord of the Admiralty at the beginning of the nineteenth century). On the coast near Aberdeen lie the ancient Viscounty of Arbuthnott and the rather more modern (1902) Colville of Culross. Lord Thurso, who is one of the first Liberals in the House of Lords, makes his home at the very tip of Caithness; Viscount Dunrossil joins the Earl Granville as the owner of a house on the sea-swept, gale-torn island of North Uist in the Outer Hebrides. Lord Dunrossil, who has a town house as befits a member of the Scottish gentry, would cost the taxpayer most of all if he chose to live in Dun Rossail, his house on North Uist, and commute each week to the Palace of Westminster; thankfully he has a senior position at the Foreign Office, which means that his visits to Scotland can be only sporadic.

There are Viscounts in Ireland, North and South, and one, Lord St. Vincent, in Jersey, in the Channel Islands. Viscount Gort lives on the Isle of Man. And there are the usual crop of expatriates: Hardinge, in Canada; Bolingbroke and St. John, sadly for lovers of living British history, now in Australia; Bridport close to his Mediterranean land-holdings in Sicily; Viscount Samuel is in Jerusalem, where he has lived more or less permanently since the Palestine War; Viscount Maugham in Spain; Viscount Lambert in Switzerland, after an eleven-year chairmanship of the Devon and Exeter Savings Bank; Lord Soulbury, whose brother was an Ambassador in Washington, in Sri Lanka. Viscount Malvern, John Huggins, who was the son of the first Viscount, ennobled for his two decades as Prime Minister of Southern Rhodesia and his three years as Premier of the Federation of Rhodesia and Nyasaland, lived where he was brought up, in Salisbury, Rhodesia, in the company of Dukes and Marquesses and Earls who had once come out to carry their share of the white man's burden and remain to display their distaste for the way matters are proceeding back in the Old Country. Lord Malvern died there, shortly before his country's name reverted to its tribal ancestry as Zimbabwe.

The mercantile zeal which so proudly raises its head in this degree of the peerage is noticeable primarily because it is so manifestly absent in the higher degrees of ennoblement. It takes a poor second place, though, to the political zeal for which viscounties have largely been given in this century. The Conservatives, in particular, directed droves of political heavyweights into the rank—Lords Ullswater, Ward of Witley, Waverley, Ingleby, Leathers, Marchwood, Margesson, Eccles, Amory, Blakenham, Boyd of Merton, Chaplin and Chilston. All these and more have strong formal links with the Conservative Party, and were made Viscount for their political prowess alone. Colonial service ranks as a splendid reason for ennoblement to this degree—providing, of course, the colony was large enough to warrant so senior a promotion. Colonial servants from the more mundane conquests of British imperial excursions usually won only baronies or, worse still, baronetcies (the hereditary knighthoods which, since they were often purchased, quite openly, for a mere £10,000 apiece, have little or no standing and conjure up little or no awe).

One office for which a viscounty once seemed a certainty, until the rules of the peerage game were changed in 1964 and the political situation in the country deteriorated, was that of Prime Minister of Northern Ireland. The first Premier, Sir James Craig, was made Viscount Craigavon; the third, Sir Basil Brooke, was made Viscount Brookeborough. (The second did not last long enough to merit a peerage.) All subsequent Premiers, Terence O'Neill, Sir James Chichester-Clark and Brian Faulkner, won life peerages for their later attempts to keep order: in earlier times those who had constructed the traditional, unsavoury hegemony of the Protestant majority, and who did so much to contribute towards the horrors that prevail in Ireland today, won hereditary viscounties, and their heirs live on today.

Of the two, Craigavon is now quite separated from the Troubles which his grandfather helped, though perhaps unwittingly, to initiate. He is a young man, born in 1944, and sporting the engaging name of Janric; his sisters have the names Janitha Stormont (the latter being the name of the Northern Ireland Parliament building) and Jacaranda. All that links him with the unhappy history of the Six Counties is his coat of arms—a member of the Ulster Special Constabulary supporting on one side, a member of the Royal Ulster Rifles on the other.

Viscount Brookeborough, son of the third Prime Minister, is, by contrast, far from being a shrinking violet in contemporary Northern Irish politics. As plain John Brooke—though he sometimes used the prefix "Hon."—he was a Stormont MP for four years, and was elected to the abortive Assembly and Convention, as a Unionist Party of Northern Ireland delegate, until it collapsed in discordant shambles. Now that power in the provincial politics is vested in a London-appointed Secretary of State, and there is in consequence no local assembly, Brookeborough has little enough to do. He lives in a splendid old Georgian mansion in the so-called Valley of the Field-Marshals in County Fermanagh—the region has produced a quite extraordinary number of senior Army officers, Alanbrooke and Alexander of Tunis among them. His official seat, Colebrooke, is a mile or so up the road, presently empty. The first Viscount's second wife, whom he married only two years before he died, lived in the mansion for a while, until it became too costly: now it glowers over the rainswept hills and bogs of this conspicuously impoverished part of Northern Ireland, empty and forbidding, like so many other of the Irish houses that decay farther south. Ashbrooke, where the Brookeboroughs now live (the word "Brooke" which appears so often, is originally just a place-name for some Ulster stream. When the family shield was devised the artists decided on including a "Brock," or a badger, as recondite pun on the word "Brooke." The practice is known as "canting heraldry," and is the sort of in-joke that keeps the heralds content in their curious task), is a perfect gem of an Irish country house. All horses and mud and dogs and deep chintz armchairs and gigantic fireplaces filled with glowing logs, an Aga in the kitchen, wellington boots, huge meals of game birds and thick puddings, large bottles of whisky (Scotch, not Irish) and constant talk of the suitability of other country families for entertainment and invitation.

John Brooke has a licence, issued by the Royal Ulster Constabulary, for firearms: it has some thirty pages, and lists a collection of weapons which any IRA functionary would be proud to lay his hands on. Most are shotguns: activity in the house revolves around the twin sports of horsemanship and hunting, and the guns, either by Purdey or Boss, stand erect and shiny among the boots and the Barbours in the gun-room. There is often a soldier staying at the house—in civilian clothes, as a guest—to cope with some of the shooting. Last time I was at Ashbrooke there was a Gordon Highlander with a month off from his regiment, there to shoot the stags that roamed the Brookeborough hills. It was from him that I learned the precise meaning of the verb "to gralloch" a deer. "Put simply, old boy," the Highlander said, "it means to take the clockwork out."

Rosemary Brookeborough, who writes sheets upon sheets of doggerel about shooting, fishing and riding, is something of a renowned expert with horses, and runs a costly, but justly famous riding school. Invariably there is a batch of girls either over from Wiltshire or Sussex, or up from Sligo or Westmeath, learning the complexities of long-reining, or jumping or dressage. The girls all look much the same: red cheeks and plump, muscular legs, headscarves and well-rounded County accents—even the girls from Ireland. The men are handsome, clean-shaven and short-haired: the talk is of other friends, memories of shows or Events or of fishes that one got up on the Tweed or the Spey or in sea locks in Sutherland. The Brookeboroughs, hugely pleasant people with infectious energies and, considering the political situation, considerable courage, are a perfect country family, ever cheerful, faintly bewildered by the unrest, constantly referring to how things once were in what is undoubtedly a beautiful country of which they are obviously deeply fond.

Few of the Viscounts are landowners, to any great degree. That does not mean they lack money. The richest of all—possibly the richest peer of the realm—is Viscount Cowdray, who manages an industrial empire from the seventeenth floor of London's first skyscraper, the Millbank Tower. It is an empire that has brought him land—some 20,000 acres in the past two decades—placing him uniquely as one of the very few peers to acquire land, rather than be forced to allow it to drain away to help meet the inexorable demands of the taxman. Of the peers listed in the Earl of Derby's "New Domesday Book" in 1874, virtually all have less land now than they did at the time of that survey. Of three who did not appear in that old list but who now own substantial estates, two are Viscounts: Leverhulme, the soap merchant, who has 90,000 acres of Britain under his belt; and Viscount Cowdray, the banker and oil millionaire, has 20,000 mostly in Sussex, with some additional acres in Aberdeenshire. The third is an Earl, the Earl of Iveagh, of Guinness fame, who has 24,000 acres in Norfolk.

Viscount Cowdray, one of Winston Churchill's cousins, is one of the most private and thus, because of his riches, one of the most legendary figures in Britain today. Cowdray is the man behind Lazards, the great merchant bankers which, together with Morgan Grenfell and Hambros and Samuels, provide the green grease that tries to keep the wheels of Britain's investments running smoothly. His personal fortune came from Weetman Pearson, his grandfather, the founder of the "Mex" that was merged with Shell to become "Shell-Mex." In the Millbank Tower, Cowdray sits at the centre of a gigantic web of property companies and trusts—S. Pearson, Whitehall Securities and the Cowdray Trust among the flagships. There is the vast Westminster Press group of regional newspapers and, to cap it all, the *Financial Times*. Cowdray has, as a consequence of the last war, only one arm: he is able, nevertheless, to describe his hobbies as hunting, polo, shooting and fishing; principally polo, of which sport he is almost an eponymous hero. His is a success story that shows no sign of ending. There is every indication that his son and heir, the Hon. Michael Pearson, will keep up the acquisitive energies of his incredible father: the boy celebrated his twenty-first birthday by becoming head of a syndicate that bought 4,400 acres of prime Gloucestershire countryside for a figure said to approach a million pounds.

If Lord Cowdray represents the apex of the modern mercantile viscounty, and if Brookeborough typifies the genteel Tory politician rewarded for services to Unionism with the title, what of the "old" Viscounts? There are few enough of these—just a half a dozen from the eighteenth century, only four from days before that.

The Viscount of Arbuthnott, a Scotsman with a pleasantly elegant house at Inverbervie, near Aberdeen, is a distinguished sample of an antique Highland family, and he wears his viscounty no more proudly than he sports the name Arbuthnott. He displays an interesting point about the Scottish attitude to titles, when compared with the attitude south of the Border. In Scotland, what matters is your name: if you are a MacNab, then all MacNabs are grand, and grander than all Frasers and all MacDonalds and most certainly all Campbells. Your leader is your clan chief—in your case a man whose title is simply

The MacNab, and you look to him as a spokesman for the interest of your family and your family name. The MacNab is not a peer; the head of the Clan Arbuthnott is, as it happens, a peer, and a Viscount at that. The head of the Clan Murray is the Duke of Atholl, the head of the Clan Bruce is the Earl of Elgin. To Arbuthnotts and Murrays and Bruces worldwide, the leadership that these men exert, as indeed they do, comes from their position in the clan, *not* their position in some "Sassenach" class system. English class, it can be neatly summarized, is stratified horizontally, with a series of layers placing Dukes above Marquesses and Viscounts above Barons and solicitors above dustmen. In Scotland all Murrays, whether the Duke of Atholl or Mr. Murray the dustman, can hold their heads equally high: stratification in Scotland is, it could be said, vertical. And the arrangement is no bad thing. There is less snobbery in the Scottish Highlands than in any other part of the British Isles. There may be fear of the Laird, or expressions of awe at the antics of the squire up from Wiltshire for his shooting; there may be resentment at having to pay exorbitant rents to a landowner who is never seen. But in Scotland the forelock tugging, if it happens at all, is done with a curl of the lip and a finger to the nose: sycophancy towards the peerage, as it can exist in Sussex or Yorkshire, is a virtual unknown.

The Lord of Arbuthnott is small and neat, very precise, very kind —and fascinated, both privately and professionally, with land. He is land agent for the Nature Conservatory in Scotland, Chairman of the Red Deer Commission and Chairman of the Scottish Landowners Federation. He took a degree in estate management at Cambridge, served with the Navy in the war, went back to Cambridge to take an MA and is now one of the country's most respected surveyors and specialists in land-management policies. He bristles at overuse of the word "feudalism": he believes landownership represents a sharing of responsibilities—the owner for the tenant, the tenant for the land— with much mutual respect and trust and benefit for all concerned. He is bitterly critical of the mismanagement of the larger estates in Scotland, but equally critical of what he regards as the unfair tactics of radicals in attempting to portray all landowners in Scotland as villains.

His house, which he has now decided, rather reluctantly, to open, is run with spare elegance. Meals are taken in a huge kitchen, beside a shiny blue enamel Aga. Rose petals, floating in cut-glass dishes, impart a fragrance in every room. The whisky before dinner is

Famous Grouse, and after is Glenmorangie. The vegetables all come from the Arbuthnott Home Farm, a mile or so down the Bervie Water valley. Lord Arbuthnott's estate wall is many miles long and noticeably one of the best maintained for a hundred miles: it is details like this that mark him out as a considerable success in holding down an ancient title with the proper application of intelligence and discipline and regard for both the past and the future. Nothing is being sold that matters; nothing is being bought that alters the character of the land or house. With his two large dogs, his elegant wife, his son, the Master of Arbuthnott, and his daughter, with his responsibilities for land and deer and forestry and the preservation of animal and plant life throughout Scotland, Arbuthnott is a man of private comfort and public duty, and he manages to blend the two functions with expertise and flair. Like Buccleuch and Anglesey and Longford in the ranks above him, Arbuthnott sets a standard of excellence that helps keep the nobility's head safely above water. He plays a subtle and considered counterpoint to the Viscounts less mindful of their charge, and more aware of their station.

The Viscounts have their fingers well enough in the pie of state. Land is not as important to their survival as it is to the Dukes, though one could never go so far as to suggest that for Viscounts to survive they do not need it. Banking, politics, beer, soap, chocolate and ships: from these rather fundamental productions and services of Britain's heyday sprang the Viscounts. But they are hardly contemporary aspects of mercantilism, not any more: nor is the viscounty a contemporary peerage. It seems, from this vantage point, merely a vote of national thanks for the principals of the country's better times. Contemporary peers, as numerous as the talents they represent, are to be found one farther step below, down in the trenches of titledom, with the humble holders of the baronies. From their level, even the Viscounts seem rather grand.

EIGHT

THE BARONS
The Broad Base of the Pyramid

My Lords, what, in fact, are we supposed to inherit? Is it some special ability or talent which enables us to function as legislators? No. What we inherit is wealth and privilege based on wealth —a principle which cuts right across every conception of democracy. Today this chamber also consists of representatives of the more recently acquired wealth, such as bankers, steel magnates, newspaper proprietors and industrialists of all sorts. It represents, in fact, the most formidable concentration of wealth. . . .

> —Lord Milford, 1963—a speech since
> circulated by the Communist Party

Sir, I have for years been intrigued by the ability of a long line of Jack Russell-type terriers to indicate the presence of a grey squirrel 40 feet above by barking up the relevant tree. Can your readers beat the experience of this January when father, son and one such terrier killed 16 squirrels within one and a half hours . . . ?

> —Lord Remnant, in a letter to *The Field*,
> 1977

The Colesbourne Arms in Colesbourne is a typically warm-looking Cotswold pub, all inglenook fireplaces and dusty lampshades, thick sandwiches of fresh bread and pints of good local beer. The arms, newly painted on the inn sign that swings outside, are those of the local landowning family by the name of Elwes—stalwart Gloucestershire country people with a mansion in the village, deep roots and a good two columns in *Burke's Landed Gentry*.

There is, however, one other figure in Colesbourne who, though not the squire and thus lacking his shield on the village-inn sign, is better known than any local. The daily woman in the pub, who bustled around followed by a large Labrador and a little boy, mentioned him first. "You're here to see Mr. Philipps, are you?" she asked. "He's a grand man. You'd never think he was a Lord. And you'd never think he was a Communist either. Fact is, I'm not sure he really is a Communist—but it's an awful pity he went the way he did."

The woman's feelings are typical of most expressed whenever the name of Sir Wogan Philipps, Second Baron Milford, of Llanstephan, Co. Radnor, comes up. That he is Britain's only Communist peer—the only Communist, in fact, to sit in either of the Houses of Parliament—has made him into something of a celebrity, to be dug from the files on a slow news day and trundled out to prove something or other about the eccentricities of Olde England. Those people who are Communists look upon Milford as an elegant sort of battering-ram, a tool for the wider dissemination of their views within the very portals of the Establishment. Those people who are of the Establishment look upon their acceptance of Lord Milford as an example of their tolerance and the excellent functioning of British democracy. Those who know Milford as a neighbour all say that he is a charming gentleman, and that you would never know by his behaviour that he associated with "those terrible people," as one Gloucestershire woman said. And those who are neither neighbours nor friends, Communists nor Establishment diehards, look upon his Lordship as a bit of a "character," not really a Red at all, just a pleasant country gentleman with a rather well-worn gimmick.

It was a foggy day in the Cotswolds when I first went to see him. To get from the Colesbourne Arms I had to double back through the village along lanes sunk deep into the meadows, up a bumpy, wet farm road, past tumbledown walls of limestone and up to a five-barred gate. Beyond loomed Butler's Farm, large and evidently pleasantly modernized from a seventeenth-century legacy to the standards of contemporary wealth. Out of the gloom heaved a huge removal lorry; from its cavernous interior trooped a small gang of men, each carrying a cardboard case filled with bottles of wine. Lord Milford, the Communist peer, wandered out from his front door, took a brief look at the mountain of wine accumulating in a distant room of the farm and waved a hand of welcome. "Sorry about the removal van," he said. "Having a few friends in over Christmas and I thought I ought to get some booze in for us all."

If Mr. Marx might have arched an eyebrow or two at seeing the removal van, he would have been struck reasonably dumb by the appearance of his best-known British Party Member's living-quarters. No humble garret filled with the reminders of proletariat asceticism here: instead, large, airy rooms crammed with paintings and books, rare vases and jewellery, bottles of fine whisky and sherry, furniture straight from the pages of *Ideal Home* and carpets thick and shaggy to the feet. Magnetic toys nodded back and forth to each other, coloured glass figures twirling in the windows twinkled when the dim morning sun peered through the mist. His first act, after running off to the kitchen to pour coffee into a cup the size of a billy can, was to proffer a copy of his famous maiden speech of 4 July 1963—a speech which the Communist Party now distributes as part of its recruiting literature under the headline: "Abolish the House of Lords." It is regarded still as a splendid piece of writing, and a thoughtful contribution to a debate on Lords reform that resulted in the decision to permit peers to disclaim their titles for life. The speech with which a new peer chooses to launch himself on his fellow peers is supposed, by tradition, to be blandly noncontentious— a tradition that Milford sternly bucked. Lord Attlee, however—the former Labour Prime Minister—rather devastated Milford's plea for abolition by noting drily as soon as he sat down that "There are many anomalies in this country. One curious one is that the voice of the Communist Party can be heard only in this House. That is the advantage of hereditary representation."

Lord Milford was born in 1902, and is a big, shambling man with a gait like a bear, mulch-grimed hands and a taste for dirty corduroys. He is the second holder of the title: his father, Sir Laurence Richard Philipps, Baronet, was related to two previous Barons Milford who had both managed through infertility or other genealogical carelessness to permit the title to become extinct. Sir Laurence, himself a distinguished businessman between the wars, a shipowner and a soft-drinks maker, the founder of a paraplegic hospital and a Governor of the University College of Wales, seemed the ideal person on whom King George should bestow a renewed barony: Philipps accepted the honour eagerly. His wife, the daughter of a Somerset parson, agreed.

But the eldest son, Wogan, was unhappy with the idea. By the time his father had accepted the title he was, in fact, preaching revolution with all the ardour of so many of his colleagues of the prewar days who went on to become trade-union officials and left-wing politicians. With his background at Eton and Magdalen College, Oxford, he may not have seemed the ideal convert: his brief sojourn in one of his father's offices in the north-east of England did the trick, however. Like the character in Nevil Shute's *Ruined City*—an industrialist who, finding himself in an industrial town in Depression days, was instantly and deeply affected by what he saw—the young Wogan Philipps saw a condition of man on Tyneside and Wearside that he had never believed able to exist. He was working then for Runciman's shipping office in Newcastle: he saw the coalminers, locked out and hungry, on their march. He complained to his father, but was told, more or less, to hold his tongue. He vowed he would do all he could to help lift the Geordies from their wretchedness; and, fired with all the zeal of a neophyte, went off to join his other new left-wing friends to fight against the present symbol of all that was wrong with European society in those days, Franco. He joined the International Brigade as an ambulance driver and fought the good fight in Spain for over a year before being badly wounded and sent home. To the immense chagrin of his father he then joined the Communist Party and remains a member to this day, the memories of Jarrow and Guernica still evident in his talk, even if it happens to be conducted beside a fireplace larger than the average sitting-room within five miles of Jarrow Slake, and with paintings on his walls that would fit easily into some grandee's drawing-room outside Madrid.

His family, uneasy at the best of times with the circle into which young Wogan had been adopted—his first wife, whom he married in 1928, was Rosamond Lehmann, the avant-garde writer; one of his closest friends at Oxford was John Strachey—promptly cut off the young man without a penny: the inheritor of all Sir Laurence's business interests was to be Wogan's youngest brother, Hanning, who is heavily bedecked with insurance and banking and industrial responsibilities and has, in turn, passed more to his son Jeremy, who, unlike most middle-aged men with Communist uncles, is a member of Lloyds and a director of an insurance company that sports his grandfather's name.

Wogan, disgraced and penniless, made such money as he now has either from farming, or from shrewd marriages. After his union with

Rosamond Lehmann ended in divorce, Mr. Philipps, as he still was then, married the wealthy daughter of an Italian Marchese, a woman who had previously been married to the Earl of Huntingdon. She died, leaving Philipps some farmlands outside Milan which, he says proudly, he managed to turn into a cooperative and thereby triple the output. He still makes a small income in Italy, a country which he regards as his second home. His present wife Tamara is the widow of William Rust, the editor of the old *Daily Worker,* the Communist daily paper that struggles along under its new name the *Morning Star.*

"My difficulty, as you can imagine, is to be taken at all seriously. They all look upon me as some kindly old eccentric who should be pointed out as an example of the extraordinariness of the institution of the peerage. I try to make a contribution by asking questions and raising debates on controversial matters—the war in Cambodia and the British Government's position on it was one that I pressed home fairly well—and I suppose that works quite well. But I have been around in the Lords for fifteen years now and I'm getting to be like the furniture: nothing much has changed, it still is every bit as bad. I take parties of schoolchildren round every so often and show them the House from my point of view. That makes them sit up."

He runs his farm along traditional lines, in contrast to his Italian properties, because, he says, the Cotswolds are not yet ready for cooperatives. He thinks that farms the size of his—about 500 acres, mostly in sheep and cash crops—should be retained: they represent efficient units, are attractive to the eye and do not represent in any sense the crushing of the neck of the farmworker by the heel of the arrogant landowner. On the other hand all the large estates should, he says, be taken over by the state—either nationalized and broken up, or the land expropriated and run on a cooperative basis. Farmers on the large estates should be the tenants of the state, with all the produce sold at state-run markets . . . ah, but he knows that is still a long way off. He is a champion of the rights of the farmworker, and helped found the Agricultural Workers' Union, with which he maintains strong links. He is one of the very few voices ever heard in the Lords on the side of farm labourers (at least, he was until the Duke of Norfolk took up the cudgels on their behalf during a debate in 1980 and managed to defeat the Conservative Government's policy towards them): he travels up to London from Colesbourne three times a week to ensure that his interests in this sphere are protected.

He is still rather saddened never to have been invited to join any of the Lords Committees, and has to allow other Socialist peers with respectably pastel views, like Lords Brockway and Ritchie-Calder, to present his views in the backrooms of Westminster. He realizes, though, that the House is still firmly in the grip of the Tory party, which he abhors with every fibre of his body: the only realistic way out of that situation, he insists, is total abolition.

So is he really a Communist? Sitting in his farmhouse surrounded by an extraordinary array of creature comforts, watching the removal van pull away empty after disgorging its ingredients for a few Bacchanalian evenings, hearing the villagers talk of him as a fellow countryman who went a little wrong in the head but nicely so, listening to his accounts of his not inconsiderable finances, it does become a little difficult to imagine him joining in the lusty singing of "The Internationale" with all the sincerity of a miner from County Durham or a Clydeside shipbuilder. The biblical aphorism about camels and eyes of needles seems at first sight to apply. And yet there is little doubt that, even muted by the passage of fifty comfortable years, the anger Wogan Philipps experienced in Tyneside in the 1930s, or in Spain in the final days before World War II, still simmers below the surface.

Whether that makes him legitimately a Communist, rather than simply a member of the Communist Party, is open to doubt. All one can say is that he does, and with total consistency, utter views in the House that are of a significantly different political shade from even those of the very few fiery members of the Labour Party there. And it is perfectly true that only an institution like the peerage, with its regard for birth, and its total disdain for the opinion of electors, or officials, or the Monarch, or even the Establishment itself, can throw up a man laying claim to such views and propel him into the legislature. In any case, the peerage can quite probably take comfort in the realization that genetics take care of such aberrance in its own way: Lord Milford's eldest son Hugo, who will inherit as third Baron before very much longer, is a member of Lloyds, a stalwart in the British National Insurance Society, a member of Boodle's Club, an Etonian with a Cambridge degree, now married to the daughter of Lord Sherfield, and living in London. There seems little likelihood that the next Lord Milford will be other than a trenchant supporter of the status quo, just like his grandfather, his uncle and his cousin.

.   .   .

The institution of the baronage, of which Lord Milford is one of the more celebratedly eccentric members, is the rock-hard foundation of the peerage system. It is huge—438 men and women who are able to call themselves, as their principal title, Baron, Lord (in Scotland) or, in the case of a very few women, "Baroness in their own right." It is quite extraordinarily variegated. Here we have a collection of Britons—and an Indian, the third Baron Sinha, of Raipur (his address, so distinguished a gentleman is he, is Lord Sinha Road, Calcutta)— with no guarantee of land or riches, "good breeding" or brains, united only by their membership of the House of Lords and their title. (And it should be noted that not even this is a truly unifying denominator of the degree. There are thirty-six Irish Barons who have the very worst deal ennoblement can hand out—not only does their Irishness deny them a seat in the House, they can never disclaim their status. Truly strangers in a strange land.)

The word Baron means "man." A Baron of the old Duke of Normandy was in principle the Man who was responsible for five knights' fees—he was, as it were, the commander of a squadron of five tanks whose duties were to protect the people and the Duke's properties. In the twelfth century a Barony, therefore, was an administrative position involving the organization of knights and the collection of fees and taxes from them and from those who lived on their lands as tenants. When the English Parliament was evolving seven centuries ago many of these Barons were summoned to take their part in the writing of the laws—so it is reasonably accurate to say that Barons, from first to last, have been created peers for the last 700 years. The last Baron with a hereditary title was created in 1965, though Mrs. Thatcher's Government held out the possibility that more may be created in the future. At present only new life peers are still announced from Buckingham Palace: men and women of distinction given membership of the Upper Chamber and all the dignity of peerage for the duration of their lives. (Their children, though, enjoy the use of the prefix "Honourable" for the rest of *their* lives, so in a sense the dignity awarded to the first generation bestows such benefits as Britain's class-ridden society offers for the second generation as well.)

There has been much regret expressed among the caryatids of the Establishment at the possible ending of hereditary titles: "How long for a Lord, how long?" asked the editor of *Burke's* in the preface to an edition reprinted in 1975. His book, he noted glumly, was being printed in a year "that coincides with the tenth anniversary of the last creation of an hereditary honour in Britain. Panegyrics on the end of such honours have been delivered occasionally in that decade and one wondered at the time whether they were not premature as it is easy to forget, amidst the flood of life peerages, that new hereditary titles only used to come in a steady trickle. It now really does seem, however, that the fountain has dried up and that Lord Margadale and Sir Graeme Finlay, Bt., are to have the melancholy distinction of being the holders of the last hereditary creations."

Of the hereditary Barons who were lucky enough to sneak under the wire in advance of Lord Margadale, more than half have been created during the twentieth century. No matter that postwar society can be said to have witnessed a revolution in attitudes—since the war no fewer than 125 men have been given honours that their children and their children's children will carry on until they are too tired or too infertile so to do. Sixteen of the eighteen Barons whose titles were announced in 1945, for example, continue today—either the original owners of the titles or their heirs.

Looking at that year is instructive of the type of award made in the wake of wartime: on 12 February, Arthur Hazlerigg, a former Lord Lieutenant of Leicestershire and member of the Wartime Committee that looked into the internment regulation, 18B, was made Lord Hazlerigg; on 2 July, Sir Douglas Hacking, Tory MP and former Tory Party Chairman, was made Lord Hacking; three days later Harold Balfour, Tory MP for the Isle of Thanet and latterly Undersecretary for Air, and just about to end his marriage with the daughter of an extinct baronetcy, became Lord Balfour of Inchrye. (So named to distinguish him from the Earl of Balfour, the former Prime Minister, and Lord Balfour of Burleigh, who was given that title in 1607 on his appointment as Ambassador to the Grand Duchy of Tuscany.) Five days on and Field-Marshal Sir Philip Chetwode was given the title Lord Chetwode; on Bastille Day Sir James Sandford, Treasurer of the King's Household, won his barony; and Edward Grigg, MP for a Manchester suburb and husband of Lord Islington's daughter, was given the title Lord Altrincham on 1 August—a title which his son John proudly disclaimed eighteen years later on.*

---

* The first Lord Altrincham had a distinguished career: he was the Rt. Hon. Sir Edward Grigg, KCMG, KCVO, DSO, MC, PC, Commander-in-Chief Kenya, Minister Resident in the Middle East, Financial Secretary to the War Office and an MP for twenty-one years.

A change in government, from Churchill to Attlee, intervened. However, peerage creation was not to stop: Sir Charles Lyle, head of the huge Tate & Lyle sugar refiners, won the title of Lord Lyle of Westbourne, with a coat of arms showing a chicken sitting on a couple of sugar canes. Later on that year, in September, Sir George Broadbridge, Tory MP for the City of London and sometime Master of the Worshipful Company of Gardeners, became Lord Broadbridge, and Mr. William Davison, Tory Member for Kensington, took the title of Baron Broughshane. Then a journalist and, to surprise us all, a devout disciple of the Labour Party, William Henderson, was given the title Lord Henderson, of Westgate, Newcastle-upon-Tyne. Admiral Edward Evans, the distinguished Polar explorer, second-in-command of Scott's fateful journey to the South Pole, and during wartime Minister for Aircraft Production, became Lord Mountevans, with a brace of penguins as his heraldic supporters. Mr. Alexander Lindsay, Master of Balliol and a distinguished Scots academic and author, became Lord Lindsay of Birker; William Piercy, the economist who was Attlee's personal assistant during the war, become Lord Piercy; Robert Morrison, the Minister of Supply, became Lord Morrison; Robert Chorley, another wartime Labour Minister, became Lord Chorley; Mr. George Muff, Labour MP for Hull and a man who had been employed as a textile mill worker when he was only a boy of ten, justly won elevation and rightly changed his name to Lord Calverley of Bradford. And to round off a year of noble excess and victory in Europe, Mr. Robert Palmer, former Co-op cashier and President of the International Co-operative Alliance, became the first Baron Rusholme.

And what of the original eighteen today? Lord Altrincham is no more, though it is entirely within the rights of John Grigg's brother Anthony to take up the title again once it is open to offers. Lord Lyle of Westbourne died in 1976 without an heir, extinguishing the title for good. The first Lord Rusholme died without an heir, terminating that title's brief life. Their Lordships Balfour of Inchrye and Henderson are the only surviving members of the originally ennobled group— both, fitness experts might care to note, are Labour men. Lords Hazlerigg, Chetwode, Chorley, Sandford, Broughshane, Lindsay of Birker, Piercy and Morrison are now into the second barony: Hazlerigg, a retired member of the Leicestershire Yeomanry who won the Military Cross for his exploits in Italy, lives in Leicestershire; Chetwode lives quietly in Wiltshire; the second Lord Chorley is a famous mountaineer, an Alpinist; Sandford had a distinguished naval career and was then ordained a priest, after which he has held a number of distinguished posts connected with social services. Broughshane is a wealthy barrister, now retired and living in Belgravia; Lindsay of Birker is Professor Emeritus at the School of International Service at the American University in Washington, DC; Piercy, who went to Eton and sent his children to Shrewsbury and Badminton and who firmly denotes himself as an Independent in the Lords, not a Labour peer at all, lives quietly in Staffordshire; Morrison was until his retirement an executive with the Metal Box Company and lives in Suffolk. He, too, does not take a party whip.

Finally, from that original group of 1945 Barons, four are separated from the title's most distinguished recipient by a generation—four of them are third baronies, even though little more than three decades have passed since ennoblements were announced. There is the third Lord Hacking, a barrister and retired sailor, former President of the Association of Lancastrians in London; there is the third Lord Broadbridge, who was at Hurstpierpoint and St. Catherine's, Oxford, where he took an MSc., and now lives in Hampshire. The third Lord Mountevans, Rugby and Trinity, Oxford, used to work for the British Tourist Authority in Sweden, and is now with the Authority in London, enticing visitors with a noble beckoning finger; the third Lord Calverley, Charles Rodney Muff, was born in 1946, married a girl called Barbara Brown and lives in a suburb of Bradford, where he works as an ordinary, beat-pounding policeman.

It all presents a curious picture of the effects of ennoblement. Those who carry a title as a consequence of their birth are in not one single case as distinguished in any field as was the first holder of the title; in every single case they are either as comfortably settled as was the first holder or are considerably more settled than was that first holder. More of the present Barons went to public schools and to the ancient universities than did those created first; the numbers who live in remote and pleasant spots in the country are far greater than those who still inhabit the more commonplace suburbs and inner cities. In short, the elevation to the peerage has brought the group firmly within the palace gates of the Establishment, yet appears to have done little to increase their usefulness, as a group, to the society that honoured their forebears. Small wonder that most peers, of recent and of ancient creation, are reluctant to give up what privileges they have: for while the right to be hanged with a silken cord (not many are in a position to claim this particular privilege: the last was the fourth Earl Ferrers, in 1760. He, "in a paroxysm of rage killed Mr. Johnson, his land-steward, and was executed at Tyburn," according to *Debrett*. No peer, save he commit either treason or arson in a naval dockyard, can be hanged these days, of course, since for all but these offences, capital punishment is no more), to eschew jury rooms and to be free from the threat of arrest may not mean very much today, the ability to enhance enormously one's standing in society, one's position in the world, one's fortunes at the bank and one's ambitions for the children is manifestly not to be sniffed at. To become a Baron, even in 1945, is no bad thing, either for the Lord of first creation or, save perhaps for Mr. Muff of Bradford, for the Lords who follow him down towards eternity.

Because the bulk of the baronage is of twentieth-century origin, because massive fortunes and mighty landholdings are not so common in this baseboard of ennoblement as among, say, the Dukes or the Earls, so the geographical distribution of the degree is startlingly different. There are a great number of Barons living in London— somewhere close to 100, or a quarter of the total of hereditary holders. There are legions of Their Lordships living in the Home County suburbs—Surrey, for example, is stiff with Barons, who fan out along the Southern Region railway tracks like so many stock-brokers, which, of course, many of them are. They stretch up and away into Norfolk and Suffolk, and cluster in the cities of Oxford and Cambridge, where not a few of them adorn ancient Colleges or are associated in other ways with the stately workings of the Universities. Barons follow the road from Swindon to Gloucester, nestling around Cotswold hideaways like Cirencester and Stroud; there are clutches of Barons in and around Salisbury, Winchester, Tunbridge Wells; with an uncanny feel for the geology of the place, they parallel the outcrop of chalk from Dover to the shores south of Studland.

They are scattered liberally through Wales—almost the only branch of the peerage that gives the Principality a glimpse of ermine and coroneted majesty: there are Lords in Swansea and Pembroke, Criccieth and Harlech, Denbighshire and Flintshire, Builth Wells, Llandrindod Wells and Usk. They are not strangers to industrial grime: three live on Tyneside, five around the Wear and the Tees, many based around Manchester and Leeds, and eight circle Birmingham, watching over the city from which so many of them drew their prestige, their money, or both. There are Scots Lords on the outskirts of both Glasgow and Edinburgh, others clustered on the southern flanks of the Grampian Hills or around the cities of Inverness and Aberdeen, and on the islands of Islay, Colonsay and Man. There are plenty to be found in Ireland—scores settled down in Dublin and Cork, ten at least in the perilous countryside of the northern Six Counties. Three live in the Channel Islands, five in Canada, two in Spain, two in Mallorca, three in Australia, three in Switzerland, three in Zimbabwe, two in South Africa, three in the United States and one each in New Zealand, Sweden, Portugal and France. The man with the distinction of being farthest from the fount of his dignity is the third Baron De Villiers, a New Zealander, grandson of the man ennobled by King Edward VII in 1910 for services as Chief Justice of South Africa. His title, though of the United Kingdom, is from the district of Wynberg, in the Province of the Cape of Good Hope. The holder has, with his colleagues of like rank, a perfect right to come and help make the laws of a country 12,000 miles away across the globe, and in which he has scarcely sojourned since taking his degree at Oxford nearly half a century ago.

The baronial creations of 1945 were, as might be expected after both a protracted conflict and a change of government, heavily political. War heroes were generally given higher ranks—Montgomery of Alamein, Alanbrooke and Alexander of Tunis, who all received viscounties (though Alexander was later promoted a degree after being Governor General of Canada)—and it was left to the Royal Air Force to collect a number of wartime baronies, in the persons of Lords Tedder, Dowding and Brabazon of Tara. (The RAF did receive one special viscounty in the person of Lord Portal of Hungerford, the former Marshal of the Royal Air Force. Portal had no son, so the peerage was, in special recognition of his services in aerial warfare, made descendable to his daughter, but as a barony. Lady Portal lives on still, a living memorial to the exploits of her heroic father). Generally, baronies have not been so dominated by purely political consideration as the degrees above, and the baronage, to a much greater extent than the viscounty, is heavily concerned with success in trade, in science and, to a very limited degree, in letters. (It is, perhaps, a rather sad fact that the peerage is almost exclusively a philistine preserve: until the life peerages came along in 1958, permitting regal recognition of musicians, actors, men of letters, painters and sculptors, virtually no peer, apart from Tennyson, was thus rewarded for his artistic endeavour. John Locke's cousin, Peter King, was given a barony—like Locke he was a Fellow of the Royal Society, though his honour was awarded for being made Lord Chancellor. Lord Napier and Ettrick is regarded as a feather in the cap of many mathematicians, despite the peerage having been confirmed in 1627 on the son of the famous Napier who invented the logarithms that still bear his name.)

Trade dominates the twentieth-century creations: there are Barons whose titles stem from their works with industrial giants like Unilever, Shell and British Petroleum. Lord Lyle, as we have seen, stemmed from shipping and sugar cane; Lord Rootes from motor cars; Lords Dulverton (of Wills) and Sinclair of Cleeve (British-American), won their spurs for selling cigarettes—an award which many might now see as rather less than appropriate, in view of the dangers of smoking proven since Their Lordships' awards. None the less, Dulvertons and Sinclairs will go on to help fashion the nation's laws. There are Barons who were bankers—Baring, Swaythling, Rothschild, Catto; there is "the Beerage"—as the collection of peers made rich by beer and porter is affectionately known. The families of Grant and Hennessy, now ennobled as the Barons Strathspey and Windlesham, had nothing directly to do with the making of whisky or cognac, as is often supposed. "It is rather like the Czechs, who persist in thinking the Duke of Portland makes cement," said one of Scotland's Heralds in a commentary published recently. There are Barons from the great British shops (Marks and Spencer have a Lord Marks and had a Lord Sieff—though the latter title became extinct in 1972). There is a potter peer (Wedgwood), a locksmith Lord (Chubb) and a Baron of baking powder (Lord Borwick). The son of "GEC"— George Edward Cokayne, the editor of the redoubtable *Complete Peerage*—became Lord Cullen of Ashbourne; and the portly, myopic and remote Roy Thomson, owner of more newspapers than are taken daily by the British Museum, was hauled into the peerage as a junior version of a press Baron. Other newspapermen eventually won themselves viscounties, like Lords Rothermere, Camrose and Kemsley. There is no ready explanation for Lord Thomson having managed to capture only a barony. Roy Thomson was a Canadian and given to eating in Covent Garden cafés—perhaps the reason was no more than that. His son Kenneth, who runs the huge family empire from his mansion in the Toronto suburbs, is clearly unimpressed by his title and unconcerned by his relatively junior status. He asks everyone to call him either "Ken" or "Mister," and affects bewilderment when the byways of titledom are mentioned.

Down in this humble company of Barons the trappings are exceedingly slim. Compare the baronial coronet and robes with those of the Duke, say: Their Graces have eight strawberry leaves on a gold circlet for their grizzled heads, a Parliamentary robe with four bars of miniver and gold lace woven halfway around. The mere Baron has but a silver-gilt coronet with six silver balls, and can wear a robe with just two bars of fur and gold lace. A Duchess attending a Coronation has a train two yards long and edged with five inches of ermine. A Baroness has a train just three feet long with ermine borders that are only two inches wide—the kind of difference easily spotted by the experts which only true snobs in the field become.

The baronage appears to encompass both the very origins of the hereditary principle of legislative activity in Britain and the first stirrings of the representative Parliamentary system. The first Barons were those who held land as direct tenants of the King—the senior functionaries of monarchical feudalism. Their resistance to the Monarch's demands led to Magna Carta, the first step on the long road of constitution; later they gathered around the person of Simon de Montfort to form the early "talking shop" that evolved, eventually, into the present-day House of Lords. In the very early stages there was no guarantee that the successor to a Baron would be summoned to the Council or the Parliament, but by the time of Edward III in the mid-fourteenth century, the right of heirs to perform the same duties as their predecessors had become firmly established: the hereditary peerage was born. Peerages that date from before the days of Edward III are still proudly recognized by their holders, but through the thirteenth century and the first few years of the fourteenth, their holding of an actual *peerage*, in the modern sense, rather than in the sense of the *membership of a class*, was rather doubtful.

We are straying into waters that go beyond the scope of this account of the hereditary peerage today, but it is worth remarking on three supposed subdivisions of the peerage that run beneath the five-way warp and woof of the nobility—the divisions into English, Irish, Scottish peers; peers of Great Britain and peers of the United Kingdom. These further three subdivisions relate to whether the peerage is held by *writ*, a direct summons by the Monarch to attend the Parliament; by *Letters Patent,* which institutionalized the writ and ensured successors of the right to attend Parliament; or by *tenure.* There are very few of the baronies by writ remaining, though those that do exist can, like Scottish titles, pass through males or females— the "heirs general" rather than the heirs male. By far and away the bulk of the peers were created by Letters Patent—impressive sealed documents usually either kept as the most hallowed of treasures in the most secure rooms in the castles, or left with the archivists of the House of Lords for safekeeping. And though many Americans may be disappointed, it is now taken as settled law in England that there are no such things as peerages by tenure—there is great confusion between peerages of Parliament, and pre-Parliamentary baronies by tenure, often leading would-be fortune hunters and titleholders to find great disappointment at the end of their, frequently, trans-atlantic quests.

One final word on the origins of the words "Lord" and "Lady." Both have their origins not in sex, but in, of all things, breadmaking. A "lord" was, in Old English, the "hlaford"—"loaf-warder"; the "lady" was, in the same tongue, "hlafdige" or "loaf-kneader." The early Barons and their ladies were, as the feudal chiefs of the King's regions, suppliers of bread to their sub-tenants, and the name stuck. As we have seen the terms apply to all the peers (in informal language) except for the Dukes. Only in communications from the Sovereign and from the House of Lords are the suppliers of bread called by their ancient title of "man." The Monarch regards a Baron as a "Right trusty and well beloved" person—there is no mention here, as distinct from all other four degrees of peerage, of the Lord as "cousin": small wonder, today, that the Throne would not wish there to be a hint of blood relationship with persons making beer, cigarettes, locks, china and petroleum spirit.

The holders of the oldest baronies are thus, as we have seen, those who were originally summoned by writ: they can be of either sex and indeed, there are six such Baronesses in their own right—Ladies de Ros, D'Arcy de Knayth, Berners and Dacre, Dudley and Berkeley. The Baroness de Ros is, in fact, the holder of the oldest barony of all—the Premier Barony of England, dating back to 1264, entitled to perform a sacred function at the Coronation of Monarchs, a senior member of a group of forty Barons who are themselves the most exalted in precedence in the Kingdom. Lady de Ros stands thus at

the head of a formidable array of walking history: it comes as something of a surprise to discover her, not permanently liveried in
ermine, surrounded by stained glass of immense antiquity and poring
over yellowed history books between a never-ending round of trips
to see the Kings of Arms, the Queen or the Lord High Chancellor,
but instead picking tomatoes from vines in a rather ordinary little
farm property on the wilder shores of Northern Ireland. The Premier
Baroness of England is neither rich, nor landed, nor particularly
grand: rather she is a pleasant countrywoman, married to a sailor
and with a daughter who once worked as a Bunny in the Playboy
Club in London.

She doesn't often hear herself called Lady de Ros, nor find her
letters addressed to her as the twenty-seventh holder of the barony.
Normally she is known quite simply as Gina, or Mrs. David Maxwell,
since she has been married for the past twenty-four years to a dashing
and rather handsome Royal Naval officer and destroyer commander
of that more prosaic name. Her children, the Hon. Peter Maxwell and
the Hon. Diana Maxwell, dislike public attention being drawn to their
special position—Peter, the heir, because he is a sufficiently radical-
minded young man to care little for the complexities of baronage,
Diana because posing naked for Hugh Hefner and waiting on wealthy
Americans while wearing a revealing rabbit suit make for a kind of
publicity that sits uneasily with the duties of inherited privilege.
Clearly, if Playboy wanted to exploit her connections it could do so
with a vengeance—ermine and silver balls would go well with
Diana's agreeable architecture. So she has changed her name to
Luella Maxwell, and does her best to forget her inheritance.

Mrs. Maxwell has as distinguished a crop of ancestors as it is
possible to have. Woven in and around the 700 years of her barony
are celebrated names like the Dukes of Leinster, Buckingham and
Richmond; and the Earls of Rutland, Shannon, Dartrey, Antrim and
Exeter. Ancestors were variously men who led divisions into battle at
Crécy, or were noted in the seventeenth century for their "profligacy
and wit," or were nineteenth-century Lieutenant Governors of the
Tower of London. The first Baron married an heiress to the Lordship
of Belvoir, the second tried to sit on the throne of Scotland, the third
married well again, winning the co-heiress of a Kentish barony, the
fourth went to Crécy. The fifth married well, the sixth went on a
pilgrimage to Jerusalem and died at Paphos, the seventh became Lord
Treasurer of England and, true to the form of the alternate Barons,

married into the peerage, in his case the daughter of Lord Arundel. The eighth served under the Duke of Clarence in France, where he was killed, the ninth married a daughter of the Earl of Warwick, the tenth married the sister of the Earl of Worcester but managed to get himself beheaded in 1464.

The eleventh Baron de Ros, still sixteen baronies and 500 years from Gina Maxwell's accession, managed to win back the title his father lost on the execution block, but was never summoned to Parliament; his successor suffered the same ignominy but, in the habit of the shrewd de Ros males, married not just well, but brilliantly well—to a widow of the Duke of Exeter and relation of King Edward IV. The thirteenth Baron managed to win the title Earl of Rutland and a knighthood of the Garter, the fourteenth was an Admiral of the Fleet, the fifteenth was a Cambridge MA who died without a son and thus lost the earldom, which trailed off to his brother and his children. He did have a daughter, who became sixteenth Baroness, her son died without children and the de Ros family found themselves united once again with the Rutlands. This son was an argumentative fellow by all accounts and managed to get a new barony created, the barony of Ros of Hamlake, but carelessly died without a son and so lost the title for all time just a few years after he had had it created.

The old title, de Ros, went charging happily on through his daughter Katherine, who married a Duke of Buckingham and so allowed her ancient ennoblement to gather dust while she went around, not unnaturally, calling herself a Duchess. Her son, the second Duke, was thus also the twentieth Baron de Ros; he, however, died aged sixty without any surviving children, and for more than a century, the title fell into abeyance. The title was eventually terminated in favour of one Charlotte Boyle, wife of the first Duke of Leinster, who became twenty-first Baroness at the beginning of the nineteenth century.

From then the title proceeded through the closing days of Georgian England and through the Victorian era until the twenty-sixth Baroness, Una Mary, died in 1956 having had a son Peter, who died in the war in 1940. He had had two daughters, Georgiana, who was born in 1933 and Rosemary, four years younger. When Una died in 1956 there was another son, Charles; but even the hazy peerage laws of Baronies created by writ dictate that the Barony shall devolve upon the oldest son, if there is one, and then to his descendants—

rather than the second son and his offspring. So Charles was denied the title, and now lives contentedly in Bournemouth; the barony was to be divided between Gina and Rosemary who, when Una died, were twenty-three and nineteen respectively.

The barony, as the rules dictate, was placed in abeyance for two years, until the Queen, with the Lord Chancellor acting as her agent, terminated the title in favour of one of the girls.

"The whole affair came up a few months after Grandmother died," Gina Maxwell recalls. "We discussed the matter one evening and decided that neither of us really cared very much—there was no land and no money or anything like that—just a vague feeling that although neither of us had any political interest it would be letting history down a bit if we abandoned the title. Though I suppose someone would have picked it up a few years down the line.

"Anyway, Rosemary (her surname was, by chance, Ross: Una had married a Northern Ireland farmer, Arthur Ross, in 1904) and I talked about it and it was decided that I would take the title—I was the older girl, but that was about the only reason. Peerage law doesn't insist on the eldest of a group of females taking the title—it is whomever the Crown terminates in favour of. So we wrote a letter to the Lord Chancellor and in due course were summoned for an examination of the claim.

"The Lord Chancellor interviewed both of us, and then took Rosemary off into a room and grilled her for a good half hour until he was perfectly satisfied that she had not been coerced into agreeing to relinquish her claim. Then I took an oath and that was that. I was the Baroness, for what it was worth. Rosemary and I never argued about it—it was all done most amicably, and all it means is that she lives peacefully in Wiltshire without any fuss, while every so often reporters come down here and ask what on earth a Baroness is doing mucking out the pigs or something."

Lady de Ros radiates civilized ordinariness. There is no fuss at all to her mode of existence. There is little money, a pleasant coastline and harbour at Strangford, Co. Down, which came into the family when Una married Mr. Ross; and there are the foundations and walls of a new country house that is being built with painstaking care to replace the ruins of a house that Irish Republicans blew up and burned in the 1920s. Her Ladyship went to a good girls' school in England, and took a National Diploma in Dairying in 1955, just after she married David Maxwell and when she realized there was a farm to look after. She has never been inside the House of Lords, save to see the Lord Chancellor in 1958, and feels she would be foolish to try and make a speech about anything. "I would only put my foot in my mouth. I don't know enough about farming to become an expert on that, and I certainly would never try to speak about Northern Ireland." Both she and her husband are concerned at the possibility of the IRA trying to eradicate them as examples of ancient English privilege, though the house has no defences and neither bothers much about taking precautions.

There are certain disadvantages attendant with the title: she dislikes the publicity, if only because it increases the family's vulnerability at a troublesome time; her land, like that of many titled families, is held in trust and so is not mortgageable when extra funds are needed; there are relics to keep (like the water-bouget, one of a pair of leather bottles used for carrying water, that was fished out of the sea by a Scotsman, and now has to be kept, at some expense, at the local bank). There is the responsibility for the land—her ownership of two magnificent beaches at Ballyhornan and Killard Point endows her with more responsibilities, but few more privileges, than the person who owns a large garden at the back of his house. "The obligations of nobility are, in our case, far greater than the perks."

And what she dislikes most of all is the snobbery. "I was at a party recently where very few people knew either David or me. There were a lot of rather grand Unionist types there—garden-party people who did Good Works and so forth. I was introduced to one of the women as plain Mrs. Maxwell, and she couldn't have cared less. But then she heard I was Lady de Ros as well, and did she gush over me after that! They were all buzzing round me like bees round a honey-pot." It matters to historians that the twenty-seventh Lady de Ros still exists; it matters more to the partygoers of County Down that a Lady, no matter of what vintage, is in their midst. The Maxwells say they couldn't care less about the latter, and caring about the former—the historical responsibility—is just another aspect of their attitude towards *noblesse oblige*.

The Baron who came second in the race for baronial seniority could hardly present a greater contrast. Here is a man who breathes, lives, eats, sleeps and dreams rank, nobility and title. While Gina Maxwell happily gets on with being a *petite dame* of the Irish countryside, Charles Edward Stourton wrestles cheerfully with all the complexities,

duties and privileges associated with wielding the combined titles of
Baron Mowbray, twenty-seventh Baron Segrave and twenty-third
Baron Stourton all at once, like juggling three heavy and jewel-
encrusted balls of immense value and keeping two of them in the
air at the same time. He does that by calling himself, even in fairly
casual conversation, by two of the titles: he signs his letters "Mowbray
and Stourton" and revels—being a faithful House of Lords man, and
rarely away from it on a weekday afternoon—in the title "Premier
Baron of England." That the official rolls place an asterisk beside his
name noting that "Although Premier Baron . . . he is not holder of
the Premier Barony, which at present is vested in Baroness de Ros"
matters little. He tends to scoff that "Her title is a bit of a fraud, you
know. If they chose to look closely they'd see I was really the Premier
Barony holder, but I can't say I'm bothered. We got to do the
honours at the Coronation." So there.*

The arbiters of peerage sympathize with Lord Mowbray's claim
to the premiership, anyway. *Burke's* notes drily that "It is . . . proved
that Roger Lord Mowbray was summoned to Parliament by one of
the earliest writs which could create a peerage. . . . Lord Mowbray
insists that as it has been decided that the writ of summons of the
49 Henry III, under which Lord de Ros is placed in the House of
Lords, could not create a peerage, he is entitled to be placed as the
Premier Baron of England." There are not many years separating the
titles: Lady de Ros claims hers back to 1264, Lord Mowbray to 1283.
From this perspective, the vanishing point permits both to share the
honours—though in fact Mowbray, whose family did, as he said, pay
the official baronial homage to the Queen at her Coronation and who
is the holder of a number of antique titles, such as Chief Butler of
England, can lay claim to many more of the perks of premiership
than Her Ladyship over in Strangford.

Lord Mowbray is a genial, hail-fellow-well-met politician, a Tory
Whip and an ebullient drinking partner. He has but one eye—the
other was shot out while he was a Grenadier during the war—and his

---

* The uncertainty over whether the Barony de Ros is senior or junior to that
of Segrave, or Mowbray, derives from the fact that the date of its supposed institution is that of the irregular Parliament called by Simon de Montfort while
in rebellion against King Henry III. Lord de Ros was thus a rebel himself at
the time he was awarded the title. Segrave and Mowbray—separately and, as
today, in the one person, would argue that this state of rebellion makes the
claim of the de Ros seniority invalid.

eye patch is one of the landmarks of the House of Lords, to be taken in with Black Rod and the square crumpets as an essential accoutrement of the dear old place. His family are Roman Catholic— an aspect of his close familial association with the Dukes of Norfolk, whose coat of arms is incorporated, along with the contentious Flodden augmentation, in the extraordinarily complicated coat borne by the present peer. (It has six quarters: those of Stourton, Howard, Mowbray, Segrave, Talbot and Plantagenet. The supporters are a lion wearing a ducal coronet and a sea-dog. His crest is a monk wielding a cat o'five tails, and his motto is, in Norman French, *I will be loyal during my life.* He has a badge too, which would be on the buttons of all the coats worn by his footmen, butlers and other servants: it is a wooden sledge of a type used in primitive agriculture.)

There is still a fair bit of land controlled by the Mowbrays—two north country estates in England and a sizeable chunk of shooting and fishing country near Forfar in Scotland. The Premier Baron also has a house in London; his wife is the daughter of Lord Deramore. His telephone number in Scotland is listed under the exchange of Foinavon; spurred on by this fact he put £2 once on a horse of the same name, to be rewarded, with all the luck of the already lucky, by a cheque in return for £1,098!

For the second time in his recent political career Lord Mowbray became, during Mrs. Thatcher's premiership, one of a number of so-called Lords in Waiting on Her Majesty. The team, though it sounds akin to the Ladies in Waiting and the Women of the Bedchamber, is not given to a peer on especially intimate terms with the Monarch; it is a formal name for a Government Whip in the Upper House—though there are certain duties expected of the group who lead, according to one of the present company, "treble and quadruple lives."

There are usually about four of this particular type of archaic creature serving at any one time: they have used the title since 1837, when Queen Victoria first allowed Lords of the Bedchamber to shake off a most unseemly and unbecoming title and suggest to the outside world that their tasks were entirely proper. They are actually members of the Royal Household, with the duty to act for the Queen at various fairly low-level formal affairs of state. They shuttle about from Westminster to London Airport and back, meeting various foreigners who are worthy of official greeting but unworthy of a truly Royal Presence at Heathrow. Lord Mowbray grinned a wicked greeting grin at innumerable more or less memorable personages during his four-year Wait: those he recalls at short notice were the King of Norway, Mrs. Marcos of the Philippines, the Shah of Persia and the Premier of Trinidad, plus one other fellow whose name and standing he forgot, but who had come from "Abyssinia." There are also various meetings with the Queen on the spot—just so that, one Lord believes, she can keep an eye on her Waiting Lords to make sure they are suitable to act as her representative at ports of entry. On top of all that, Lords in Waiting act as spokesmen for various Government departments in the House—Mowbray spoke on transport and the environment and housing—and are on call as Whips for the Government in the organizing of debates and divisions. All this for about £5,000 a year—money which Mowbray might not miss, but which a few of the life peers could well use. At the time of writing, with a Conservative Government in power, the six political Lords in Waiting are Tories; the Permanent Lords in Waiting, with more strictly Royal functions to perform are courtiers and thus in most cases cross-benchers, without any specific party attachment—a good example of a nominally apolitical Permanent Lord in Waiting is the present Lord Charteris, the former Private Secretary to Queen Elizabeth.

Mowbray is a skilled defender of his sanctum: he believes that the Lords display "far more responsibility, far less frivolity than you would expect—there's a lot of hard work done here." The peerage was not above criticism, "but frankly it is a body of men and women that are 99 percent good, and only 1 percent bad." He doubts that Socialists will manage to stir up enough dislike of the peers to bring about the demise of the system. Everyone, he claims, is looking out for ways of bettering himself: "What better a goal to seek than a peerage, the highest honour a nation can bestow?" He then proceeded to take me on a tour of his friends in the Lords bar, ending with Mandy Pitt, the pretty daughter of Lord Pitt, the black peer from Grenada who had been Chairman of the Greater London Council and a distinguished doctor. Lord Mowbray is a great fan of Mandy Pitt, and acted towards her in a manner that was affably lascivious and full of bonhomie. With his roguish eye patch and his whisky glass, his outrageous flirtations and his roaring laughter, Lord Mowbray seems far distant from the *gravitas* one might associate with the holder of the premier barony but one. It is rather akin to the discovery that the Marquess of Cholmondeley, the Hereditary Lord Great Chamberlain of England, collects toy soldiers. Something which, Lord Mowbray pointed out, the noble Marquess does with extraordinary zeal. "One of the finest collections in England!"

At the other end of the spectrum, 700 years removed from the date of creation of Lady de Ros's title, is John Granville Morrison, the first Baron Margadale, who was given the title by a grateful Conservative Prime Minister (via the Queen, of course) in 1965. The announcement was made on New Year's Day, without any sure indication that, saving Royalty and their possible self-ennoblement some time in the future, Lord Margadale was at risk of being the very last hereditary peer to be created in the United Kingdom—and thus the last to be ennobled and given legislative powers and guaranteed ennoblement for those descending from him in the male line, in all the world. He is a man who takes the distinction lightly, though he looks very much the part of the English peer, and lives the life of a Lord to the very hilt.

The MacBrayne's ferryboat that runs from West Loch Tarbert to Port Ellen on Islay, in the Hebrides, is rarely crowded in the winter. One Sunday in a recent mid-January the little steamship chugged away from the Tarbert pier with a shooting-party of half a dozen from Carlisle; a wild Canadian gentleman wearing a cowboy hat and two bandoliers, who had flown over from Calgary for the simple purpose of shooting geese; and a finely chiselled, tweedy pair from Wiltshire who turned out to have the name Heywood-Lonsdale and be related to Lord Rollo. They, too, were going for the shooting—indeed, everyone on the boat had some interest in the sport on Islay, virtually all of which belongs, as does most of Islay itself, to the first Baron Margadale.

The Heywood-Lonsdales were, in fact, going over to stay with His Lordship. They were near neighbours of his in Wiltshire, and he invites them for the shooting every winter once he has managed to get himself and his retinue up there. They were planning to spend a week—Colonel Heywood-Lonsdale to shoot, his wife, the sister of Lord Rollo, to paint watercolours of the plant life and perhaps pick up the odd gun. Their presence on the steamer turned out to be invaluable—not least because they corrected the pronunciation of Margadale (it is *Mer*gadale) and managed to win for me a dinner invitation from a peer generally regarded as one of the most private of men.

Conversation during the three-hour run across the sea and past the Island of Gigha (owned by Sir John Horlick, maker of one of Britain's best-known bedtime drinks) turned to the usual topics of the county aristocracy—the difficulties of getting nannies, the outrageous wages for which servants ask these days, the fact that Colonel Heywood-Lonsdale had managed single-handedly to persuade an entire German regiment to surrender, and that his wife would do her bird-watching through binoculars that the gallant Colonel had taken from a dead German soldier.

The Canadian approached at this point to tell of his ambition to shoot the geese on Islay. "You do know that Lord Margadale *protects* his geese, don't you?" asked the Honourable Mrs. Heywood-Lonsdale. "Oh yeah?" said the man, obviously deeply disappointed by the intelligence. "Well, I guess I'll just have to shoot woodcock or something. Damned pity, though."

"Lord Margadale," Mrs. Heywood-Lonsdale continued after the interruption, "is an absolute dear. And his wife, too—you know she is a Hambledon?" I blinked. "You know—W. H. Smith, the newsagent. Piles of money made out of bookstalls. Well, that's the family he married into. All absolute dears."

We looked at a chart of the Hebridean waters through which we were churning: Mrs. Heywood-Lonsdale pointed out the tiny island of North Uist, in the chain of the Outer Hebrides. It was owned by Lord Granville, she said. Callernish House, a dot on the green island, was the family seat. The Queen and Prince Philip had stayed there recently—just pulled *Britannia* alongside the quay and walked up to the house, the Granvilles being "rather down-to-earth people, you know."

And so the conversation meandered on. Since the Heywood-Lonsdale's eldest son had gone skiing with the young Duke of Roxburghe the year before, they knew something of Floors Castle. "Super place. Very grand. Lots of staff—simply heaps of butlers and things. Makes us look pretty small with our daily woman." On the social stratification of Perthshire: "It's stuffed with peers. You go to the Perth Ball and you'll trip over them, there are so many. You really have to watch your manners there—it's not so bad in Inverness, it's quite a lot more relaxed. But Perthshire can be a bit sticky." She hates snobbery: speaking of a mutual acquaintance, she said that he was, "in my view, one of the worst snobs around. I simply cannot sit at the same table as him. The only thing he wants to know about you is who you are the daughter of and who your father's grandmother was, and if the answer's not right he won't talk to you." She loves grand living: "My husband went to dinner once recently where there were footmen in white gloves, the whole thing. And they were using the gold dinner plates—the hostess said she preferred to use the gold ones because they didn't need any polishing. You just washed them up in Lux and then stacked them away, just like china." (This tale turned out to be apocryphal, but none the less illustrative.) On the employment of daughters of the gentry: "Our eldest girl is secretary to the owner of the General Trading Company. Such a nice shop and used by the nicest people too." On motor cars: "We always use Rovers. They're just as comfy as Rolls-Royces, only rather cheaper."

Such was the scene-setting for a visit to Lord Margadale, the last man to slip under the portcullis before the realities of egalitarianism halted, at least temporarily, the creation of any further members of this very special class. It seemed perfectly appropriate, and Lord Margadale, host that evening to the Heywood-Lonsdales, Lord Muirshiel and one or two other octogenarian Scots Lairds and a wealthy metropolitan stockbroker, did nothing to lower the tone of the day.

He is a gigantic man, six foot six of solid bone and muscle, and very deaf. A friend says he can outstalk most people of his own age on the hill. He won his peerage from a grateful Sir Alex Douglas-Home who, with the then Tory MP John Morrison, had been defeated at the polls that put the new Socialist Government in power in October 1964. For the previous twenty-two years he had been Conservative Member for Salisbury, and retained his formal links with the region in which he lives for most of the year by being Her Majesty's Lord Lieutenant in the county. He is also a Wiltshire magistrate and, during those periods when he is in residence on Islay, magistrate for the county of Argyll. He is the only peer to have a whisky created especially for him:* when he came of age, in 1927, the distilleries which his family owned on Islay came up with a subtly flavoured delight known as Islay Mist, which still sells well. At the coming-of-age party in Islay House, Margadale remembers: "The estate workers drank thirty-six dozen bottles of the stuff. I

---

* Other peers, such as the Duke of Argyll, have had private whiskies made for them, but none in so large a quantity—or, they say, of such good quality— as that distilled in Islay for Lord Margadale's coming-of-age.

remember the men were left outside overnight and lay there stiff as boards and totally insensible until their wives came and collected them in the morning." Margadale's distilleries produce one special whisky now for the private use of the family—a malt called Bunnabhein, which is nearly as peaty as the better-known Laphroaig of Islay and not quite as sweet as the popular Bowmore. It is a slightly cloudy drink, but no one complains at Islay House, since the Excise men permit His Lordship to have a nine-and-a-half-gallon cask of the stuff duty-free every year.

Islay House has 365 windows, one for every day of the year, "and I am told it is possible to find one for a Leap Year too," said Lady Margadale, a white-haired and friendly old lady who until her death in 1980 happily entertained the great shooting parties for which the mansion was built. Stags' heads line every room—Margadale complains sadly that the antlers are not as good on Islay as they once were, but is able to point to a magnificent specimen that was taken only three years before, showing that "all is not quite lost." He likes to take visitors out walking in the grounds at night, to hear the sky-filling din of ten thousand barnacle geese talking to each other in the sanctuary at the end of the river. Back in the house vast log fires burn in each of dozens of rooms used each evening—the dining-room, the drawing-room, the various studies and bedrooms and guest rooms. To keep the fires burning is evidently one of the more formidable undertakings for the staff who serve at Islay House.

"And it is a rather small staff these days," sighed Lady Margadale. "They really are just too expensive. In fact we have to keep most of the house shut up all the time, otherwise the heating bill would be unthinkably big." The family usually make the trip from Wiltshire to Islay about twice a year now: until a couple of decades ago the journey was a major undertaking. Staff came two days ahead to prepare the house: the family followed by train to Glasgow, by ferry to Greenock and again by ferry to Tarbert; by motor bus across the narrows of Bute to West Loch Tarbert and thence by ferry again to Port Ellen, where a fleet of cars from Islay House would be waiting. "It used to take two full days to get up here," said Lady Margadale. "Now we just fly up from Heathrow to the aerodrome on the island; it takes a couple of hours if there is no fog and we make the connection at Glasgow."

Margadale's interests are those of many of his friends in the Wiltshire squirearchy—horses, hunting, gentleman farming. He was

once one of the Tory Party's pre-eminent "Mr. Fix-its"—Chairman
of the 1922 Committee and a power to reckon with in local politics.
He has three sons, of whom the two younger are Conservative MPs
(one for Devizes, the other for Chester) and his heir the High Sheriff
of Wiltshire. His daughter, Mary Morrison, has been a Woman of the
Bedchamber to the Queen since 1960, and was given a Companion-
ship of the Victorian Order as a personal note of gratitude by Her
Majesty. All things considered, the Morrison family have done very
well for themselves.

In the company of 438 there is, as would be expected, a bewildering
variety of sorts and conditions. Lady de Ros and Lord Margadale
present as great a contrast as do Lords Milford and Mowbray, and
all manner of degrees of poverty, politics and principles can be found
among the noble Barons. Lord Saye and Sele, who lives in a huge
moated castle outside Banbury (and who is quoted as saying that
the hereditary principle was "ideal" for the House of Lords because
every other method of selection suffered "by virtue of relying on
someone's opinion"), is not at all well off: he has to allow all sorts
of people to use the castle, and quite recently agreed, for a fee, to
allow a breakfast-cereal company to dress men up in the guise of
monks and have them do a cornflake commercial in his undercroft—
a kind of crypt.
    There are author Barons—Lords Egremont and Kilbracken; and a
racing-car Baron—Lord Hesketh; diplomat Barons—Lords Harlech
and Sherfield; and whiz-kid baby Barons who attract the ever-open
eye of the popular press. Lord Melchett, born in 1948 to a family
steeped in the more majestic branches of British industry—Imperial
Chemical Industries, the International Nickel Company and the
British Steel Corporation—is one such: he was still impressing his
contemporaries in 1977 as the brightest star in the Lords for years.
The young peer, at one time an expert writer on drugs for London's
alternative press, is of Eton, Cambridge and Keele Universities, was a
Government Whip and prime mover in the Lords of much of the
Labour Government's industrial legislation. He was made an Under-
Secretary for Northern Ireland in late 1976 and projected himself
ably in the embattled province as a man considerably keener and more
dedicated than many of his fellow politicians. He is almost the
youngest politician in either house—another indication, as Lord
Atlee remarked of Lord Milford's Communism, of the democratic

benefits of the Upper House. Not only does the hereditary system bring the only representation for the Marxists: it also permits the only real representation of youth.

Variety continues: there are intellectually gifted peers, like Lord Rothschild, one time head of the Downing Street "Think Tank"; there are playboy Barons aplenty (Lord Moynihan, described as a "bongo-playing liberal" is only forty-five, but has managed to acquire three wives so far, one English, one Arabic and one Filipino); there are irrepressible publicity-seeking Barons like Lord Montagu of Beaulieu, who maintains his lead among the most popular stately-home owners by diversifying in the most zealous manner. His last project was to sell his own, Hampshire-grown wine—a very pleasant German-style white wine that can chase off a Blue Nun any day of the week. Lord O'Neill, who runs a steam railway in the grounds of his Shane's Castle, in Northern Ireland, can trace his ancestry back to a King of Tara who lived in AD 360; he is married to a granddaughter of the seventh Duke of Buccleuch and has a passion for model railways.

The Barons are the *sine qua non* of the two great gossip columnists of the daily newspapers, Nigel Dempster and "William Hickey," and of their pale imitation in the Sunday's Lady Olga Maitland—a woman who, as daughter of the present Earl of Lauderdale, should know what she is talking about. Scarcely a day goes by without reference to some mayfly figure who would provide little interest to most readers but for the title appended to his or her name. And there is "Jennifer" of *Harper's and Queen* magazine—a plump, late-middle-aged dowager named Betty Kenward, who writes about, nay lists, the herds of socially significant Barons and Baronesses with all the fascinating literary qualities of the Belgravia telephone book. It is easy to sneer at the strivings of the British gossip columnists, but Olga Maitland and Nigel Dempster merely reflect the constant fascination of the average Briton for the rare and costly figures of the nobility. The only difference between the American and the British scene is that in America the aristocracy of which the columnists write—the Hollywood nobility—is actually attainable by the little girl in deepest Iowa and the budding star in Muncie, Indiana. The aristocracy of Britain—and, more especially, the hereditary nobility of Britain—is in a class that is for ever out of reach of the common herd, except by virtue of an unlikely marriage. Perhaps that is why the British columnists have developed the industry of gossip to the heights of possible perfection—because they are for ever writing out a fantasy, of life in a world that must remain, and indeed tries desperately to remain, exclusive and inaccessible.

The Barons, then, feed the multitudes with the occasional tantalizing glimpses of nobility. Dukes and Marquesses, Earls and Viscounts are, with certain singular exceptions, remote and lofty, of a kind with the Monarch and much more private. The Barons are the point of contact between nobility and normality—and provide a contact which is strong enough to prove a constant fascination and temptation to those on the other side, but which is too weak ever to provide a bridge. The chasm that stands between barony and banality yawns wide and deep, and now, since 1965, is quite unbridgeable—unless a Tory government decides on creating more hereditary titles, of course. But even then, the bridge would be a frail one, a structure few would ever succeed in crossing.

NINE

THE IRISH PEERAGE
Alone in the Wilderness

"Who shall I say called?"
—Lord Dunsany's butler, supposedly to the
Black and Tans, as they left after sack-
ing Dunsany Castle, Co. Meath

To have been given an Irish peerage—and an Irish peerage only—is the ennobling equivalent of having been damned with faint praise. Few, however, have to endure the unique miseries of an Irish peerage for very long: a year after Pitt ennobled his banker, Mr. Smith, as Lord Carrington as a consolation for not letting him drive through the Horse Guards, he promoted him another degree to a barony of Great Britain. This is the condition in which most holders of an Irish title happily find themselves today. There is an Irish Duke—Abercorn; but he has subsidiary titles, including a marquessate of the same name, that are of the United Kingdom; there are many Irish Earls—Longford is one of the best known—who have other titles lacking the singular millstone of Irishness; there are thirty-seven Irish Barons, like Rossmore, Sheffield and Henniker, who own "respectable" British titles besides. Only a very few keep the questionable distinction of a solely Irish title—and they, as one recent editor of *Burke's Peerage* noted, remain unblessed and "in the wilderness."

A man who has an Irish peerage only is very different from a man or a woman who can sport a title of England, Scotland, Great Britain or the United Kingdom. He may have a coronet and robes—but he has no use for them. He may sound to the untutored like a part of the ruling Establishment—but he has no right to sit in the House of Lords. He cannot join his peers across the waters and remain aloof from the undignified demands of democracy—he votes in an ordinary election, while his brother and sister peers are restricted, along with lunatics and prisoners. And if an Irish peer happens not to want his title, as Richard Needham decided when, in 1977, he was supposed to succeed to the Irish Earldom of Kilmorey, then that is very hard luck. Mainland peers can, under the terms of the 1963 Act, disclaim their titles for life. Irish peers do not benefit from the law. Richard Needham can protest as much as he wants, but in the eyes of the House of Lords, which denies him membership, he is now the sixth Earl of Kilmorey, and shall remain thus until his passing, when a seventh Earl shall arise from his ashes. (But Irish peers can belong to the House of Commons, unlike other peers, who are specifically excluded. And Richard Needham, sixth Earl of Kilmorey, has made full use of the perquisite: he was elected MP in the 1979 General Election, and sits happily in the House next to the "other place," as the Commons refers to the Lords, which has denied him membership.)*

All things considered, to be an Irish peer is to be an extremely odd animal—you are neither fish, flesh, nor good red herring, not noble enough to help make the laws of the land that ennobled you, not ignoble enough to be able to shake off the obligations of titledom. You fall untidily into some noble no-man's-land and, not surprisingly, you are often eccentric, mad, or extremely obscure.

The dilemma of the Irish nobility stems from the fact that the Republic of Ireland is no longer formally associated with the Crown from which the honours spring. Before 1921, when the Irish Free State declared its independence from the United Kingdom (and the United Kingdom shrank back from being "of Great Britain and Ireland" to "of Great Britain and Northern Ireland" only), Irish peers enjoyed rights similar to the peers of Scotland. Neither group was composed of quite full-dress members of the House of Lords. The Scottish nobles met whenever necessary to elect some of their own to a committee of sixteen to represent them in the House; whenever a General Election was held, sixteen "representative peers" were elected to sit in the House of Lords until the next election. But unlike the peerage of Scotland (which was necessarily created while Scotland

---

* The most celebrated example of an Irish peer taking his Commons privileges seriously was Lord Palmerston—Viscount Palmerston, KG, MP—who was Prime Minister from February 1855.

was entirely separate and independent from England, before the 1707 Act of Union), peerages of Ireland were often granted to Englishmen who had no connection with Ireland whatsoever—they were given Irish peerages in much the same way as others were awarded baronetcies, so they had the honour and dignity of a title, but did not clutter up the House of Lords.

This group, who were *not necessarily Irish at all,* nor necessarily in any way connected with Ireland by the ownership of land or by marriage or sentiment, were allowed to elect twenty-eight representatives for life in the House of Lords.

The establishment of the Free State undid that arrangement. The Upper House that the stripling Republic's architect constructed dismissed the notion of any inborn rights to legislate—it was to be an elected Senate. There was to be no further recognition of the Monarch: the English Ulster King of Arms at Dublin Castle was to be replaced by the native Chief Herald of Ireland. No further hereditary honours were to be created for Irishmen, and no elections were to take place among the peers of Ireland for the benefit of the Parliament in London. The abolition of the office of Lord Chancellor of Ireland removed all machinery necessary for the election of the twenty-eight representative peers. In short, the Irish peers became walking anachronisms overnight, like obscure Irish chieftains such as The O'Conor Don, or like French Dukes or Austrian princes—useful men made history with the stroke of a politician's pen.

The House of Lords, sorry to see so distinguished a body of men go, permitted those twenty-eight who were then serving as representatives from Ireland to continue so to do; but one by one they fell by the wayside until, in 1961, the fourth Earl of Kilmorey died and the House was left without a single Irish peer, except for those who sported other titles. From the time of Kilmorey's death, on 11 January of that year, the anachronisms lost what little power of official speech they had, and they have, of necessity, remained silent since.

(It is, incidentally, pure coincidence that brought the Kilmorey name to the fore again in 1977. The fourth Earl had been succeeded by his nephew, Francis Needham; his son, Richard Needham, declined to use his courtesy title, Viscount Newry and Mourne, since he came to regard it on his seventeenth birthday as an encumbrance. The fifth Earl died suddenly and unexpectedly at the age of sixty-two, in April 1977, and the unwilling Viscount, a Somerset County Councillor, objected to having to wear the title of sixth Earl and tried to disclaim it. As we have seen, he was refused—but informed that no one would really mind if he hid his nobility under a bushel for the rest of his years, so long as he let his son into the secret when the boy came of age.)

The House of Lords has not, it should be stressed, forgotten totally about its Irish colleagues. According to the standing orders of the House, Irish peers, in common with eldest sons of noblemen, retired Bishops and the Dean of Westminster, may sit on the steps of the Throne and listen to debate in the chamber; if an Irish peerage falls into abeyance, claims are made to the Committee for Privileges; while most of the perks enjoyed by the mainland nobility—the freedom from civil arrest in Britain and the exemption from British jury service among them—can be enjoyed by the Irish peer. But he is not excluded from voting for Parliament, nor from sitting there. Indeed, Earl Winterton was an MP for forty-seven years, and Father of the House, no less, despite his Irish title. When he retired from the Lower House he was given a United Kingdom title, but two degrees lower (the Barony of Turnour) to entitle him to sit on the benches, rather than merely the Throne steps of the Lords.

The Roll of the Lords Spiritual and Temporal, published each year by Her Majesty's Stationery Office, currently lists 1,075 men and women who are technically officially recognized as of the peerage. It curtly omits the Irishmen—seventy-one men who have become, in many senses, the pariahs of the peerage system, left stranded by the hasty separation of Ireland and her former Monarch. The seventy-one—twenty-one Earls, fifteen Viscounts and thirty-five Barons—do their best to keep up the standards demanded by their rank.

The names are redolent of the West Britons: Bandon, Carbery, Doneraile, Dunboyne, Gort, Inchiquin (who is recognized by the Chief Herald of Ireland by the magnificent appellation of The O'Brien of Thomond, head of the Dal gCais who gave several High Kings to the rain-washed Ireland), Muskerry, Portarlington and Rathdonnell. Critics of the phrase "West Briton" warn that "proud Inchiquin may not let the insult rest. The hereditary banshee of the Dal gCais, the terrible *Aibhinn,* may come to haunt you." For the sake of neatness, the unintended slur must stand. Their titles are, by and large, respectably ancient: the premier peer of Ireland, Lord Kingsale, sports a barony that was first given in—well, a year "shrouded in the mists of antiquity." The Irish are great yarn-spinners, of course, and so the sober acolytes of the House of Lords have not always believed the Kingsale claim that the sixth Baron was already sitting in his castle as far back as 1309! There are suggestions that the barony was created in 1223 or even earlier, which make the titles of de Ros and Sutherland seem mere babies by comparison. Certainly the present Kingsale (descended from the cousin of the Lord Kingsale who, it will be recalled, claimed his right to remain hatted before William III) suggests he is either the thirtieth or the thirty-fifth in line, which sounds extremely impressive. The registers record the Baron's birth as having been "posthumous" (meaning, of course, that he was born after his father's death). The twenty-ninth Lord Kingsale died in 1969. His eldest son predeceased him—he was killed in 1940 —and of the two sons he left one was killed in 1953. The younger, surviving son, John, who was born posthumously, succeeded his grandfather. He was a soldier, in the Irish Guards; his home is in Somerset.

One of the more recent Irish peerage creations is that of Lord Fermoy, awarded the distinction for his services to Liberal politics in 1856: he sat as MP for Cork, then became ennobled and sat on as MP for Marylebone. His descendant, the fifth Baron lives in Berkshire and runs a bookbindery near the town of Hungerford. There are more recent creations still: Lord Rathdonnell was created in 1868, and Lord Curzon—whose title, lovers of the old Indian empire will regret, is now extinct—was created thirty years later.

The senior Irish peer and the junior Irish peer live in England: so, in fact, do most of the others. Only eighteen still soldier on in Ireland, usually in crumbling old mansions beset by weeds and the dank vegetable growths that feed on the warm Atlantic mists. Some are rich, of course; but the Irish peer who has retreated to an Ireland his predecessor probably never knew is, generally speaking, in as peculiar a position as can be imagined: not only does he take no part in the legislation of his country, a Republic that owes nothing either to him or his forebears, but he is also regarded with grave suspicion by many of the older Irishmen as one of the former rulers of Ireland, one of the sahibs behind the anti-Catholic phrases, "Croppy lie down" and the rest.

Many of the remaining members of this little group prefer to live on in southern England—in London, or within easy reach of it by train. There is an Irish peer in France, another in Australia, one in Florence and another in Canada. The group can count a novelist, a civil servant, a secretary, a judge, a busy executive, a member of the

United Nations secretariat and a member of the Isle of Man's Parliament, the House of Keys, among its numbers. One is related to a former headmaster of Eton, another to the writer Terence Prittie, another is also a French Count; one, Lord Lisle, sports a coat of arms festooned with swords, coats of armour, spears and angry-looking lions with the motto "Wars! Horrid Wars!" They are, indeed, a rum bunch.

Three—the Earls Belmore, Caledon and Roden—live buried in the countryside in Northern Ireland, remote from the troubles that beset the province. Indeed, the fact that most Irish peers (or "peers with Irish connections" as a newspaper put it) have consistently taken little interest in easing the strains of political life in their country, at a time when all their good offices could possibly be put to use, has made them a ready target for respectful criticism. Why, the *Belfast Telegraph* wondered in two articles in January 1977, did not Northern Ireland have greater representation in the House of Lords? Was it right that so few of the titled nobility with links to Ireland should so consistently ignore its fate? Was there not, as Lord Massereene and Ferrard had argued in 1961, after Kilmorey's death ended the Irish representation in the Lords, a case for allowing the Irishmen back in, if only to redress the balance for a Northern Ireland that was ill served by the politicians who generally championed its cause at Westminster. "The Irish situation in the Lords is one of the most compelling reasons for abolition of the Upper House," a noted Northern Ireland lawyer, Brian Garrett, has said. "The Irish peerage is an historical mess and a political slum."

One of the classic ironies of the modern Irish scene is that the village that was the crucible of all the present Troubles—Caledon, County Tyrone—has sported three generations of Irish Earls who, through all the nightmare goings-on outside their castle walls, have managed to keep their families and possessions nicely aloof from the whole unpleasant affair.

Caledon, the village that saw the first protest marches in the late 1960s; Caledon, where the first Catholic Member of Parliament was arrested by armed policemen under the television klieg lights; Caledon, the barely remembered birthplace of it all . . . and three Earls of Caledon have lived there during the first years of the Troubles, with, until very recently, little interest in or sympathy with the violent struggle going on around them. The walls of Caledon Castle might have been a thousand feet high for all the Fifth, the Sixth, or the Seventh Earls have known—in an intimate sense—of events beyond.

Erik James Desmond, the Fifth Earl, barely lived through the Overture—he died in 1968. Nicholas James Alexander, the Seventh and present holder of a title first awarded in 1800, assumed his post only in 1980, and spends a good deal of his time—perhaps not unreasonably—in his town house in the more peaceable climes of London, SW1. The man who stood to during the grimmest years of all was the Sixth Earl, Denis James Alexander, a one-time officer in the Irish Guards, a kindly, thrice-married, somewhat tragic figure who died at a particularly sad time for his part of the Province—a time when many of his friends and kinsmen in the ancient castles of Ireland were being murdered by gangs from the IRA. The Earl, it is some small comfort to relate, died peacefully, in his own bed.

I knew him fairly well, and liked him. Denis Caledon was one of the most courteous countrymen it was possible to meet, a large man with engineer's hands and a soldierly manner, with an upper lip that jutted over his lower and gave the faintest impression of the legendary receding chin of the true British aristocrat. He was forever tinkering with the farm machinery that trundled over the more distant reaches of his 1,700 acres that abut directly on to the Free State border. He was an oilfield mechanic when he realized he would inherit the title. "I am sorry to say I lost interest in staying in Arabia right there and then. I knew I would come back to Caledon, where I spent the butterfly-net stages of my life. There seemed little point in going on mucking around in the oilfields," he said.

So he came back to Ireland and waited for his elderly uncle to die—not, it should be stressed out of greed or ambition, but simply because he felt drawn back home when he knew that eventual succession would force a return anyway. "There is a fundamental feeling of belonging here. It is primeval instinct, such as lions and deer have. They will always go back to the point of origin. This is my point of origin."

And the point of origin of the Troubles, too. Lord Caledon, like so many of his noble colleagues, was no student of the alleged complexities of the politics of Ireland. He avoided all discussion decorously. He continued to use his Army training by commanding a unit of the Ulster Defense Regiment: he rarely got into uniform, but would drive around the winding border lanes in a fast sports car, visiting senior officers of brother regiments for a "bit of a chat" about the night's activity. Once while driving thus with His Lordship we stopped for a few whiskies at the Officers' Mess of a Guards regiment in a small police station close by the border. We drank deeply until past one in the morning: when we rose late next day back at the Castle the newspapers were full of reports of gunfire that had been blazing from the Free State side of the border towards the same police station in which we had sampled the Guardsmen's whisky. We had not heard a thing: it is possible to be insulated from the miseries of Ireland, if you have the connections.

So what did Lord Caledon do—given his already reported comment that nothing urgent awaited him? He took his white Land-Rover around the park, examining the deer and seeing to the planting of new groves of trees; he wandered down to the little village he mostly owned to see his secretary at the estate office and to put a perfunctory signature on one or two routine letters. He took the aeroplane to London occasionally to see the estate trustees, to discuss the income from his farmlands in Hertfordshire. And from time to time he would get into his Alfa-Romeo (his "motoring car" he called it, with delicious Victorian embellishment) with his wife and drive across to Ashbrooke to dine with his friends the Brookeboroughs. Most evenings he stayed in one of the small, warm sitting-rooms in the Castle, reading books about deer, while his wife watched police dramas on the television. The couple slept in a four-poster bed; hares cavorted at night on the gravel drives that were illuminated brightly by arc lamps that blazed to help keep the IRA at bay. A man with a rifle stayed up on the castle roof at night, with a thermos flask of tea. "We are rather vulnerable, you know. We have to take some precautions."

The Earl saw no social problems arising from his standing, nor did he seem to encounter them. His estate workers did address him as "Your Lordship," but did so while they sat on tractor wings, sucking away at their old pipes. There was little bowing and scraping, no forelock touching (a custom rarely observed outside the fictional romance, anyway). There was respect, but the respect of countrymen for a fellow countryman, whose interests were the birds and the deer and the sheep; in the contouring of the hills and the planting of the next generation's forests were their interests too. "Do you realize those firs we are putting down today," the Earl asked as we gazed over at a group of men digging holes in a sodden-looking field, "will be tall and beautiful long after these troubles are over? There is continuity out here in the countryside of a kind that transcends mere politics. It transcends people's lives, too. So many will be killed here, and yet the trees will go on growing, thanks to what we are doing now. They will be beautiful, they will be good for the economy, and they will be here long after I've gone, however I go."

That is more than can be said, though, for the Irish peerage as a group of seventy-one. Two titles—the Viscounty of Templeton and the Barony of Teignmouth—totter on the verge of extinction, after nearly two centuries of existence. The Caledons are well provided with heirs, but the Earl is probably well aware that, unlike the trees his father was so busy planting, his peerage is not a permanent fact of life; one day it will vanish into the mists for ever. In the case of the Irish peers it is perhaps sad that so little worthy has emerged from their number—little in the way of true talent, or wisdom, or foresight, or art, or politics, or even fortune.* Lord Caledon's trees provide a splendid memorial—how much better some tangible contribution from others of the troupe towards the betterment of life in their beleaguered little island. That they have proved so comparatively bereft of corporate beneficence is perhaps the price one pays for damning them so harshly with the faint praise of such a miserable ennoblement.

Small in number and in stature they may be, but the Irish peers are a vociferous bunch. Back in 1966 a sprightly barrister, Lord Dunboyne, decided to help form a lobbying organization to wage war on the unfairness meted out, as he believed, to those with titles recognized as beyond the jurisdiction of the British Crown. The Irish Peers' Association—the IPA, a splendid set of initials for men of such beery reputation—fought an unsuccessful battle in the House of Lords, to be told that no, they could not have seats in the Upper House and that yes, the only place they could settle themselves was

---

* Some worthies have emerged from their ranks, of course. The Iron Duke of Wellington, the son of the Irish Earl of Mornington, made something of a mark in the last century; so did Field-Marshal Earl Alexander of Tunis, son of the late Irish Earl of Caledon. Lord Dunsany was a celebrated poet and author. Lord Curzon, Viceroy of India, was one of the last Irish peers created. Air Chief Marshal the Earl of Bandon, GBE, CB, CVO, DSO, who died in 1979, was one of Britain's most remarkable war heroes. And, as noted above, Lord Palmerston, Foreign Secretary and Prime Minister under Queen Victoria, was an Irish peer who never sat in the Lords in all his life.

on the steps to the Throne, and not an inch more.* One might have thought that Dunboyne, who was later promoted to judgeship would retire gracefully from the scene and let the IPA slip serenely beneath the foam. But no: under the chairmanship of Viscount Mountgarret and with the active support and encouragement of no less a memorialist than John Betjeman, the Association flourishes, preparing, like the Army on the Rhine, for a war that may never come.

"Perhaps one day the House of Lords will be reformed in such a way as to admit elections from within the body of existing peers," said one member of the IPA. "In that case, why should we be excluded? We've been dealt a very poor deal already; surely it is unfair to deny us one more chance." And so the Irish Viscounts and Earls and their exalted cousins wait for the reform to come, their briefs composed, their arguments finely honed, their expectation of a joyous return to the fold undiminished by all the suggestions that Lords reform, if it ever comes, will be a very different affair indeed.

"To deny us access means that men like Bandon [the fifth Earl], who's our best expert on air crashes; and Antrim [who has died since the conversation], head of the National Trust, can never come and give the benefits of their experience. So we'll continue hammering away, ever so gently, until we are let back in.

"In the meantime we are a very good dining club. Rather irregular, of course. But all sorts of people are members. It's only a couple of pounds a year, and the chaps are very good fun. Dinner's usually at Fishmongers Hall, except we had it on the terrace at the House of Lords in 1976, during that terribly hot summer. A lot of Irish peers didn't come, it was so warm. And those that did wilted in the sun. It was rather sad to see them all there, outcasts really, all perspiring in the heat. We must have looked a little pathetic."

---

* Irish peers feel a strong sense of injustice—one to add to the list is that many peerages for what one calls "typically Irish reasons," too, were given to people who had no connections with Ireland whatsoever on the promise that they could elect twenty-eight representatives to sit for life in the Lords. "This contract has been dishonoured in a peculiarly hole-in-the-corner way because," an IPA member wrote to me, "of the emotive use of the word 'Ireland,' and without constitutional consideration."

TEN

THE FOUNDATION OF LORDLY EXISTENCE

The resident squire . . . cared for the village on his estate, built the parish hall, presented the playing field, contributed largely to the upkeep of the church, expected to be, and was consulted before any major improvements were put in hand by the vicar or any other local persons downwards. In rural districts his guiding hand was everywhere apparent. . . .
— James Lees-Milne, in *Burke's Landed Gentry*, 18th edition, 1965

When one of Gladstone's daughters, staying at Drumlanrig Castle, a Buccleuch estate in Dumfriesshire, asked the fifth Duke "Where are the park walls?" he replied by pointing to the distant mountains.
— From Mary Gladstone, *Diaries and Letters*

For sale: fine Georgian-style mansion in complete seclusion. Formerly a home of the second Earl of Iveagh. 27 bedrooms, 9 bathrooms, 6 reception rooms, domestic offices. Oil-fired central heating. Swimming pool. Coach house converted to six staff flats.
— Advertisement in *The Field*, 1976

In spite of evasion, deliberately induced confusion, obfuscation, an obsession with secrecy, a bewildering selection of estimates of wildly varying authority and reliability and a fairly total lack of cooperation from the owners, it is just about possible to arrive at a rule-of-thumb figure for the amount of land that belongs to members of the hereditary peerage in the United Kingdom. It is something like four million acres.

There is no suggestion at all that the figure is meant to display the kind of accuracy needed for a detailed polemic on the future of land-ownership; the estimate that the peers own or control this area of the surface of England, Scotland, Wales and Northern Ireland is suf-ficient only for making the most general points arising from the central and ancient thesis relating to the uniquely successful survival of the British peerage. That thesis asserts that the principal reason the British peerage has managed to keep extinction at bay for so long is because of a combination of the principle of primogeniture, skilful compromise, and the ownership of land. The British peerage, unlike so many of its counterparts in other corners of the world, is firmly wedded to and deeply rooted in the fields and forests, the meadows and machair of these islands' precious land; so long as that situation is permitted to obtain, so long will the peers continue to enjoy their peculiar standing in the nation.

The figure of four million acres, dubious in itself, will mean even less to those for whom an acre is a measure difficult to imagine. English countrymen have a marvellous way with acreages: they drive their Land-Rovers past fields studded with grazing cattle, allow their eyes lazily to tour the hedges that surround it and will pronounce, with practised ease, "Damned good twenty acres, that!" with no difficulty at all. The word itself is ancient and in early times signified a size of a piece of land that depended on all kinds of variables. It could be a piece of land that was sown with a certain amount of seed; then again it could be land that had taken a certain number of men and beasts a certain time to till. Irish acres and English acres were not the same in the seventeenth century; and even as this is being written, area measures are in the process of being changed in England to the hectare, which, in spite of being anagrammatically *the acre*, is actually ten thousand square metres, a measurement relating to a specific, un-changing, scientifically worked-out unit. But at one time an acre was the size of a parcel of land which the average yoke of oxen could plough in a day; it later became institutionalized as thirty-two furrows, each a furlong in length. Edward I put the force of law behind a measure of forty poles long by forty poles broad, and this it remains today—4,840 square yards or, as any English countryman will tell

you, a square, seventy yards by seventy yards. So long as you think
of an acre in terms of length of the side of a square you won't, they
say, go wrong.

Even then, the four million squares, each seventy yards by seventy
yards, which fall under the control of the hereditary members of the
House of Lords are not easy to envisage. Put simply, it more or less
equates to the Principality of Wales from the south coast to a line
drawn between Harlech and Oswestry. The Scottish Highlands north
and west of the Caledonian Canal make up about the same acreage as
is owned and controlled by the peers. All Northern Ireland and a good
chunk of County Donegal would be needed to fill the required
amount. Or in England, the great bulge of East Anglia, with the finger
of Cornwall and the heel of Kent thrown in for good measure, would
indicate the size of the landholding. Only an American would regard
the estate as puny: four million acres is roughly equivalent to the
ownership of all of Connecticut and Rhode Island, and four Texas
farms the size of the King Ranch would prove equal, in terms of area,
to the entire landholding of every Duke and Marquess, Earl, Viscount
and Baron from Muckle Flugga to the Seven Stones. Looked at from
the viewpoint of a Texan, the landholding is laughably small; from
the perspective of a hill farm outside Selkirk or a leasehold terrace
house in Belgravia the territoriality of the British peer is a power at
once immense and intimidating, giving unequal distribution of power
and wealth, but endowing the countryside with much of its unspoiled
beauty, and rural society with much of its peaceful stability.

Whether the situation that allows such relatively vast ownership—
ownership of a third of Britain by a mere 1,500 families if the other,
non-noble landowners are counted—is an arrangement either to be
applauded or to be permitted to continue has provided material for
debate for centuries. The only difference now is that a system of
taxation has for the first time been recently introduced which seeks
without doubt to diminish savagely the wholesale ownership of large
tracts of land. "Two generations more, I give it," says a despondent
Duke of Devonshire. "Unless matters change soon, we will see, not
just the splitting up of the large estates into smaller ones, but the
total extinction of any sizeable landholdings whatsoever. The day of
the big estate—even of the fairly big estate—is nearly over. I only
hope they think they know what they are doing." By the end of the
century, the Duke, and most other landed nobles besides, believes
Britain will be fortunate to sport any estates larger than 300 acres.

"This time," concluded an article in the *Spectator* in 1977, "the fox's earth is properly blocked at all its exits."

Blocking the earth, if in fact that is what has been done, has been frustrated through the years by a simple lack of information on the central point—what land do the landowners own? It is all very well to say that the Duke of Devonshire has property in Barrow-in-Furness or Lord Calthorpe in southern Birmingham, that Lord Seafield has control over most of the Speyside Hills or that Lord Margadale owns much of the western Islay beside Loch Indaal. But what about some precise figures, some maps, some aerial photographs or some rent roll books? The answers to such queries are invariably vague, if not wholly negative.

Surprisingly, Central Government has no real idea—or is unwilling to say—who owns what when it comes to the surfaces of the nation. The Treasury, the Land Registry of the Department of the Environment and the Department of Agriculture all have a collection of official statistics, but they regard the information as being held in trust, and in confidence. And not even Members of Parliament manage to find their way through the maze. Jim Sillars, the Labour Member for South Ayrshire, made a valiant attempt (which largely paid off, though through unofficial channels) to compile a set of statistics relating to landownership in Scotland. He wrote:

"No one is willing to provide an accurate estimate of how much land is held by private owners, because the Establishment has made sure that no modern register of land ownership exists and has successfully resisted all pressure to create such a register.

"When I served on the Select Committee on Scottish Affairs which dealt with land use (the House of Commons Session 1971/72) I found it impossible to get the facts of land ownership in private hands. Up against muddle and vagueness it was possible only to extract the odd piece of information such as that the Countess of Seafield held 216,000 acres, Lord Lovat 200,000 acres and the Duke of Buccleuch 500,000 acres and Sir Alec Douglas-Home 60,000 acres. These figures were the product of private digging. . . ." (Mr. Sillars was wrong about Lovat, who made all his land—far less than 200,000 acres— over to his four sons.)

Private digging has its attendant risks, of course: in the last fifteen years there have been three, and maybe more, "authoritative" estimates of the holdings of the Duke of Buccleuch: Sillars says half a million acres; Roy Perrott, in *The Aristocrats*, says 220,000; and the *Weekend Telegraph*, in its issue of 2 December 1966, quoted a figure of 336,000 acres. My own researches suggest that the Duke owns around 256,000 acres. There are maps at Bowhill, one of the Duke's principal houses, which bear out this last figure.

A writer for the *Spectator* ran up against an elegant smokescreen from aristocratic territorialists when he was compiling a 1977 version of the Domesday Book for his journal. The only way to win the necessary information, he concluded, was to ask the owners in person:

"This was usually attempted on the telephone and naturally entailed difficulties. Often, the landowner was out shooting; once he unfortunately turned out to be dead; and once he was drunk. One landowner could not decide whether he owned 10,000 or 100,000 acres: 'I do find it so difficult to remember what an acre looks like when I drive across the estate.' The younger ones tended to be fairly candid, the older ones suspicious. When reminded that the *Spectator* was a Tory paper, one replied: 'Ah, but we lost them a long time ago.' There were those, too, who sheltered behind half-truths: they would say that they did not own any land at all when in fact their estates were owned by trusts of which they, or their families, were the sole beneficiaries."

The *Spectator's* aim, on this occasion, was to provide a reasonably accurate summary of the landholdings of the nation's giant estate owners. It had been noted that in 1873 the Earl of Derby, angered by what he termed "the wildest and most reckless exaggerations" about landowners and their power, decided to compile a "New Domesday Book" of estate ownership that would, he prophesied, display that land was held much more widely than was suggested, and that it was nonsense to suggest that only a few men owned the greater portion of the land in Great Britain. The noble Earl in fact had to eat crow: he found, much to his embarrassment, that only 7,000 people held title to a mighty 75 percent of the land surface of England, Wales and Scotland. The mere fact that he was able to compile the survey is interesting in itself: in the nineteenth century (indeed, up until just after World War I) local valuation rolls prepared for the levying of rates on agricultural land gave all the necessary information. Today, rates are not levied on farmland, there are no valuation rolls, and no budding Lord Derbys eager to defend their peers' ownership of the countryside by publishing the facts.

Three years later, in 1876, the *Spectator* prepared its own survey of the 700 largest landowners—those who controlled more than 5,000 acres each. It found more or less the same display of immense territorial holdings that Derby had discovered and, defending its own (the Tories had not been "lost" in those halcyon days), the journal commented that only by confiscation or deliberately punitive taxation could the landholdings be substantially diminished. It also made a remark that was not to become prophecy until almost exactly a century was over: the system could be altered, it said, with a shudder of aristocratic distaste, "by an *impôt progressif* upon land—that, by a breach of the national faith, which commands that taxation shall have revenue, not the pillage of class, for its first end. And it could be altered by an abolition of the freedom of bequest which would completely revolutionize the condition, not only of English society, but of every family within it." That *impôt progressif* which mandates the "pillage of a class" is with us now, in the shape of the Capital Transfer Tax. More than any other single aspect of Socialist legislation since World War II, the imposition of CTT is seen by the landowners as the sounding of their death-knell: as we shall see, the levy is the machinery which has managed to block the fox's earths at all possible exits.

In its survey of 1976, set to parallel the 1876 list of the 700 largest landowners, the *Spectator* discovered, as has every other investigator since the 1920s, that landholdings are falling substantially. True, Lord Leverhulme, awarded a viscounty in 1922 for making soap so successfully, owns more land now than his family did in 1876—he owned nothing to speak of then, but controls 90,000 acres today; the Earl of Iveagh, made a peer in 1919 for making good Guinness, owns 24,000 acres of good Norfolk farmland; and Lord Cowdray, of polo and banking fame, owns 20,000 acres. But they are exceptions. New promotions to aristocracy rarely come with large landholdings these days: either they have owned land for centuries, or they are landless now.

It should be noted, of course, that the peerage is far from having a monopoly of large landholdings: *Burke's Landed Gentry* contains the names of some 2,000 men and women who have owned 300 acres or more for scores of generations. The "gentry" regard themselves as infinitely more patrician than the "mere nobility": they have land and money, in many cases a prescriptive right to be known by some truly ancient title, and not one awarded out of monarchical gratitude for the cavortings of a mistress—names like the Knight of Glin or the

LANDHOLDING
(in acres)

SURVEY / NAME	1876 (Spectator)	1877 (Sutherland)	1883 (Bateman)	1966 (Sutherland)	1968 (Perrott)	1976 (Spectator)	1976 (Scotland)	Increase (+) or decrease (−)
D. Abercorn		65,500						−
M. Ailesbury	53,362					5,500		−
D. Argyll		175,500		81,000	96,000		73,400	−
D. Atholl		194,500		120,000	120,000		130,000	−
E. Ancaster	67,638				10,000	22,680		−
M. Bath	41,690					10,000		+
D. Beaufort		51,000		52,000	52,000			−
D. Buccleuch		459,000		252,000				−
D. Bedford	87,500	87,500		21,000		11,000		−
M. Bristol	31,974					16,000		−
L. Brownlow	57,798					10,000		−
E. Carlisle	78,541					3,000		−
E. Cawdor	51,517				80,000	76,000		+
L. Cowdray					17,500			−
E. Derby	56,597					22,000		−
E. Dunmore			78,620					
D. Devonshire	132,996	199,000		72,000	72,000	56,000		−
E. Durham	30,472		30,471			30,000		−
L. Feversham	39,312					12,500		−
D. Grafton		29,500		10,500	11,000			−
E. Howe	33,656					2,500		−
D. Hamilton		157,500		13,000				−

Owner							
E. Ilchester	30,716						—
E. Iveagh					24,000 °		
L. Egremont	109,900	[As L. Leconfield]			13,000		—
E. Leicester	43,024			24,000	27,000		—
E. Lisburne	42,666				3,230		—
L. Londesbrough	67,457				72,000		+
L. Leverhulme				99,000	90,000		
E. Mansfield		49,074		37,000			—
D. Marlborough		23,500	11,500	11,500			
L. Middleton	34,701			13,500	13,500		—
D. Norfolk	40,176	44,500	15,000		25,000		—
D. Northumberland	186,397	186,397	80,000	80,000	105,000		—
E. Pembroke	40,447				14,000		—
D. Portland	53,771	162,000	64,500	64,000	17,000		—
V. Portman	31,969				1,000		—
E. Powis	61,008				19,000		—
L. Redesdale	30,247		18,000	1,000	1,000		—
D. Rutland	58,943	70,000	12,000		18,000		—
D. Richmond		286,500	18,000				—
D. Roxburghe		60,500					—
E. Seafield				21,300		186,000	
E. Spencer				60,000			—
E. Stamford	30,792				3,500		—
E. & C. Sutherland		1,358,500		137,000	150,900		—
D. Somerset		22,500	7,000				—
D. Wellington		19,500	10,000				—
D. Westminster		20,000	138,000	78,000		120,800	+
E. Yarborough	55,272				30,000		—

twenty-third Dymoke of Scrivelsby mean immensely more on the
secret tablets of snobbism than a simple barony or an Irish earldom.
That this account is restricted to the titled landowners should not
disguise the fact that they are not alone: it simply happens that peers
occupy most of the top positions in the rankings of aristocratic
territorialists.

The new *Spectator* survey, in common with surveys in a number
of recent books, displays then the general atrophying of the private
landowner. Its figures are included on pp. 216–17 with other, older
sets of statistics compiled by among others Roy Perrott (*The Aristocrats*), Douglas Sutherland (*The Landowners*) and John McEwan
in his paper "Highland Landlordism" in *The Red Paper on Scotland*.
The general picture is of disintegration; the wild variations in the
figures bear out the difficulties of establishing the truth with any
precision.

The evidence may be suggestive of katabasis, but it also betokens
the stability of the landed Establishment. Only Lord Ilchester seems
to have permitted his holdings to wither completely, and that was due
to the unfortunate lack of heirs that afflicts some titled families from
time to time. The seventh Earl was one of those rare creatures who,
in the inimitable abbreviated style of *Burke's*, "d.s.p.m.s."—"*decessit
sine prole mascula superstite*"—or died without surviving male children. Both his children died, one after an accident, the other in
Cyprus, in 1958, while making war against Eoka—it was left to a
distant cousin to inherit the land. Thus while the title and the acreages
have been forced to part company, a relation of the Earl's is still a
force to be reckoned with as a landowner—she has some 15,000 acres
in Dorset and South Yorkshire, half of what the fifth Earl had in 1876.

Of the remainder, all still have some landholdings and remain
within the major league. The lands of the Duke of Sutherland now
belong to the Countess; the holdings of the Duke of St. Albans, once
a big landowner, were turned into liquid assets and paintings; but
generally speaking the highest echelons of nobility remain staunchly
praedial. As we have seen, 1,500 families, a great many of them
titled, still own one-third of Great Britain. Such land as has been
lost by the grandees has not been assiduously redistributed among
the commonalty. Far from it. The major beneficiaries of the reduction
of noble landholdings are the various offices of the state—the Forestry
Commission, the Crown, the Church and the National Trust. Large
financial institutions own great tracts; one piece of land sold in Sussex

in the past decade went to the Post Office Superannuation Fund, to be salted away in case of a rainy day. The small farmer has benefited to some extent, of course: the Ministry of Agriculture shows that while in 1876 about nine-tenths of farm land was leased to tenant farmers, a century later only one-third was let—the rest was owned.

Not all the ground they own is worth a great deal: farms sited on the hills of Scotland and Wales make very poor returns, and there is little to be won in either rent or farm income from ten thousand acres of windswept heather, however pretty it may be. The Seafields and the Atholls, then, with dozens of square miles of Scottish upland under their belts, cannot count their fortunes in millions of pounds unless—like the late Countess of Seafield—they see to it that their holdings are developed to the full. Nina Seafield saw her precious plots of Speyside worked for the skiing industry, with the result that she profited by unimaginable sums of money and, till death duties and other circumstances drained the funds away, was a very wealthy woman indeed.

Most of the land owned by Britain's peers is, though, good and rich farm country, worth a substantial amount intrinsically, bringing in a considerable income from the tenant farms. Currently, the price of an acre of respectably arable land is reckoned to be about £600— meaning that the Duke of Devonshire, should his trustees ever dispose of the 56,000 acres over which they have absolute control, would profit to the tune of £33 million. And yet in June 1965, when Lord Cowdray's heir, Michael Pearson, bought 4,400 acres of prime meadowland in Gloucestershire, he paid somewhere in the region of a million pounds for the tract—little more than £200 an acre. In the mid-seventies the price of land tripled—giving the lie to suggestions that the landowners are worth less than in the heyday of the truly mighty estates. In 1876, when the seventh Duke of Devonshire owned 133,000 acres, his total worth (excluding all his goods and chattels, the massive houses, the paintings, the priceless furniture) was then around three-quarters of a million pounds. Today the eleventh Duke's fortune, on paper, has increased by some fifty-fold, while his actual holdings of land have dropped to nearly a third of his predecessor's.

In terms of land-endowed wealth, the Duke of Buccleuch and the Duke of Westminster struggle for first place, though Buccleuch's holdings have diminished marginally over the years, while those belonging to the Grosvenor family have burgeoned by the year. Thus far we have only been discussing agricultural land: in those terms

alone Buccleuch is probably worth marginally more than Westminster
—around, say, £100 million; but when Westminster's urban owner-
ships, especially those in the very centre of the most fashionable part
of London, and his foreign holdings, are added, then the fortunes of
the Duke far outstrip those of Buccleuch and all his Scots kin put
together. It would not be unreasonable to place Westminster's total
worth at £400 million, and it is quite probably considerably more.

All these figures presuppose, of course, that the landowner is likely
to sell his holdings—and this happens only occasionally, whenever
there are taxes to meet, or new roofs to put on the mansions, or farm
buildings to construct (Buccleuch, for example, had to put new lead
on the roof at Bowhill: it cost £250,000). Rarely does an owner sell
land for the simple pleasure of allowing liquid assets to trickle through
his well-manicured hands: the only such money that percolates
through to him in regular fashion is that other great source of wealth
for the landowner—farm rents.

Currently, decent farmland rents are about £9 per acre per year,
so a farm of 500 acres, which is around average for the better arable
land on a well-managed agricultural estate, would thus pay £4,500
annually to the landowner. But here the passage of the years has not
meant a concomitant increase in true wealth: the increase in rents
over the past century has only been about seven-fold, while the
inflationary pressures of the past hundred years have been very nearly
as great. And in the nineteenth century rental income went untaxed:
today it is mightily taxed, and regarded in much the same way as
normal income. The landowner still reaps vast sums in rentals—but
they usually only manage to cover the costs of improvements to the
estates and general maintenance. No Duke is able to affect a grand
style by virtue of income from his farms: for that he has to rely on his
income from investments and such business ventures as are indulged
in by his estates company, or by his other associations.

Nevertheless, the gulf between a landowner and his tenant is a
spectacularly deep one, albeit their relationship is largely symbiotic.
The owner, though his troubles may be vast, still manages to live in
assured and pleasant style. His tenant, though supposedly cosseted
from cradle to grave by the benevolence of the owner of the "big
house" on the hill, invariably finds life a good deal more difficult than
one would suppose.

John and Janet Robinson are in their fifties—a quiet, stolid couple whose faces, both constantly exposed to the chafing winds whistling down the moors, are lined with purple veinlets, earning them the description of "rosy-cheeked." They live in an ugly square farm building, half a mile from the village of Beeley, one of three Derbyshire villages owned in their entirety by the Duke of Devonshire. They have been with the Chatsworth Estates since 1953, and will remain tenant farmers for the Duke until they retire in another ten years or so. And then—"Well, there's no hard-and-fast rule, but we'll probably be offered a cottage in one of the villages and we'll live out the rest of our lives there, paying just a little rent."

John Robinson, son of a policeman in a nearby town, had always wanted to farm—though he knew that, with a mere £300 in his savings account, he could never hope to own his own land. So he applied to the Duke's agent to rent a small farm: he was eventually offered one, high up on the short-grass hills above the village—twenty-four acres, for which he paid a mere £72 a year. The Duke gave him a four-bedroomed house and a cowshed for eight head of cattle. John Robinson spent his £300 on a single cow (which cost him £45), two suckling calves, four weaner pigs, a chick brooder and fifty day-old chicks. From the beginning he built up—well, to be frank, he built up nothing. His farms got larger and larger; his rents got steeper and steeper; his herds bigger and bigger. He now makes a comfortable enough living but, save for his furniture, his livestock and his tractor, he owns nothing. Perhaps, if he sold everything, he would be worth a couple of thousand pounds, but would have nowhere else to live and no means of making a livelihood—save as the hired tiller of another man's estate.

Not that either he or his wife minds. They display a certain stoic acceptance of living their lives wedded to the estate. "Ownership brings with it responsibility, doesn't it?" John Robinson said. "I know the estate will take care of me. The people up at the House are not out to ruin me or anything like that. It's for the good of both of us— the Duke and me—that this system is preserved. I trust them to be fair to me, and I go on farming well and making as much as I can, and paying my rent on time."

Little by little the tract for which the Robinsons are responsible has grown—ten acres here when a nearby smallholder died, fifty acres there up on the hill when the estate office decided to "rationalize" the Beeley holdings, another patch and some more buildings when a neighbour retired. There were problems in restoring some of the dilapidated buildings—the Robinsons complained that too much of the burden was being placed upon them, and that the estate was doing too little. The reply came that the Duke had consented to build a new farm for the family and consolidate the package of land into a discreet 220 acres, which the Robinsons could farm with efficiency and profit for the rest of their years.

The structure which the Chatsworth Estates erected was built with more of an eye to cost than to aesthetics—which, in view of the painstaking attitude of every one of the ten previous Dukes towards the great houses, the parks and the gardens, seems rather odd. The new building, set back from the valley road, looks like a Monopoly house, finished in a dull sandy brown. It is constructed in an appallingly ersatz fashion: no matter that Derbyshire houses are traditionally stout and hearty structures of massive stones and slate and seasoned woods; no matter that Chatsworth, though a gloomy mansion from the outside, has been finished with care and attention worthy of a watchmaker. No matter that the Devonshires have over the centuries, kept a weather eye on the development of the surrounding countryside to ensure, by their benevolent use of influence, that it remains pleasing to the eye. Here it was principally money that counted: the house, which resembles a box made of wood, fibreglass and concrete, faced with a thin shell of artificial stone, clashes rudely with the older structures nearby. "Her Grace came down to look at it when they were starting to build," said John Robinson. "We told her that the way it was planned, it would get neither the morning nor the afternoon sun. So she had a word with the agent and the whole house was turned around a bit so we get the morning sun in the bedroom and the evening sun in the kitchen. She was very gracious about that."

The family moved in during the spring of 1970. They were paying around £2,000 for their right to farm the Duke's land—their livestock and milk sales brought in about £7,000 a year. After all the outgoings they were left with rather less than the average factory worker "except that I'm doing what I like, and it's a good, healthy life. I like the Duke's people at the estate office, and, though we don't see much of His Grace, he seems a very nice chap. Very kind, although a bit standoffish." Early in 1977 Mr. Robinson had a letter from the agent: rent was having to rise to £3,600—an 80 per cent increase. "I just don't know how we'll pay the difference. Everything else is going up—all the chemicals we use here have doubled and tripled in cost. All we can do is hope for a rise in the milk price, otherwise we will suffer a bit. But I suppose everyone is suffering these days."

Very occasionally the two worlds of Duke and tenant collide, ever so gently. The last time was in 1965, when the Robinsons were invited up to Chatsworth for the coming of age of the Duke's eldest son and heir, the Marquess of Hartington. The Robinsons still keep the engraved invitation, and can recall every detail of the evening. "It was so lovely," said Janet Robinson, looking into the distance. "They had the house floodlit, and there was a great buffet laid out on tables on the lawns. There were servants in livery, and the food was wonderful. Late in the evening there were fireworks that they say could be heard and seen away over the hills. There must have been two thousand people at the party—tradespeople, doctors, all sorts. Of course they had held another party the night before, a private one for the high-ups. Harold Macmillan was there, I think, and there might even have been someone in the Royal Family. But of course we couldn't go to that." By the early 1980s the whole Chatsworth estate was experiencing financial troubles—titled and untitled were having to tighten their belts.

There is still some residual irritation at the circular letter that arrived at the Robinson farm a few weeks before the Marquess's party. "The agent asked us if we would like to contribute for a present for His Lordship, and suggested that we might like to send money according to the acreage we rented. The bigger the farm, the bigger the contribution, you see. The more rent you paid to the Duke, the bigger the present you were supposed to give his son. It seemed a bit odd." Anyway, the Robinsons did contribute, and received, some weeks later, the page-long letter from the Marquess, which the Hodkins also received, thanking them for their generosity in helping to buy him a "beautiful wristwatch." The letter looked real enough, but had in fact been photocopied: the Robinsons keep it, though, among the few other family treasures, including the invitation to the party, and Mrs. Robinson's invitation to a summer garden party at Buckingham Palace, which she won for her sterling service to the Women's Institute.

The relationship between Duke and tenant is, though economically intimate, socially remote. The difference between their styles of life is vast. The respect held by one for the other is deep; in the Duke's case Mr. Robinson is regarded as a faithful member of a happy band; in Mr. Robinson's case His Grace is always regarded as someone before whom one makes a slight bow of the head, addresses by title and invariably fears. To the outsider the ties that bind the pair appear outdated.

In his ceilidh play *The Cheviot, the Stag and the Black, Black Oil,* which John McGrath wrote for his 7:84 Theatre Company (so named because "7 percent of the nation own 84 percent of its wealth") to perform in Scottish towns and villages in 1974, a particularly bitter sketch denounces the English landowner in the Highlands, his "love" of the "quaintness" of the Scotsman and his utter joy at returning, year after year, to kill the stag on the heather hills and fish the trout from the swift rivers. The sketch has all the malice that can be summoned by a Scotsman who, in those early straining days of nationalistic fervour, sees himself as having been mercilessly exploited by such English landowners as "Lady Phosphate of Runcorn—she's very big in chemicals, you know" who own the lands, and the people, of the remoter glens of the Highlands.

> But though we think you're quaint, don't forget to *pay your rent*!
> And if you should want your land, we'll cut off your grasping
>   hand!
> You had better learn your place, you're a low and servile race.
> We've cleared the straths, we've cleared the paths,
> We've cleared the glens, we've cleared the Bens,
> And we can do it once again.
> We've got the brass, we've got the class,
> We've got the law, we need no more:
> We'll show you we're the ruling class!

Not entirely fair, maybe, but it illustrates by exaggeration.

In all the large estates, the agent (or in Scotland, the factor) stands firmly between owner and tenant, insulating the one from the other and perpetuating and institutionalizing the rural caste system that keeps owner and tenant on two very separate social planes. The agent, a man of many parts indeed, can best be looked upon as the lubricant of the rural class system: it is he who deifies the landowner in the eyes of the tenant ("You should have proper respect for His Grace, you know," he will advise a recalcitrant tenant) and who keeps the workers and the tenant farmers in a proper ducal perspective

—it was quite probably an agent who first brought the phrase "the natives are restless" back from the Colonies and applied it in the Home Counties.

Derrick Penrose, agent for the Chatsworth Estates, stands astride the different worlds represented by the Big House and the Robinson farm. He is educated and highly intelligent, part businessman, part lawyer, part social worker—a management man who would fit in well in the boardroom of a medium-sized provincial manufacturing concern with somewhat Victorian attitudes. He is the Duke of Devonshire's representative at the occasional meetings in the Grosvenor Office in London—meetings which, as the then Lord Grosvenor, now the sixth Duke of Westminster, admits, "aim to improve the image of landowners, both rural and urban." Penrose is not terribly forthcoming about the rationale, though he accepts, with the new young Duke, that landowners are "going through a bad time at the moment. The taxation system is horrendous; the Socialists are against us and are managing to whip up sentiment against us; we have to do something to keep our end up." The group of discreet businessmen-agents from the twenty-five biggest estates assemble to discuss how best to proceed against the tide of public opinion. "We make it known that we are available for consultation by academics, civil servants, politicians and so on, to give our point of view. We are not so much a lobbying group as a self-help organization, giving each other advice on tax problems, whether or not to open up our houses, how to combat the prevalence of envy among the general public—that sort of thing. It is all very informal, but we hope in the long term it will prove effective."

Penrose is not as certain as some of the landowners themselves that the Labour Party, which instituted the dreaded Capital Transfer Tax, is solidly against the large estates. "One or two party members are rabidly against us, but I detect a deeper feeling that responsibly and benevolently run estates are still going to be all right. The civil servants we have talked to seem convinced of the benefits of continuity of ownership, and they are aware that in nearly all cases actual ownership is by trusts or estate companies—not by wealthy individuals. It is rather more difficult for them to rail against an efficient estate company running the affairs of a large tract of land and a few villages. Socialists find that easier to take than to see a gigantically wealthy Duke running his farmers into the ground to make a profit so that he can buy more port, or something. That is something we have managed to convey to the civil service, and I think the view is accepted. There is great national affection for the preservation of the estate, if not the preservation of the owner of the estate."

He points with some pride at the manner in which the Chatsworth Estates Company has looked after its workers—the swimming pool behind his office teems with children who have been driven for miles from the villages all around. "We didn't have to build it. It cost well into six figures for us. It just seemed right that the children round here should have something that they would get if they lived in a city. The only difference is that we built it, rather than the local council." There were other benefits for the Duke's workers: the club, in the same old coaching inn that now houses Penrose's offices, has bars and billiard rooms; there is a golf course and a bowling green, a cricket pitch and a football ground—all provided by the Duke. "The council announced it would close down the school at Beeley quite recently, so we built an extra classroom on to the school we own at Pilsley and arranged for a bus to take the children there. We thought it was important to keep the children at school on the estate—it breaks up the community if they have to go over into the big towns away from the estate. We look upon our job, in a way, as maintaining a community, as well as making money. It would never do if the people were allowed to drift off."

Most of Devonshire's land is let for farming, though extra profits are creamed off by the sensible working of the sporting possibilities offered by high moorland and wood. Sporting lets are arranged—supra-tenancies that overlie the farming lets and which bring businessmen over from the cities for the shooting of game birds that are specially reared at various parts of the acreage. The man who has the farm tenancy is allowed, under legislation of the 1880s, to shoot "ground game and vermin," like rabbits and hares: the man who has the sporting tenancy has the right to dispose of the rest. A gamekeeper, employed by the sporting tenant, looks after the individual rights of the two men: the position is regarded as one of the plum jobs on an estate. One letter a week comes into the estate offices asking for the job: since the Duke has only six permanently installed within the ring fence of his Derbyshire lands, Penrose has to turn down nearly every application.

So far we have looked only at the rural landowner. Urban holdings have, in many cases, made the principal fortunes of the more astute members of nobility and have added the glitter and opportunity to the stability and continuity offered by the ownership of acreages in the country. The pre-eminent urban landowner is, as we have noted, the Duke of Westminster who, by virtue of the lucky marriage of Sir Thomas Grosvenor to the twelve-year-old heiress, Mary Davies, in 1677, collected a parcel of land in what was to become Central London, and which proved of inestimable value.

The story is well enough known: how the grandson of that union, Richard Grosvenor, drained the land near the newly built Buckingham House and constructed an elegant London suburb, Belgravia; how Pimlico and Mayfair were developed, how Pimlico was later sold in the 1950s to provide funds for further purchases, how Grosvenor Square was redeveloped and how the American Government fought in vain to win the freehold of the prime site in that square for their handsome flagship embassy. The 300 acres in London—200 in Belgravia, 100 in Mayfair—have been justly called the jewel in the coronet of the Grosvenor family. Efforts over the past several decades by a shrewdly managed Grosvenor Estate office have ensured that the exquisite architectural character of the most agreeable parts of West One and South-West Three has been rigorously defended and maintained. Though controversies develop with monotonous regularity to place the Grosvenor managers at the centre of new storms, it cannot be denied that it has been largely through the influence of their sensible and far-sighted policies that the character of such gems as Belgrave Square and Eaton Square has been maintained, while squares in the more remote corners of the metropolis have become, in many cases, cluttered with uninspiring shops and glass monoliths of little architectural merit. So vast are the London holdings of the Dukes of Westminster that mistakes do occur from time to time: generally, though, the family's beneficial influence on London as a visual asset cannot be doubted.

There have been detailed studies completed in recent years of the influence of the great landed aristocrats on the cities they owned, both in political and physical terms. To delve too deeply into the historical aspects of nobility's influence on urban character would be to depart from the terms of reference of this book: two examples, none the less, are provided by the work of a Cambridge social historian, David Cannadine, who has studied in great detail the influence of the Calthorpe family upon the development of Birmingham, and the Dukes of Devonshire upon the jewel of the Cavendish crown, the

elegant seaside resort of Eastbourne. The conclusion to which Cannadine comes runs counter to one accepted historical canon: that, as Asa
Briggs once wrote, the influence of the "protected estate" (i.e., an
enclosed region, owned by a large landowner of power and wealth) in
a provincial city was "strategic," presenting a formidable "conservative
interest" that dominated the development of the city as a whole, no
matter the political tendencies of the city inhabitants. Cannadine
found, from his studies of Birmingham and Eastbourne, that the
conservative influence of the titled landowners—who were actually
leaders of the Liberal Party of the day, so the use of the word "conservative" here is not meant strictly in its political sense*—was only
formidable when the inhabitants beneath them were themselves set in
the conservative mould. The influence of the Lords Calthorpe, who
developed the pleasant suburb of Edgbaston, upon the stoutly mercantile and radical folk of Birmingham, was not, he concluded, as
formidable as most historians had assumed. In Birmingham, while
the Calthorpes' financial interest was gigantic, their "conservative
interest" was small—had they lived in the city permanently (the
present Baron Calthorpe lists his address as a ship, the *Fantôme de
Mer*, off the Channel Islands) they might have had more political
interest: as it was, Birmingham never turned itself into a Calthorpe
company town.

With Eastbourne, however, the situation is considerably different.
Here the Dukes of Devonshire have been successively lionized and
almost worshipped by the city burghers. From 1847 onwards the
Cavendish family, and their family solicitors, Currey & Co., have
exerted the kind of influence over the development of Eastbourne that
the Dukes of Argyll have had over the development of Inveraray. At
the height of the building boom, in the early years of the Edwardian

---

* To underline the point that the Calthorpes and the Devonshires can hardly
have exerted politically conservative influences on the towns under their control, it is worth noting that the third Lord Calthorpe (1787–1850) was "a
Whig for many years," the fourth Lord (his brother, 1790–1858) was a Whig
MP and a Palmerstonian Liberal in the Lords, and the fifth Lord Calthorpe
(1826–93) was a Liberal MP from 1859 to 1868.

Similarly, the sixth Duke of Devonshire (1790–1858) was a prominent
Whig, the seventh Duke (1809–91) was a Liberal MP from 1829 to 1834,
the eighth Duke (1833–1908) was better known as "the Silent Lord Hartington" and was an important Liberal Cabinet Minister, Leader of the Liberal
Opposition and three times refused to be Liberal Prime Minister.

era, this "Empress of watering places" expanded vastly, to the mutual satisfaction of the Duke, 200 miles north in Chatsworth, and London's fashionable or retired elite who swept into the town in such droves that "buildings are occupied almost before they are completed." When the brilliant and accomplished seventh Duke died, Eastbourne Corporation deluged Chatsworth with flowers and telegraphic messages of sympathy and condolence. Corporation officials went to his funeral, memorial services were held in two Eastbourne churches, businesses closed for the day, black shutters were put up in windows, a statue was later erected to the "Father and Founder of Eastbourne." The eighth and ninth Dukes, though rarely resident in the city, each served terms as Mayor and were asked, unanimously, to serve second terms. And all this despite the admission of the Dukes that when they visited Eastbourne it was "for the purpose of obtaining rest, recreation, fresh air and health," and most certainly not for dealing with the irritation of running so sordid a business as a municipal corporation. The only details which evidently concerned the Dukes were trivial—the amount of wine to be provided for a local orchestra and whether invitations from the Duke in his capacity as Mayor should include the ducal coronet of strawberry leaves.

David Cannadine concludes that, during the heyday of Eastbourne's development, the simple fact of the ducal connection was sufficient a selling point to permit rapid, though tasteful, expansion of the town; in themselves the Dukes were "the town's greatest asset." Cavendish money, in far greater amounts than the town could raise through taxes, built schools and hospitals, drains and parks, and kept the people supplied with every amenity normally provided at public expense—water, gas, sewerage, all these came courtesy of the Cavendish family. Not, it was later admitted, that the Dukes did all this for purely altruistic reasons—far from it, as the eighth Duke pointed out in 1903. "What we have done has been done naturally to a large extent for the purpose of improving our property and increasing its value." His vision was essentially of the long-term kind reserved for families who can be certain that their riches and their status will continue for century after century: just as the Duke of Buccleuch argues in favour of permitting agricultural land to be retained privately because of the benefits of long-term planning to the countryside's aspect, so the Dukes of Devonshire can say that their long-term financial interests act for the long-term benefit of the population in their urban property. "Long-term benefits" is a phrase that crops up again and again when hereditary nobles discuss the advantages of the existing system.

The elements which contributed to the development of Eastbourne as one of England's most pleasing seaside towns were, Cannadine wrote, "the reflected glory of ducal ownership; the careful supervision by ducal employees of planning, zoning and development; the massive provision from ducal coffers of money for amenities and the infrastructure; and the extensive control by a ducal oligarchy of the town thus created." Little has changed over the years: the social tone of Eastbourne has remained steadfastly haughty, the provision of the kind of pleasure domes that would appeal to "the cloth caps" as one writer noted, was left to nearby resorts like Brighton and Bognor Regis. When the tenth Duke died in 1950 "there were wreaths and flowers from no fewer than ten Eastbourne voluntary societies . . ." A vast industrial scheme was started in 1973, on the orders of the present Duke, and Eastbourne saw no reason to doubt the "spokesman" for the family when he said: "The Duke has taken a personal interest in the scheme. He is not so much interested in maximum profits as he is in the high standards that have always been maintained as the guiding principle of the Chatsworth Settlement." The fact is, however, that revenues from the Eastbourne properties more than help to offset the £100,000 loss which Chatsworth House sustains each year. Without Eastbourne, as without John Robinson and his colleague tenant farmers, the Dukedom of Devonshire and the grand houses in which those sporting the title languish, would founder in double-quick time.

The picture, in summary, is of a nobility still firmly based on land-holding, both in the city and in the country. City properties provide the wherewithal that permits the noble life in the country to be maintained—and thus it is in the continuing interest of the owner to maintain the excellence of his urban property so as to extract as much revenue from it as possible. Developers in Central London place their faith in the revenue possibilities neither of huge office blocks nor of great battery-farm apartments: to construct such monsters might profit them in the short term but, since they would reduce the attraction of the inner city as a dwelling site, would ultimately have the effect of lowering value. Thus the present Duke of Westminster, the sixth, has absolutely no intention of turning Eaton Square into a paradise for bankers or faceless thousands from the multinational corporations:

people will always want to live in elegant houses, he feels certain, and thus for the eventual good fortune of, let us say, the tenth Duke, elegant houses will stay there and plans for office blocks will be quietly set aside. Similarly with Eastbourne and its like: doubtless conference centres and *Clubs Méditerranées* would flourish where the wide avenues and serried ranks of town houses stand now, and doubtless the present Duke would be rapidly enriched and the Chatsworth accounts speedily brought back into the black if the construction crews moved in tomorrow. But the present Duke is comfortably enough off to permit himself the luxury of thinking of some long-distant heir who is not yet a twinkle in a grandchild's eye: that, in sum, is the "long-term benefit" he seeks.

The spectre that confronts them all, and which threatens to confound the long-term planning of the present landed nobility, is taxation. Not, it should be said, that noble and rich Britons are any more averse to tax than is any other subject: it is simply that changes in the tax structure made in the mid-1970s have, as the *Spectator* imagined in 1876, now set "the pillage of a class for its first end." That fact, to the class affected, appears a monstrous development.

When Sir William Harcourt, Lord Rosebery's Chancellor of the Exchequer and an impassioned enemy of the House of Lords, rose in the Commons on 16 April 1894 to introduce his famous "death-duty budget" he was announcing the invention of a tax that had as its intention merely the increasing of the efficiency of raising revenue, not the ruination of the members of the House he abhorred. The tax he announced was to be called "estate duty," and it was being put into immediate operation to replace the cumbersome armada of probate duty, succession duty and account duty which had raised revenue from the passage of riches until then. The single, graduated tax was to be levied, on death, on a scale that today seems derisory—from a minimum of 1 percent on estates worth between £100 and £500, to a maximum of just 8 percent on estates valued at more than £1,000,000. The duty, Harcourt announced, was to be levied on the new owner— the "tenant for life under a settlement"—the person who, in the case of the hereditary peerage, was invariably the eldest son and heir. There was opposition, but never of any great volume: in fact Harcourt's finance bill for 1894 passed through the Liberal-dominated House of Commons by the fairly respectable majority of twenty; when the Tories, under Lord Salisbury, replaced the Liberals the following year they left the provisions for death duties untouched. And so little did the high priests of Establishment discount its importance to their futures that, in 1902, Harcourt was offered a peerage. He declined; it was left to his son to accept a viscounty fifteen years later. (And the last Viscount, betraying the Liberal principles of his grandfather, took the Conservative Whip. The viscounty is now extinct.)

The reason that the wealthy classes in Britain never took estate duties too seriously was that they regarded it as a purely optional tax. It was a tax you could quite easily avoid, and after an uneasy start, most of the more skilled members of the landed and ennobled classes took great pains to avoid paying a single penny. However, there were some who noted the probable effects of the legislation if they failed to take care. As Lady Bracknell commented, in *The Importance of Being Earnest*: "What between the duties expected of one during one's lifetime and the duties exacted from one after one's death, land has ceased to be either a profit or a pleasure. It gives one position, and prevents one from keeping it up. That's all that can be said about land."

So they took care to avoid the duties exacted after death. A few of the weaker estates went to the wall fairly early on: in the closing years of the nineteenth century and the first decade of the twentieth land sales jumped by an order of magnitude as hard-up landowners attempted to raise capital. Some of the nobility began to cut down on their expenditure; the first signs that the aristocratic tradition might one day be permitted to wear threadbare started to become apparent. Charity payments dropped slightly; the London Seasons of the day had rather more absent friends than was customary. The exigencies prompted by the imposition of the duty can very well be regarded as one reason for the sudden interest taken in commerce by members of an aristocracy who had hitherto regarded "trade" as a vulgar occupation fit only for the great unwashed. By 1912 a dozen large estates were on the market: financial expertise was badly needed by the noble classes. Forty-nine direct heirs to peerages were killed in the Great War, prompting further huge sales. World War I was instrumental in the demolition of almost as much property at home as overseas, as great houses were savaged in their dozens afterwards to pay the accounts of the previous decade.

The upheaval initiated by Harcourt's invention was soon to be calmed: all manner of complex devices were constructed to alleviate the burden of death duties, the rates for which rose relentlessly as the

Government's need for revenue became ever more pressing. It would be tedious to list all the many financial bolt-holes devised to accommodate the noble rich: the estates company, an invention of the 1920s, was one such. The various types of trusts—blind, discretionary, and so on; the so-called spendthrift settlements that actually urged some heirs to spend all they could before Chancellors could get their hands on the lucre; and the practice of avoiding duty by the simple device of giving everything dutiable to the heir seven years before death—all these managed to lighten the burden, and, for a while, the tidal wave of sales receded. Agricultural land values, which had sunk during the 1920s, started to rise again; rents were increased; the revenues from meat and milk started up once more. The financial outlook for the landed few began, slowly and steadily, to improve. By the end of the 1940s investment in land was running at a decent rate once more: some newly ennobled gentlemen of substance—like Lord Rootes—were able to buy up tracts of Scotland and to consider they had done something shrewd.

But rich men do not have a monopoly in good fortune—and some very rich men have had to pay staggeringly high bills for estate duty. When the second Duke of Westminster died, for example, the bills sent in by the Inland Revenue amounted to some twenty million pounds. An entire subdepartment of the Revenue had to be established to deal with the massive financial empire His Grace left for his inheritors. He took precautions, before he died, against this kind of a financial disaster happening again: in his will he divided the family fortunes into a twenty-part trust fund, limiting the amount of wealth that could be held by any one person and thus be vulnerable to taxation. It was one of the measures that has helped the Grosvenor Estates in their present unparalleled fortunes. With investments in land and property from Hawaii to South Africa, immense landholdings in the British Isles and, as we have seen, the most valuable privately controlled block of property in London, the Grosvenor family are the senior members of a very small band of aristocratic entrepreneurs who have succeeded, and succeeded brilliantly, in these harshly egalitarian times.

Much of their success is due to expert planning; much also to tough bargaining. There was a fourteen-year fight, for instance, over the death duties assessed against Gerald, the fourth Duke, who died in 1967. It was reckoned that the Estates should pay between ten and fifteen million pounds duty on his worth: the Grosvenor family claimed, though, that despite his death taking place in 1967, he actually succumbed after a twenty-five-year lapse to his war wounds—wounds he gallantly collected while serving in Europe with the Ninth Lancers. With several million pounds at stake, the trustees could afford to pay the very best lawyers in the land to meet the ever-inquiring minds of the Revenue—and the trustees won.

The legislative loopholes which made estate duties the "optional tax," derided by zealous Socialists (and there have been innumerable stories of men dying a month before the seven years were up, and being kept pickled in bed by their heirs, and the doctors bribed with a few thousand to keep their mouths shut and sign the death certificate with a more appropriate date), eventually led to the famous 1975 Finance Act, the Act that replaced the eighty-year writ of estate duty with the tax that well and truly blocks all the exits—the Capital Transfer Tax.

This tax is a Socialist's dream, aimed quite plainly, not just at the raising of revenue, but at the positive redistribution of the national wealth. (Discussions on an even more swingeing form of redistributive taxation, a wealth tax, continue. Recent attempts to prepare the legislation have been continually frustrated, but there is little doubt that a Socialist Government armed with a respectable Parliamentary majority, would introduce a wealth tax beside which the present horrors of the CTT would seem to the victims mere pinpricks.)

The basis of CTT, which in its application and taken with its varying exemptions sounds massively complicated, is actually very simple: it places tax not only on property when it is handed over at death, it also prevents the avoidance of taxation by the simple measure of handing over the money some years before death, by levying duty—albeit at a lower rate than at death—on any gifts made during a person's lifetime. Thus if the Duke of Buccleuch had decided to settle a million pounds on his eldest son, the Earl of Dalkeith, when the latter reached his twenty-fifth birthday on Valentine's Day 1979, he would have been heavily taxed on his gift—no less than £700,000 would have been snapped up by the Chancellor and placed in the national treasure chest. To enable his son to have benefited to the tune of one million pounds the Duke would have had to have made his gift one of four million pounds—a powerful disincentive, one might think.

There are, of course, all manner of exemptions and loopholes—though the latter are small and exceedingly difficult to find. There is certain relief for farmland, handed on by a working farmer to his son; there is relief (thanks to the vigilance of Lord Montagu of Beaulieu) for the owners of stately homes to which the public has ready access; there is relief, too, for gifts made to political parties, to listed heritage bodies like the National Gallery and the British Museum; and works of art can be transferred if they are made to institutions that do not conduct a business for profit. Generally, though, the effect is numbing: small wonder the Duke of Devonshire does not believe his fortunes and his landholdings will survive more than two generations—unless, of course, the rates are reduced substantially, as a Conservative Government might have been expected to attempt to do.

Tax lawyers, accountants and solicitors to the landed nobility are, not unnaturally, having a field day, advising their clients on how best to proceed with the distribution of their wealth. The kind of advice that might be given to a nobleman worth a cool seven million came in one gloomy lawyer's letter sent early in 1977:

"When we last spoke I explained the deleterious effect that Capital Transfer Tax will have on the Estate if matters are left as they are. But then I was naïve enough to assume that there was a pretty good chance that the Government might be persuaded, by our friends, to alter the CTT rules to rid us of what we all consider a monstrous inequity. . . .

"I regret to say, now I have had a chance to study the new 1976 Finance Act, that the new law is no help at all to us. So far from easing the rules as I had expected, it has actually stiffened them in some crucial respects. . . . since I first learned of this I have been waiting to see if some previously unnoticed loophole might be found. But not so. Hence my advice is to get moving before the deadline of 1 April, 1977, even though this will mean paying out a pretty vast sum to the taxman: by acting quickly we will at least safeguard the Trusts and the other funds for the future.

"As you will no doubt have noticed, the full CTT bill is very nearly one million pounds, which would be totally crippling. . . . " [A strange choice of phrase: it would actually leave some £6,000,000 behind, a sum which many of those who voted for the Finance Bill would be quite content to have in their pockets.] ". . . at present I know of no way in which we can avoid it . . . but I think we can delay having to pay it for a while. . . ."

The letter then continues with a list of the choices open to His

Lordship, and concludes: ". . . meanwhile, I have warned the other Trustees that we may have to raise £150,000 for CTT later this year (it will be payable in October 1977), and they are shaping their savings and investment arrangements accordingly."

A list appended with the letter shows the costs that lie ahead for the nobleman: some £990,000 to be paid to the Revenue if he transferred the Trust as he had planned; a periodic charge of £300,000, payable every decade; a reduced rate if the terms of the Trust are changed before 1980. In any case the hapless peer who had to read advice like that one spring day in 1977 had to grapple with the knowledge that, no matter what steps he took short of leaving the country, the Labour Government had passed a law that was destined to take away at least an eighth of his fortune every decade, and could "cripple" him long before his children are in a position to accede to his title. One cannot wonder at the anger, bitterness and frustration expressed by virtually every really wealthy member of the House of Lords, or avoid speculating what debate might have taken place had the Upper House been able to frustrate the progress of financial legislation; instead, Their Lordships, under the rules of parliamentary procedure that govern them, could only gnash their gums and wail soundlessly at the tax that seeks to pillage their class and sack their surviving castles.

The first effects of CTT upon the landed estates have not yet been noticed. The stately workings of the taxing machines have ensured that the legacy of the old estate duty remains with us for some time. An example of the effects of estate duty on collections of nobly acquired treasure came in 1977, with the solemn announcement by the seventh Earl of Rosebery that the grandly castellated Victorian masterpiece of Mentmore (just north of London) would have to go on sale to meet a bill of £4 million in estate duties. The Government of the day had turned down Lord Rosebery's offer of the house in lieu of duty: it refused even to accept a bargain-basement offer of just £3 million for the house—an astonishingly low price, considering the value placed on the structure and its bewildering variety of *objets d'art* collected, in the main, by Baron de Rothschild, father of the fifth Countess. The press, almost to the last serif, was angered to white heat by the Department of the Environment's decision to allow the sale to proceed by default, and thus place part of "Britain's heritage" at risk of going overseas. Even the *New Statesman*, a journal that cares little for the extravaganzas of wealthy ennobled Jews like Baron de Rothschild and the plaintive whines of those who inherit such fortunes, thought the Government's attitude rather parsimonious. That the present Lord Rosebery, a little-known figure and the heir of a man whose claim to fame came from the breeding and owning of racehorses,* owns two other sizeable houses besides Mentmore— one in Scotland, the other in Suffolk—and was most certainly not short of a few pounds, was largely ignored. That the Government was facing the most devastating period of public expenditure curbs seemed, to the critics, quite irrelevant. That collections of furniture and paintings far superior to those assembled by the Rothschilds and handed down to the Roseberys are still in good hands and good shape was discounted by the Government's critics. And few seemed to consider whether in fact the Mentmore collections were truly a vital part of British heritage and of crucial importance to our national wellbeing.

In fact one might almost have suspected that the campaign to try and persuade the Government to help Lord Rosebery out of his dilemma by buying the house (and selling it later, for a profit of perhaps £7 million) was orchestrated from behind the walls of estates faced with similar problems in the future. The Twenty-Five Invisibles, meeting each month at the Grosvenor office—could they have had an interest in promulgating the view that Mentmore was a citadel of importance equal to the Tower of London and St. Paul's Cathedral? It was a perfect vehicle for their views, a perfect example to enable the other large landowners to look back and say "I told you so" in another decade's time. And the Twenty-Five had long said they operated "under the cover of an established organization"—might their link not be with one of the energetic groups which unsuccessfully master-minded the Mentmore appeal early in 1977?

As it turned out only a very few writers tried to put Mentmore into its proper perspective. One, William Feaver, a distinguished art critic and author, wrote in the *Observer* a series of remarks that, considering the attitudes of his colleagues, appeared faintly heretical. "Cue for lamentations," he said, referring to the widespread protesta-

---

* Winston Churchill's Government was supposed to have chosen the late Lord Rosebery to command the whole of Scottish Region had there been a Nazi invasion of Great Britain during World War II. He therefore had obviously impressed Downing Street as having more to him than the mere breeding and training of racehorses.

tions made immediately following the Government's announcement that it was not buying:

"The house and collection, the argument went, were a priceless, irreplaceable, unrivalled whole. The Government have spurned a bargain. But, scanning the lists and actually examining the most prized or, in auction parlance, 'important' pieces, it is hard to find anything that qualified indisputably as British heritage material.

"You couldn't count Venetian state barge lanterns, however big and gilt, or a Louis XV clockwork orange tree, however perfect in every detail.

"Only a perfervid Jacobite would be distraught at the prospect of the export of a large and lofty Masucci of the Old Pretender's marriage and a matching Chezzi of Bonny Prince Charlie's baptism. Yes, one might opine, Gainsborough's painting of hounds streaking in for a kill should be acquired by the nation at all costs. But François Drouais' portrait of Mme. de Pompadour, late in life and awash in silks? Regretfully, no."

Mr. Feaver's article came at the very height of the debate over Mentmore, which occupied the headlines throughout a spring otherwise devoted to bleak stories about disputes at British Leyland motorcar factories. Two days later the Government, after even more anguished thought, it said, than had preceded the original decision to tell Lord Rosebery "thanks, but no thanks," made up its mind once and for all: it would definitely not buy Mentmore, and if Lord Rosebery was to pay his bills in full, then the sale would have to go ahead. A delighted Sotheby's sprang into action, and the auctions began in May. One imagines there will be many further Mentmores once Capital Transfer Tax begins to take its intended bite.

Although the County Landowners' Association, with its forty thousand members and a fairer knowledge than any other body of precisely who owns what land, and how much they own, stays obtusely silent in order to protect its members' interests, there were recommendations in the mid-1970s coming from within the lobbies of landowners for the establishment of National Registers of Land. Lord Rothschild, wearing his hat as chairman of an advisory committee on agricultural strategy at Reading University, made a formal recommendation that, in order to make the best possible allocation of the nation's hard-pressed land resources, such a register would have to be compiled. "Many landowners may be appalled by the suggestion that there should be more bureaucratic probing into their affairs," commented *Country Life* in November 1976, but there were "good reasons for supporting this proposal." Then again, Lady Stocks was writing in a Fabian Society pamphlet in 1976 that inherited wealth should be "taxed out of existence" and all reference to people by titles or modes of address should be abolished—and her suggestion was not drowned out by the cries of abuse that tended to accompany such disagreeable offerings a few years before.

There are growing indications like these that taxes on wealth for which no work has to be performed are becoming politically acceptable in Britain; that national treasures may be, to most people's certain knowledge, sufficiently well accumulated and guarded by now to require no further additions or "saving" by the taxpayer—in short, the landowner and the stately-home owner are becoming further and further isolated as the century wears on. The Conservatives blustered, when in opposition, about their certain abolition of Capital Transfer Tax—the promised unstopping of the fox's earth. But given the public mood—the acceptance, albeit grudging, that inherited land, property, wealth, is not, perhaps, something one has to worry about preserving any more—given that, one wonders if even the Tories will succumb to the evident appeals of masterly bodies like the Twenty-Five Invisibles. Somehow it seems rather doubtful.

The corollary, of course, is the ending of the unique economic status of the hereditary nobility. Whether their Grandisonian manners will go too, and whether the dwindling band will fight to the last as a disgruntled rump of privilege cannot yet be known. All one can say with certainty is to utter the reminder that a titled, constitutionally emasculated and decadent clique can only remain if the people wish them so to do. With CTT, with widespread insouciance over their future and with new and ambitious plans for curbing the powers of— and even abolishing—the House of Lords, it does rather seem as though peerage in Britain is entering its most critical phase in its seven-hundred-year history.

There was a memorable article in *The Times* of 19 May 1920, entitled simply, "Changing Hands." "We all know it now," it began, "not only from the advertisements, not only from various attractive little descriptive paragraphs, not only from the numerous notice boards with which the countryside is disfigured, but from personal experience amongst our friends, if not actually of our own: 'England is changing hands.'

"For the most part, the sacrifices are made in silence. 'The privileged classes,' to use an old name, take it all for granted. It had to be. Only the background of their lives is gone. The historical associations need not be enumerated: they are all in the beautiful illustrated book to be had on application to the land agent. What will not be found there are the intangible things: the loving care the estate has received from each successive owner: how each in turn grew to know every nook and corner of his vast possession, from his earliest days when as a nursery child he played with the acorns under the trees. . . .

"Now, such is the minor consequent tragedy of all we have gone through, all this . . . must be swept away—'England is changing hands.'"

The "tragedy" was World War I, and the changing of hands came about because of the nightmare killing of so many of the nation's heirs across in the mud and gore of France. But what that *Times* writer noted then could equally apply today. England is on the verge of changing hands once again—only this time it will not be a change from the hands of the landed rich to the mercantile rich; if the Exchequer, and the people, have their corporate way, it will change from the hands of the rich to the hands of the masses. Whether that kind of redistribution will be for the general benefit of that England remains to be seen. The proposition that such reworking of England's acres will be for the greater good of every Englishman is, to be fair, open to a great deal of doubt. Who, one wonders, will look out for "the long-term benefit"?

ELEVEN

OF MEN AND MANNERS

If he was a sage in business hours, he was always a boy at heart. The heart was given over to birds, beasts and flowers. He was an eager field natural-ist and gardener, a still keener shot. And like most great English killers of birds he was a merci-ful man who cherished the victims he slew so cleanly.

—Obituary in *The Times*

The middle, lower middle and working classes are now receiving the King's Commission. These classes, unlike the old aristocratic and feudal classes who led the old Army, have never had "their people" to think about. . . . they have largely fallen down in their capacity as Army officers.

—R. C. Bingham, letters to *The Times*, 1941

All the obvious things have been done which were fought and argued about. And yet, myster-iously enough . . . the ideal, the pattern of values, has not been achieved. We have done them, we have created the means to the good life which they all laid down and said "If you do all these things, after that there'll be a classless society." Well, there isn't.

—Richard Crossman, in Fabian Tract No. 286, 1950

Despite Mr. Macmillan's dinner-table remarks that many of the peers created by Mr. Pitt "were unspeakably middle-class," it cannot be seriously doubted that, *en masse*, the hereditary peers of the British

Isles represent the very apex of the undying class system of the kingdom. The Monarch, in the person of Elizabeth II, gamely tries—though with little actual success—to radiate the image of a middle-class Queen, only slightly distant from her subjects, dogged by the same problems that afflict the herd beyond the Palace railings. But the peerage have had to make few such concessions. Public approbation has only recently become of import to Their Lordships. If like the Duke of Buccleuch or the Duke of Wellington, peers choose to remain remote and awesome, then they brook no familiarity or lack of respect. If they choose, like Lord Cowdray, to advertise their riches for the world to see, then they can still do so with impunity. If they wish to remain aloof, like the late Duke of Portland, or snobbish, like other Dukes, they can proceed as they will, safe in the knowledge that their quaint political views or their eccentric behaviour will excite a degree of interest and condemnation that will never harm them nor cause them to alter their ways. The Monarch of today has to accept a proportion of the dictates of public opinion; so long as the hereditary peers continue to be recognized, so they can turn their backs on the demands of the public, and stand icily ignorant of their *gaucherie*. Or at least, that was so until recently.

The habits of the peerage, and the institutions which their names help to preserve, are thus still a fair constant in the shifting sands of modern British society. Like the peers and their estates, the institutions they support and which support them are battle-scarred—but they still stand and, unless a violent upheaval dislocates the genteel manners of the British people, it looks quite likely that they will remain standing for some time to come.

It is not easy, for example, to change one's accent—even though Tony Benn, the former Viscount Stansgate, who relinquished his title for life, tried hard to drop the unmistakably clipped tones of his London public school, he has found the task well-nigh impossible. Accent, though, is only the half of it: inflections of the voice, the very words used, the degree of interest one affects in subjects of conversation—these seemingly trivial matters all can mark one for life as a member of the upper classes, and all prove as hard to discard as they do for novitiates to learn. Nancy Mitford's essay on "The English Aristocracy" in *Noblesse Oblige*, though written in 1956, remains the standard work on the mannerisms of the nobility. "Dinner" is eaten in the evening, "luncheon" (not lunch, and most certainly not dinner) is eaten at noontime; port is passed to the left, never lifted from the table surface ("Slide it, man! Slide it!" one crusty octogenarian Earl bellowed one evening when, in my presence, an unfortunate guest happened to allow the decanter to rise a millimetre or two above the shiny oak surface); Stilton cheese is always to be sliced, never scooped (though silversmiths still market elegant cheese scoops, little trowels with mechanical pushers for removing the cheese, which evidently sell to some of the pretentious lower orders). Argument at dinner over whether you are a slicer or a scooper is still considered an excellent choice of topic by some aristocrats. The consensus view seems to be that since scooping ruins the cheese, the practice is only for the vulgar rich; slicing is elegant and gentle to the cheese, and altogether combinative of economy, prudence and politesse. A similar argument over whether porridge should be eaten standing or sitting was allowed to run in the letters columns of *The Times* in 1976: observation suggests that few Dukes eat their gruel on their feet—it tends to frustrate their attempts to open their morning letters.*

Other mealtime observances: the provision of a separate, silver, set of pepper, salt and mustard holders, very sharp knives, the pouring of the cream and sugar into coffee cups first, but of the milk into tea last—all are marks of social rectitude that have come down from the arbiters of manners in the stately homes of England. The noble families manage their faultless behaviour without noticeable effort. "I never have to think about saying 'writing paper,' instead of 'note-paper,'" says the Duke of Devonshire. "I may think it is foolish to make a fuss about what you say, but on the other hand I can be sure I would never put a step wrong. Everyone I meet talks about 'writing paper'—'notepaper' is just not in the language."

Writers on the subject of upper-class mannerisms have often remarked that the true Upper Classmates are perpetually on the lookout for mistakes made in speech from aspirants—the inadvertent use of "serviette" instead of "table napkin," or "Scotch" for "whisky," "relative" for "relation." (Some use the word "kinsman" for any relation more distant than a third cousin or so. Sir Iain Moncrieff of

---

* Eating porridge standing up is said by a Scotsman to be an old Scottish custom that has nothing to do with Ducal ennoblement. It has more to do, one imagines, with Scotsmen being unwilling to submit their sub-kilt regions to the icy woodwork of night-chilled chairs.

that Ilk says he would use the word to describe C. K. Scott Moncrieff, the translator of Proust, who was his thirteenth cousin twice removed, and with whom he last shared a common ancestor in 1496.) Frankly, I doubt if the upper classes really care all that much for such niceties. A conversation overheard at one stately house in County Fermanagh suggests why: the family were discussing whom they might invite to a forthcoming Christmas party for their eldest son. "Well, there are some O'Haras, *they're* bound to be all right," said Her Ladyship. "And there are some Craigs, we've heard of them so they'll be fine. What's this name—Morton? Can't say I know anything about them. Don't think we'd better have them along. Stourtons, Smyths, Stockfords—yes, they'll all do. . . ." and so on. The intelligence network that exists to provide subtle information on the suitability or otherwise of potential guests is discreet and vague. It cares little whether those it rejects say "riding" instead of "horse riding," or "lounge" instead of "drawing-room"; it cares less that members of one distinguished family may ask to use the "toilet" or that members of another may put milk into their tea before anything else. The latter will be people "one will have heard of" and of whom the intelligence network will have taken good care; the former remain cast out in the wilderness, somehow vaguely different from the truly noble, and never really suitable.

"No gentleman ever wears brown shoes with a blue suit." "Gentlemen lift the seat." And there is the question, as Evelyn Waugh put it, of ichthyotomy. "Some years ago a friend of mine, in a novel, described the wife of a Master of Hounds using a fish knife. I warned him that this would cause offence and, sure enough, the wife of a neighbouring MFH got as far as this passage and threw the book from her crying: 'The fellow can't even write like a gentleman!' "

Peers of the old school like matters to proceed slowly and decorously, it is often assumed. If sea mail is slower than air mail, they use the former—it is more dignified; if the man can be reached by letter rather than by telephone, they write instead of calling; they journey by train rather than aeroplane, by horse rather than by car. Long live the ocean liner, the airship, the four-in-hand—swift death to Concorde, the Channel Tunnel and the mass-produced car. But what nonsense these assumptions are! Peers fly by Concorde, send telegrams, babble on the telephone like everyone else. When petrol became expensive, the old Duke of Portland was to be found driving the ultimate in popular motor cars, the Mini. "Just picked up a couple when the fuel got too much," he explained. "Easier to get around the parks, you know."

And again it is said they prefer to talk in terms of circumlocutory vagueness, disapproving of direct attention to a topic, finding argument based on fact tedious and rather vulgar. From the cavernous interior of the bath chair, the angered mumbles of elderly noblemen protesting dully at the machinations of Socialist governments on the performance of England in the last Test have become lasting caricatures of noble conversational habits. That true peers should talk in detail and with deep knowledge of the complexities of such topics as the Joint European Torus, the genetic characteristics of Sika deer, the prospects for trade with Saudi Arabia, or the mating habits of African elephants strikes at the heart of the accepted notion of noble behaviour. Yet these were all conversations into which I was drawn at various times during the winter of 1976, and I heard not a whisper from a single bath chair, nor a gouty grunt from beside the inglenook as an ancient Marquess protested at the length of hair on a footballer spotted on the sports page of the *Telegraph,* or the decline in the quality of claret.

Progress is, in short, being made. The titled apexes of the class system are dropping their more archaic mannerisms, retaining only those that imbue them with charm and isolate them a little from the lower orders. A man that insists on sliding port and slicing Stilton, but who can discuss with intelligence and interest the development of European politics is, one would assume, more at one with his fellow countrymen than one who slides, slices, grunts, grumbles and bellows in a cobweb-covered world of vague and faded elegance and determined insulation from the world beyond his park's fine sandstone gateposts.

Speech and manners are one thing; education, and progress in the nation's great institutions, is quite another. Here, while progress is undoubtedly being made, and equality of opportunity far greater a factor in British society than, say, two decades ago, the habits of the ennobled upper classes, and the ennobled middle classes whom Mr. Macmillan so despises, are hard to break. Preparatory schools, Eton, Christ Church, the Grenadiers, the older London clubs—all still prove immovably central to the world in which the truly noble feels most at ease and in which he finds it most comfortable to flourish.

Not all prep schools meet with the approval of their victims. One

Etonian reported for *Harper's and Queen* magazine on the terrors of his school in Scotland:

"Most of the pupils were sons of Scottish farmers, and owed more to the croft than a civilized home. Everyone was mad on rugger. It was played six afternoons a week, through rain, snow and hail, and was the yardstick against which everything was judged. The headmaster was almost fanatical about it, even to the extent that discovery with a football was a beatable offence. Twice a year there was a school film, and invariably it'd be a New Zealand v. Scotland rugby challenge. Days out always coincided with the Edinburgh rugger international.

"The staff had to be seen to be believed. They were the dregs of their profession—unqualified, untalented, and unsympathetic. The Latin master suffered from St. Vitus's dance. The rest were convinced Conservatives of the most bigoted nature, so when I foolishly admitted my father was standing as a Liberal candidate I was openly ridiculed by them, and blue Tory stickers were gummed to my desk.

"I can see no possible excuse for this type of school, which serves no purpose but to encourage vice, squalor and brawn, and exists only for the convenience of parents' social life."

And then Eton—still, along with Winchester, reckoned the finest training base for the Establishment in Britain. Not, that is, by the measures of academic attainment alone—Manchester Grammar School still wins more scholarships and exhibitions to Oxford and Cambridge colleges than any public school. Etonians can be, and often are, extremely stupid men, or evil-mannered beings unworthy of the worst slum school—Lucan was one such, as were many of his friends. Generally, however, men lucky enough—or titled and rich enough—to undergo their education within the pleasant confines of the huge old school in the shadow of Windsor Castle, emerge well suited for the comfortable rigours of managing Britain in its stately decline. Eton is not the most costly school—Winchester, Westminster, Stowe, Shrewsbury, Millfield, Cranleigh and Worcester College for the Blind will set parents back considerably more than will Eton; it is far from being the gaudiest, or the loveliest, or the best at sports or scholarship. But its products—assured, confident, well mannered and intellectually solidly based, in the main—are a sure commodity of which the peerage, and the class it dominates, like to avail itself. Of the present members of the House of Lords 432 were schooled at Eton. In 1977 no fewer than ninety-three sons of hereditary nobles were being educated there; and while some peers, like the thoroughly modern Marquess of Queensberry, preferred to send their offspring to comprehensive schools in Central London, the majority of the well-founded families to be found in *Burke's* cling resolutely to the older schools of which Eton remains the finest paradigm.

From Eton the stately caravan still proceeds, as it has for generations, to either the ancient universities of Oxford and Cambridge, to the Royal Military Academy, Sandhurst, or to the Royal Agricultural College at Cirencester—the RAC taking the heirs to prepare them for the duties of managing their estates, the RMC taking more of the second and subsequent sons for training in the martial arts. In 1977, Cirencester sported the sons of the Earls of Radnor, Harrington and Iddesleigh, of the Viscounts Allendale, Falmouth and Monckton of Brenchley, and of the Lords Stafford and Wynford. Lord Elphinstone, then twenty-four years old and eighteenth in line, was the only Cirencester student who was already a peer in his own right. Nearby girls' schools, which regard the Cirencester students as the most eligible bachelors for miles, believe the college to be the repository for the dunderheads of the nation's nobility—and it must be said that while the college has an excellent reputation in its field, the young men it turns out are more likely to become aristocratic versions of the horny-handed sons of rural toil than the great movers and shakers of the realm.

The same cannot be said for the dozens of sons of peers who make the trek up to Oxford and Cambridge for their three years of polishing and finishing. A senior don at Christ Church, Oxford—a place known colloquially as "The House," and a college to which most of the young Hons. repair—refutes any suggestion that his distinguished institution is actually "the Oxford college to which titled families still like to send their brighter sons"; rather "if we are offered a bright boy of a titled family in our entrance examination we certainly have no prejudice against him." He noted that at the time there were five sons of hereditary peers among the body of scholars at the college, a proportion of 1.5 percent. To suggest that this represents "as wide a range of backgrounds as possible," as the don does, is going a little far: were the nation composed as is the present student body of Christ Church, there would be three-quarters of a million men entitled to be styled either "Hon." or "Lord"—there are in fact only about 4,000. Christ Church thus has some

200 times as many members of the peerage in its ranks as has the rest of British society and this is a proportion which can hardly bear out the don's assertion.*

To suggest that the proportion is correct because the sons of peers just happen to be cleverer than the sons of commoners is to begin treading on extremely dangerous ground: that of the importance of the genetic factor in the degree of intelligence. It would be far safer for colleges like Christ Church simply to forgo the humbug and admit that yes, they have an enthusiastic appreciation for the cleverer sons of British nobility and like to include them on the rolls if at all possible. It is a mark of the sensitivity of the guardians of such institutions that they feel reluctant to admit that they strive to perpetuate privilege—why, if it causes embarrassment, do they simply not alter their ways?

The question of the possibility of the hereditability of intelligence will allow us to digress, briefly, and consider the effects, if there have been any, of the fairly ruthless interbreeding that has been practised over the years by the majority of the hereditary peers. All the Dukes, for example, are fairly closely related to one another; marriages between cousins, the closest relationship that is permitted in marriage by most races and religions in the world, are fairly commonplace among the British peerage. (The nobility do tend to stick to their own when it comes to choosing mates—as the Dukes display. The Duke of Buccleuch's mother was granddaughter of the Duke of St. Albans; the Duke of Buccleuch's sister is Duchess of Northumberland; the Duke of Northumberland's mother was a daughter of the Duke of Richmond, his grandmother was daughter of the Duke of Argyll and his sisters are Elizabeth, Duchess of Hamilton, and the Duchess of Sutherland. The young Duke of Roxburghe is now safely married, to give a more up-to-date example, to the sister of the Duke of Westminster, daughter of the late Duke). There have been occasional marriages out of the class—to actresses, especially, mostly in

* One aristocrat who went to "The House" bristled at the thought his old college might allow membership to men solely because of their titledom. His own son, he said, went to Christ Church after winning an Oppidan Scholarship at Eton, had been Captain of the Oppidans there, and went on to get a rowing Blue at Oxford. "It is not hard to observe that the sons of talented families are often talented too, and there's a lot of talent in families that attain peerages," he wrote.

Edwardian times—and the peers have been shrewd enough to do what budgerigar breeders recommend for improving the quality of that avian breed: they "dip in the green" every so often, by marrying rich American heiresses. (Even this course is not certain to improve the stock; the very existence of an heiress suggests some weakness in the stock of the American families unless the heir was killed or died before inheriting.) American families with only a single daughter are regarded with some suspicion among the noblest British families, however affluent they may be. Sometimes a marriage is effected, and for years the words "bad blood" are whispered *sotto voce* when the consequences of the union are examined and found wanting. Consuelo, Duchess of Marlborough, commented with asperity once on the facial similarities of the various European families—the Trautt-mansdorffs, the Lobkowiczs, the Auerspergs and the like—who were all so deeply interrelated as to render them one giant family. Consuelo noted sourly that breeding "could be too much of a good thing."

Professor John Maynard Smith, the noted Sussex University specialist on inbreeding, doubts that any of the known deleterious effects of consistently close matings are discernible among the British peerage. "Of course there will be features like receding chins and prominent noses that will be passed around a bit—just like the Hapsburg lips in all the Velasquez paintings. Those kinds of features, which are hereditable of course, do tend to become noticeable if there is a good deal of intermarriage. You would expect that." (A Duchess de La Rochefoucauld, noticing the striking nasal resemblance between a prominent French nobleman and an unknown young woman, commented: "God forgives and the world forgets: but the nose remains.")

The damaging effects of inbreeding—infertility being the most dramatically deleterious—would not, Maynard Smith asserts, become evident unless two conditions had been met: that the group of peers had *only* bred among themselves, and that they had bred for the same number of generations as there are members of the peerage. Thus if the sons and daughters of the present 900 or so peers, let us say one of each per peer, married with the group of 1,800 eligible men and women; and if their offspring did the same; and if the whole group continued to behave so for 1,800 generations—then, it can fairly be said, the infertility effects of the inbreeding would demonstrate themselves. But not until then; under present conditions "only noses and lips and chins, size and hair colour and so on can be expected to show any similarity."

The sensible marriage policies of successive noble families have had other effects than the mere transmission of facial effects—transmission that has brought about the unfortunate term "chinless wonder" for the most aristocratic young men around. They have created a small group of Britons who are undoubtedly taller, lankier and better-looking than the average. That an upper-class Briton is so often so easily recognizable in a crowd owes much to his breeding: his clothes will represent his budget, of course; but his height, his slim elegance, his handsome face, his rather pointed, perhaps slightly receding chin, his longish nose, his wavy hair, his blue eyes—all these will have been handed down as the result of generations of sensible weddings between the prettiest representatives of older generations of gilded youth. Ugly, fat, balding peers are rare—save for the life peers and peers of first creation; flaxen-haired, pink-cheeked and impossibly beautiful children still tumble from the noble loins of England. It is a situation that will obtain for many generations more, so rigid and impervious are the rules of the class system in the reaches in which the peerage swims.

Handsome, dashing young men—the phrase "Guards Officer" seems quite naturally attachable. Why is it that the sons of the British peerage still prefer the Guards to any other division of the British Army? And why, in the Guards, is the Grenadiers still the favoured regiment? Among the present officers of the "First or Grenadier Regiment of Foot Guards" there are six sons of hereditary peers, more than in any other unit of an Army that is still heavily dependent on the landed and titled families of the country.

Why the Grenadiers? Why not one of the glittering cavalry regiments, like the 14th/20th King's Hussars or the 17th/21st Lancers? Why not the traditional sentries to the Monarch—the Household Cavalry of the Life Guards and the Blues and Royals? The latter has the Army's only non-Royal Duke in uniform as a member—the young Guy Roxburghe; in 1977 when he was a captain, he served a grim four months in barracks in Londonderry. Why not one of the principal infantry regiments—the Royal Scots, say, First of the Line and immensely proud of the tradition?

From a number of Grenadier officers came admirable and fascinating suggestions for the regiment's peculiar position. The following explanation should be regarded as an amalgam of many conversations within, and without, the Grenadiers' messes.

A lot of the young officers like the fact that they are generally garrisoned in London, and the informality—no uniforms, no insistence on officers' mess routine and so on. They have a tradition of always having a Colonel of the Regiment who is a member of the Royal Family, which lends a certain tone. There are old and long-standing connections with the great families. The Grenadiers run themselves in a way that allows a man to indulge his outside interests.

Ironically, the recruiting policies they use to attract "other ranks" are considerably easier than even among the socially "unspeakable" Army units like the Engineers and the Signals, since there are no special technical skills needed to be a guardsman in the Grenadiers. Whether the consequent difference in background between the officers—well-bred, rich, suave young bloods, filled with confidence, loaded with social connections and potential activities in and around London—and the men—invariably poor unemployed from Walsall and Stoke and grim old towns of the mucky English Midlands, men of much lesser intelligence and of a social standing approximating zero—has any effect on the efficacy of the regiment as a fighting force, one cannot say. They insist they have "quite a name for battlefield excellence."

London clubland is another institution in which the peerage is heavily grounded. Yet while Eton and Christ Church, the Grenadiers and the better City stockbroking firms that often take the brighter but more peaceable sons of the shires are managing to maintain a certain stability, clubland is all at once becoming tired and seedy, full of old stories, never of new tales. Time was when a noble Lord could not move for annual accounts from Brooks's or White's, the Turf, St. James's or Boodle's. Nowadays the changed social tendencies of the British upper classes, the relative impoverishment of some of their number and the widespread movement of nobility away from the metropolis have started the death-watch beetles ticking away in the woodwork of some of the more vulnerable clubs: many members prophesy that the London club is dying on its feet, and that before another two decades are up the streets south of Piccadilly will be filled with shops and offices, and bereft of the bow-windowed mansions heavy with tobacco smoke, the bouquets of fine clarets and all the atmosphere of masculine privilege.

Before World War II there were about 120 of these sacred preserves in London. Today there are fewer than forty, many of them suffering from peeling paint and a diminishing membership. Entrance fees range from the £150 of Boodle's and the 100 guineas of the Turf to the £30 of the Beefsteak, where all the waiters are called Charles and the existence of only one table in the dining-room ensures that you have to talk with your luncheon neighbour. The Beefsteak is, like the Garrick, essentially a clubbable man's club; the Travellers is a reserved, bolt-hole club. Lord Mountbatten, who was the most clubbable of the peers, to judge by his membership of no fewer than sixteen of the institutions, belonged to neither. He, instead, was a stalwart of the Savage, the Arts, Marylebone Cricket and a host of other sporting and recreational institutions; the clubland clubs to which his fellow peers still belong in droves were oddly absent from his list. Harold Macmillan, who declined a peerage with the sniff that there were "better clubs in London than the House of Lords," belongs to eight; the Beefsteak and Pratt's for food and conversation, the Athenaeum for gathering the fruits of national wisdom, the Turf for mixing with his horsey pals, the Carlton and Buck's for mixing with his Tory cronies, the rest for escaping from the common herd.

Although the clubs have special characters which endear them to Britons of various persuasions, there is a certain similarity about most of them which is evidently proving less and less charming to their memberships. Masculinity, now officially frowned upon, still dominates their operating style: until Mrs. Thatcher became leader of the Conservative Party only female members of the Royal Family were allowed to use the staircase at the Carlton; until quite recently females were forbidden even from telephoning one of London's more celebrated dining clubs, and were brusquely told so by an irate steward if ever they did. Today the deep-brown and cream rooms still display essentially male accoutrements: octagonal card tables, half-played games of backgammon, cigar holders and snuff boxes, moustache combs in the bathrooms. Tales invariably relate only to male members—Michael Faraday, dead for three days under his copy of the newspaper before he was discovered by the Athenaeum staff; the colonel at the Oriental who set the same chair on fire with his cigar fourteen times in a single year; the porters whose task it was to wake sleeping peers each hour to assure them they had not died while asleep; the plate washer who only wore his false teeth on special occasions and who insisted he was the rightful Marquess of Queensberry and had to be given a week off so that he would not badger Princess Anne's fiancé, Mark Phillips, when he stayed at his club in the days prior to his wedding.

At Brooks's the venerable Whig Club which has continued in business on St. James's Street since 1764, membership stands at a fairly healthy 1,200—though the number was boosted somewhat by the closure of the St. James's Club and the transfer of some of its members to Brooks's. Four Dukes belong, and the peerage (with seventy-three Lords, at the last count) is generally more heavily represented than at any other institution except White's, its High Tory relation, or the Turf Club. White's, in 1980, had 144 peers, including six Dukes; the Turf had 120 peers, including a round dozen Dukes—nearly half of the total number on the rolls. But the age of the members is worrisome for the club officials: three of the committee members are nonagenarians, and the average age of all the members is fifty-five. Watching the early morning activities of the determined Brooks's men is to witness something like a Serengeti ritual: the ponderous progress of the old bull elephants as they stroll around the game reserve, some distance from the main herd, walking endlessly till they die. Ancient and grizzled men, their scraggy necks hanging down over boiled and starched collars, indolently read from the columns of *The Times* or *Sporting Life*. They talk not, neither do they hum: deadly silence prevails, except for the ticking of the clocks and the crackle of the coal fires. A few club servants wander listlessly about, polishing brassware and setting dusty pictures straight. The bar opens with just three members tempted in. The card tables are unoccupied. No clatter of backgammon chips disturbs the peace. London busies herself outside; inside Brooks's, privilege slumbers on.

"Mind you, luncheon is always pretty crowded," coughs Colonel Warner, the breezy librarian, "and dinners aren't bad now, especially since ladies are allowed in. In fact letting the ladies in has been very beneficial for the club: we have all sorts of coming-of-age parties, golden weddings and suchlike; they wouldn't have allowed that in the old days."

The Society of Dilettantes meets five times a year in the Brooks's famous Great Subscription Room, preserving the mystique of literary and artistic nobility and breeding; it is a more secret coven than the mere Brooks's membership, and dislikes publicity. But one gathers it is in almost as poor a condition as the club in which its members meet—sad, ruminant, sunk in a brown study of nostalgia. The club is still exclusive, of course, the membership is "very limited: it's not a question of money, you know, more of one's reputed conduct and one's merit." But it is ages since there was a seven-year waiting list at one club—there is none to speak of at Brooks's these days, and the time when potential members trembled at the thought of those two black balls being cast into the pot to bar them from membership are long gone. The black ball is as unnecessary as a revolving door at Brooks's; and at nearly every other London club besides. The peers still haunt the sombre halls and idle by the Zoffanys and the Reynolds portraits when on their monthly three-day visits for an appearance at the House; but other members who might have lent style, if not rank, are now called home to the suburbs of an evening, and can only drop in for the occasional luncheon now and then; and anyway the food is not so good, and the staff is getting pretty slipshod, and there was that bomb set off outside by the IRA in '74, old boy. . . .

"Staff is a problem, I must admit," said a club steward. "You just cannot get servants these days. Why, we've got a Nigerian here now— he's kept downstairs, you know—and there's an Israeli, and a girl from Egypt. Even so, staff costs run to £100,000 a year, and go on rising all the time. It is just not the time to run a gentleman's club any more. If the peers left us, we'd be in a proper fix."

If their institutions are in disorder, the traditional pastimes could hardly be in better shape. Foxhunting, despite the attempts of the anti-bloodsports group, continues on its merry way. Polo, helped to no small extent by Lord Cowdray and until recently by the Duke of Edinburgh, flourishes. Shooting, stalking, salmon fishing—though made expensive by the need to cater to the game-hungry Americans and Germans—ride a never-breaking crest. The hobbies of the individual nobles are allowed their fullest expression: the Duke of Hamilton can afford to collect motorcycles and racing cars; the Lord O'Neill can build mighty model-railway layouts and play with them from dawn till dusk; the Marquess of Cholmondeley can collect his tin soldiers and fight mock battles; the Duke of Devonshire can scour the London auctions for exquisite paintings; the Marquess of Bristol can continue his associations with the fallen monarchs of Europe. Self-indulgence is an understandable right of the members of a group, many of whom have little else left with which to occupy themselves— only hobbies, pastimes, sport, and worrying about the future of their fortunes, their lands and the titles.

Such is the face of the British nobility. It is a face somewhat wrinkled with age and care, but full of the old character that lent it its original allure. Some of the cosmetics are becoming a little more expensive, and the cracks in the make-up more difficult to hide. But the accent and the tone is still just about right, the teeth are in fair shape and the eyes are only a little dulled in the harsh lights of the plangent demands for equality, the plaintive whining of the body politic below. It is a face cast down with concern for the future, occasionally cast back to spot the pursuing enemy, yet often held high again with a toss of fierce pride. But it is probably not the face of nobility that needs so much attention; more sickly still is the ennobled body, and most vulnerable of all the heart—the ancient engine that has hitherto given such impetus and drive to the titled few, the Chamber of the House of Lords. That, if true diagnosis be made, is where the real sickness has its root.

TWELVE

THE FATAL WEAKNESS

> Mankind will not always consent to allow a fat, elderly gentleman to fill the first place, without insisting upon his doing something to deserve it. I do not undertake to say in what particular year hereditary distinctions will be abolished: but to the philosopher . . . the ultimate fate of such distinctions is already decided.
> —John Stuart Mill, published anonymously in the *Examiner*, 1832

> To rid Parliament of the hereditary principle would be a big advance towards rational democracy.
> —*Guardian*, 1968

> Heredity no longer commands assent as a sufficient condition for a seat in Parliament.
> —*The Times*, 1968

> What's wrong in Britain is more what's wrong at the top than what's wrong with the bottom. They haven't been served very well by their elite.
> —William Pfaff of the Hudson Institute, quoted in the *New York Times*, 1976

Their Lordships are an amazingly stubborn crew. For more than a century and a half their ancient rights have been subjected to the fiercest challenge, their futures plunged into the deepest doubt, their excesses and their activities held up to scorn. The whole character of titledom has been changed during the twentieth century, and more and more exemplars of mercantilism have been promoted to noble status, while the reign of the landowners has been scissored to a minimum. The House of Lords, bastion of the peerage power, has

been all but emasculated, its power successively cut back, its membership vastly widened, the degree of respect it commands sadly diminished. The influence of the peerage on the daily lives of Britons is
very much less than it was only fifty years ago, even though there
are far more titled men and women on the boards of directors of the
country's largest companies than either mathematics, or the strict
exaction of talent, would suggest. The institutions which these privileged few hold dearest—their land, their exclusive educational and
recreational preserves, the business of the state's defence, or its
diplomacy—are no longer so exclusive and reserved for the higher
ranks of titledom.

The hereditary peers are, in short, the victims of a massive attack
of well-seated woodworm, riddled with Dutch elm disease, thick with
the death-watch beetle. And yet, as Richard Crossman might have
remarked in that celebrated Fabian tract noted as an epigraph to the
previous chapter, here they all are still; here, in the centre of a
London dominated by the interests of extra-territorial efficiency and
wealth—the Arab sheiks, the Eurocrats, the American bosses of the
multinationals—is the only legislative assembly remaining in the
modern world where the majority of the members are selected by
right of birth, and birth alone. Here despite the constant strivings
of zealous Socialists who have brought the Welfare State and the
nationalized monopolies and the emerging systems of comprehensive
education; yet here repose privilege and pomp, ermine and velvet
breeches, Gold Sticks and Hereditary Great Almoners, Falconers and
Butlers, Ladies of the Bedchamber, Orders of Precedence, courtesy
titles, words and phrases like "Honourable" and "Your Grace,"
forelock-touching, feudal rights, the third penny, the Keeperdom of
Dunstaffnage Castle, the right to remain hatted in the Monarch's
presence, butlers and footmen, square crumpets and House of Lords
cigarettes, Masters of the Horse and the right to maintain, as successive
Dukes of Atholl insist, a small private army deep in the wilds of
northern Scotland. All this remains, arranged decoratively around the
bejewelled, creaking, cosy, scarlet-and-gold, stewarded and Black-
Rodded, tiny, stained-glassed and bright-brassed floral centrepiece, the
House of Lords.

It was as long ago as 1905 that the Monarch and the Prime
Minister of the day started a programme of the wholesale creation of
peerages from among deserving multitudes who did not own vast
acreages in the shires. Three years later Mr. Asquith took over in

Downing Street as the first Prime Minister who was similarly unblessed. In 1911 the powers of the House of Lords, hitherto equivalent to, or occasionally greater than, those of the Commons, were severely circumscribed: from that year on the House was merely an advisory body with some powers of delay or obstruction, designed only to reject laws if there was sincere and overwhelming belief among Their Lordships that passage of the legislation would be inimical to the common weal. By the end of World War II peerages were being handed out even to men without large incomes, heaven forfend—the ancient rule that one had to have sufficient private wealth with which to maintain a peerage and keep it nicely groomed and presentable went into oblivion. By 1958 men and women of special merit were being allowed into the House of Lords as if peers, able to give the benefits of their wisdom to the process of such legislative activity as the House was permitted, yet restricted from offering their privilege in the lottery of parenthood. In 1963 peers were given dispensation to renounce their titles, so they could enjoy the concomitant rights of commoner status: the right to vote and, more especially, the right to run for a seat in the House of Commons. Just over a year later John Morrison's elevation to the peerage as Lord Margadale was announced, and with it, the suggestion that his was to be the very last hereditary peerage to be created. Since then not one such honour has been announced and, saving the possibility of a wholesale return to the old system by some entrenchedly Tory government with a vast majority, or a very occasional award out of affection, or the use of the Monarch's rights to create hereditary titles for the elevation of some future Royal offspring—aside from these possibilities—hereditary peerages seem destined never to be created again.

But still the country seems unwilling to curb any further the powers of the House of Lords—curbs which would, of themselves, go some long way towards removing the anachronism that Their Lordships, in more candid and port-soaked moments, admit themselves to be. A writer in the *Observer*, Rudolf Klein, summed up the essential reasoning in an article in 1965:

"The need to reform the Lords is accepted, in theory at least, by all parties. But in practice, it suits both the Tory and the Labour parties to keep the present ramshackle structure more or less intact— with just the occasional repair to the mullioned windows and a touch of paint to the crumbling façade. . . . [A crumbling façade,

Mr. Klein might have noted, had he been writing a decade later, that was costing more than four million pounds a year to maintain.] Labour is terrified in case a reformed House of Lords becomes respectable: the fact that it is so obviously an anachronism ensures that the Conservative peers will use their powers circumspectly. The Tories have no strong incentive to change a situation which suits them well enough. . . . [As well it might, with their built-in majority of about ten to one.] But of course, all this was as true in 1910— the first occasion when a clash between Commons and Lords produced a curb on the Upper Chamber's powers—as it is today. And it may be over-optimistic in the extreme to hope, that should there be another crisis, anything more than an emergency repair will be carried out to the Gothic structure of the Lords."

How right Mr. Klein's predictions were. Time and again the legislative machinery of the country has become embroiled in "new" programmes for reforming the House of Lords. As recently as the winter of 1976, when Their Lordships had the temerity to obstruct the nationalization programme of a Labour Government for the basic reasons that the Government was in a minority and thus, in the view of the Lord's Conservative bosses, not representative of the true feelings of the people, the row broke out again; as this is being written both parties have committees wasting their time discussing new proposals for reform. Little is expected to come of either, so firmly wedded is Britain still to the unwritten principles of disguised oligarchy and to the God-given rights of the upper classes.

It would be tedious to run through either the history of various reform measures, or the proposals of today, so chimerical do they look in the harsh glare of global realities. In summary, the Labour Party objects, not just to the existence of an hereditary right to legislate, as one would expect, but to the continued existence of bicameral parliament. An Upper—or a second—Chamber is always bound to be a force for the dilution and obstruction of radicalism, the Left contends: thus real change is slow to eventuate, is perpetually frustrated, and legislation becomes distant from the popular will. Real socialism will not be permitted to attack the problems inherent in British society until one Chamber, elected by the people, sets in motion tough laws to allow such battles to begin. Abolish the House of Lords, abolish the second Chamber, bring the process of lawmaking back to the people to whom the law belongs.

The Tory argument is less distinct. There are those of the right, like Enoch Powell, who question the prerogative of twentieth-century man, a mere upstart, to tinker with the constitutional arrangements of the foregoing seven hundred years. What, he wonders, if we are wrong? What a terrible responsibility, to have wrecked the machinery that has served this island kingdom so very well for so very long. A timid argument, perhaps, a template for Conservative philosophy, but, not surprisingly in a country so weighted down with historical responsibilities, a persuasive one. It was in fact an "unholy" alliance between Mr. Michael Foot, of the Labour Left, and Mr. Powell, that effectively wrecked the last real plan for "democratizing" the Lords in 1968. Foot did not want a reformed Chamber that had such wide powers as to result in the dampening of radical ardour in the resulting combined House; and Powell did not want to tinker with a House that had been operating so well and so blamelessly for so very long. Moderates of both parties who agreed in principle with the need for some reform thus saw the whole mass of their proposals torpedoed by the conflicting conservators of the extreme wings.

There are other Tory positions, though. A Conservative committee, chaired by Lord Home of the Hirsel (whose political ambitions have necessitated his sporting three sets of names—The Earl of Home, Sir Alec Douglas-Home, and Baron Home of the Hirsel—in rapid succession) looked into such questions as what to do with the life peers and peers of first creation (i.e., those who are still the original title holders—few of these have titles originating much before World War II, since they were usually made peers while fairly elderly); whether to allow the hereditary peers to continue to sit until they die off; whether to allow them a vote in proceedings, whether to include a leavening of appointed men of distinction and so on.

If matters do begin to move again, and reform becomes a matter for parliamentary debate rather than mere committee study and press comment, then it seems probable that an all-party agreement will somehow be forged to create a revising Chamber of fairer composition than at present. Of the reforms that have so far been introduced—the creation of life peers; the removal of the longstanding prohibition of women, even peeresses in their own right, from attending the House; the limiting of the delaying powers of the Lords and so on—that which has excited most comment, but surprisingly little activity, is the agreement to permit peers to renounce their titles for life. This radical step, taken as the centrepiece of the 1963 Peerage Act, was feared by many critics as likely to hasten the demise of the Upper House: young and able peers, the critics said, would cast off their titles and run for the Commons, leaving the Lords drained of its political energies and peopled with senile representatives of a vanished age. They need not have worried. Britons have a deeper love affair with titledom than the authors of the Act imagined, and of the seven hundred-odd who were now legally able to disclaim, a paltry fifteen have: the remainder either claim they can fight more adequately to reform the Lords from within, or they claim that the Lords needs no reforming and they love the situation in which they find themselves. The latter view may be defensible; the former, held in many cases by one-time radicals who are now happily ensconced in the comforts of Victorian ivory towers and display as much radicalism as one would expect from converts to the Establishment, is less so.

The fifteen who have disclaimed are headed by that most celebrated advocate of the sovereignty of the people, Tony Benn. He was born plain Anthony Neil Wedgwood Benn, son of the wealthy Baronet, but totally lacking in title or official dignity. His father became, however, a successful Government mandarin and an equally successful MP for a variety of constituencies and for two parties—first Liberal, then Labour. In 1942, when Anthony was seventeen and just on the verge of leaving Westminster School and taking his place in the Army, his father was given the Viscounty of Stansgate in the county of Essex; from plain schoolboy Anthony, Benn went to war as the Honourable Anthony, and proceeded, thus dignified, to New College, Oxford, and eventually, to the House of Commons as Labour MP for Bristol, South East.

In 1960, the first Viscount Stansgate died and, such was the unshakeable process of dignification in those days, the Honourable Anthony Wedgwood Benn became the second Viscount, instantly debarred from the House of Commons. He unsuccessfully petitioned the House of Lords to be allowed to renounce his title. He was ousted from his Bristol seat. There had to be an election in May 1961. The new young Viscount stood and was handsomely reelected by his people. The Election Court, however, took a dim view: it was illegal, the Court ruled, for a peer to sit in the Commons, and Stansgate must move over. The incensed Viscount did indeed move over, but began immediately to campaign for the law that was eventually to be passed in 1963, permitting him and his fellow peers to disclaim for life. The very moment the Act received the Royal Assent, Stansgate requested his common title back, became Anthony

Wedgwood Benn, stood for Bristol South East, and won. His political career with the Labour party proceeded almost as fast as he was able to discard the trappings of his old honours: first he pared his Christian name down to the more familiar "Tony"; then petitioned the almanacs of distinction—*Who's Who, Burke's, Debrett's*—to delete his name, or at least delete references to his public-school background and his entitlement; and finally made an abortive attempt at "democratizing" his accent, rendering it classless. His most recent scheme aims to achieve the creation of 1,000 life peers who will then take their seats only to vote for their own extinction. He remains the determined champion of the meritocrat, firmly set against hereditary privilege, and, unlike many of his party colleagues who are awed by Royalty and nobility and the trappings of archaic elegance, a stalwart to his principles, unshakeable and isolated.

Well, not quite isolated. There is the Earl of Durham, who disclaimed his title so he could sit in the House of Commons— except that he wanted to call himself "Lord Lambton" rather than the "Antony Lambton" he should correctly be. The *Daily Telegraph* was alone in pointing out that Lambton could not enjoy the best of both worlds, and be both a Lord (his courtesy title, and the one under which he was elected, he claimed) and a commoner at the same time. In any case Lambton's political career came unstuck for other reasons in 1973, so the debate became moot. (And actually the whole question of how the children of peers who have disclaimed their titles should be known is still very much open. Should they forgo their courtesy titles, or the style "Hon." or "Lady" because their father is no longer a peer? Or should they retain their precedence and take up their courtesy titles if they like, since they will have the right to reclaim what is essentially only an abeyant title once their father has died? The Earl Marshal of England actually devotes his time to such pressing matters and has recently ruled that children can use their titles and precedence if they like—but that peers who disclaim may not revert to courtesy titles they used before they acceded to the peerage which they later disclaimed. It sounds complicated, but is merely pointless.)

And still not alone: Lord Altrincham, an eminently sensible writer with a celebrated distaste for the hereditary principle that once managed to earn him—for making a mildly disrespectful remark about the Queen—a slap across the face, became and still is John Grigg. The Earl of Home became Sir Alec Douglas-Home to stand in a by-election and take up the Premiership in 1963 and now, no longer electable but still comparatively active, has reverted to his rightful hunting ground in the House of Lords as a resurrected life peer, Lord Home of the Hirsel. Viscount Hailsham did much the same—turned to become Quintin Hogg, then reverted to the life peerage of Lord Hailsham of St. Marylebone. When he expires, his present title will go with him to the grave; his former title, the viscounty, will arise again in the person of the Hon. Douglas Hogg who, unless he wants also to disclaim, becomes the third Viscount. The Earl of Sandwich disclaimed so that he could pursue his Commons career as Victor Montagu, but didn't; Arthur Silkin, son of the Labour peer who introduced the amendment that resulted in the passage of the 1963 Act, did the same for similar reasons.

Others disclaimed for reasons that had little to do with politics: Sir Max Aitken declined to become another Lord Beaverbrook, out of "respect for my father"; Sir Hugh Fraser decided not to become the second Lord Fraser of Allander for the same reason, "filial respect." Charles FitzRoy decided against taking up the title of fifth Baron Southampton because he had, he said, an eighteenth-century reluctance to support an "appropriate style of life"—and instead supports his third wife at home on the island of Malta. Larry Collier, a thrice-married doctor living in Essex, says he has a radical distaste for calling himself the fourth Baron Monkswell; Christopher Reith allows that he could not possibly match the legendary image of his father, the BBC's first and unforgettable manager, Lord Reith. And another doctor, Alan Sanderson, quotes his "retiring disposition" as the reason for not accepting the title of the second Lord Sanderson of Ayot. In April 1977 Mr. Trevor Lewis decided that the 1,500 acres of Pembrokeshire he inherited on the death of his father, the third Lord Merthyr, was quite enough—the title would only make him feel "rather a fraud." His father, a guiding light in legal and rural circles, spent the best part of ten years campaigning for Parliament to fix the date of Easter: Trevor Lewis has no such ambitions, though admitted he would not stand in the way of his son one day reclaiming the title: at the time of the disclaimer, Mr. Lewis's son was seven weeks old.

It is unlikely, then, that the Act really altered the composition of either the Lords or the Commons to any significant degree—and the rapidity with which men like Hailsham and Home crept back into the Lords after their Commons career had ended might well suggest that the interest of some politicians in the Act's provisions was more for the supplying of a platform than the reform of British parliamentary democracy. One peer, Lord Avebury, had in December 1970 to make the agonizing decision between renouncing his title and standing again as a Liberal MP in a very narrowly marginal seat, and keeping his title and going to the House of Lords. He took the latter course, joining the small but vociferous band of Liberals there, a band that included the fourth Earl, "Johnny" Kimberley (in 1979, he left the Liberals for the Conservatives), a relation of the late P. G. Wodehouse, a man who has been five times married, a recovered alcoholic who is now a leading light of the National Council on Alcoholism, and father to a policeman. Lord Avebury is not politically notable to any great extent—though, given the appalling electoral fortunes of the Liberal Party, all the Liberal peers are probably more noticeable in the Lords than if they were merely unsuccessful campaigners for the Commons once every five years, at election time.

The inclusion of women—both as life peeresses and as peeresses in their own right—in the Upper Chamber had to come, of course; and it is true that women play a greater part in the House than their still small numbers might suggest. But their efforts, rarely reported in the press and scarcely noted if they speak outside the chamber, could almost be called wasted. Their inclusion has proved as meaningless as the dissenters' right to disclaim. It cannot be suggested, in summary, that the provisions of the 1963 Act, so trumpeted at the time, have accomplished more than the repairing of the hull of the *Hindenburg.*

There have been innumerable reasons for the supposed decline of the Lords—Lords who nevertheless still do exist, and still do have influence on the running of the country out of all proportion to either their numerical or their deserved power. Honours have proliferated to the extent that they are of less value than once they were; death duties and income taxes have reduced some peers to near impoverishment; Capital Transfer Tax will hasten the withering process. World War I removed scores of heirs to the grant estates; the mass parties have largely taken the political initiative from the Dukes and the Marquesses and the Earls of old.

One can go on and on citing reasons for the increased egalitarianism of the nation—and yet, and yet . . . class is still there, noble influence is still rampant, the House of Lords still presides with supposed fatherly benevolence over the hasty and impetuous activities of the common populace and its elected representatives. Maybe the House does enjoy some small advantages from being unelected: its members are beholden to no one (save themselves); there is no special interest (save the perpetuation of advantage); there is continuity (despite possible popular will to the contrary); there is good debate from established experts (like the directors of the country's four biggest banks, directors of twenty-three of the others, directors of twenty-eight insurance companies and twenty-five of the top fifty companies in the country—but few experts on poverty, or criminality, or immigrant life, or Scottish crofters, for example); and so on. Its principal disadvantage—that it represents a formidable, eternally Conservative bulwark against the theoretical will of a people who should be longing to be unshackled from the millstone of the class system—goes persistently unheeded.

Britain may yet have to learn a lesson from Japan. After her ignominious defeat at the hands of the Allies in 1945, Japan was forced to accept a new constitution from her conquerors that, among other tenets, abolished not just the House of Peers, but the very recognition of peers by the remainder of the people. When the MacArthur constitution came to be voted on by the Diet, only five votes were counted against the proposal—Article Fourteen of the document still stands today: "Peers and Peerages shall not be recognized."

Well, of course, not everyone will agree that Japan is a healthier place to live in now. It is firmly bound to the ugly excesses of consumer insanities, its cities are unbelievably polluted, physically ugly, its peace and sanctity are threatened. But on the other hand the country is enjoying prosperity undreamed of two decades ago; with the peers safe in their old clubs, stripped of their power and their wealth and rendered into political eunuchs, the old Japanese class system is nearly dead. The Emperor continues, revered and respected as a symbol of continuing Japan; but the legions of ennobled Princes, Marquesses, Counts, Viscounts and Barons are no more—to the general good, it is now accepted, of modern Japanese society. Pollution would have happened, peers or no peers.

Could Britain not look hard at what an equally old and wise society on the other side of the globe has achieved, and learn, however bitter the pill, a lesson? What, indeed, would be the real effects of passing laws stripping our peers of any special rights or recognition? If all honours were to be dropped, if the House of Lords were to be abolished, if taxation were to bring ownership of property down to levels of reasonable equality and trim the fat from the mighty holdings of land and treasure enjoyed by a tiny minority now—what really would happen? Would the Monarch be threatened? Certainly not. Would the great houses tumble down and the splendid gardens regress to weedy jungles? Not if some national institutions were established to prevent it. Would there be revolution in the towns and shires, widespread grief at the upsetting of the hymnal doctrine that:

> The rich man in his castle,
> The poor man at his gate,
> God made them high and lowly,
> And ordered their estate . . .

or would, on the other hand, matters that suffer from the class system improve out of all recognition? Would the barriers that separate "us" from "them" come down almost overnight? Would the kind of divisions that make many an Englishman experience a feeling of bitter envy when he sees a Rolls-Royce, while an American admiringly gloats at the possibility that he might one day own one—would those kinds of attitudes and divisions gradually fade? Would the sovereignty of the people become rightly absolute, and would the law pass totally into the hands of the masses, rather than some portion of it be retained in the jealous guardianship of a highly titled few? Quite probably the answers to all these questions would be yes—Britain would be made healthier and more vital by the abolition of its peerage system, and the sooner the better.

It is hard to have to utter sentiments like these. Throughout my researches and travels I have come across men and women who, while ennobled and symbolic of ancient prerogatives and comely elegance, have been unfailingly kind and courteous, whose lives are in many cases pillars of responsibility and dignity, who look after their acres, or their houses, or their people with cheerful love and affection. There are few robber Barons, few evil Earls, few damnable Dukes. I agree entirely with the remark, from *Iolanthe,* quoted at the beginning of Chapter 1: "the Peerage is not destitute of virtue." Far from it. But it does not belong here any more. Privilege based on birth is a concept more akin to mediaeval times, when the known world was smaller in extent, when political development was limited, when the peasantry could, perhaps justifiably, have been regarded as in need of being looked after.

But, naïve and unseemly as it may be to say so, the world is not like mediaeval England any longer. For Britain to retain respect among the thrusting, grasping, assertive countries of the globe that now surround her, for her to win the admiration of the Bangladeshi and the Venezuelan, the Kenyan and the Michigander, and for her to win the friendship of the new generations of leaders springing up from every classroom of the twentieth century, she must develop a machinery of government that is in tune with the demands of the century, and to the needs of the people—not just of Perthshire or the Borders or Wiltshire, but of the world at large. On Spaceship Earth, ennoblement by reason of fortuitous birth has no place: the British nobility, decent a body of men and women as well they may be, have outlived their usefulness, and must go quietly, out by the back door.

BIBLIOGRAPHY

REFERENCE

Almanach de Gotha (final edition). Paris, 1944.

The AA Guide to Stately Homes, Castles and Gardens. Drive Publications, Ltd., 1977.

Burke's Landed Gentry, Vol. I, II and III (18th ed.). Burke, 1965.

Burke's Peerage and Baronetage (105th ed.). Burke, 1970.

The Complete Peerage, Vols. I–XII. St. Catherine's Press, 1910–1959.

Debrett's Peerage and Baronetage. Kelly's Directories, London, 1976.

Dod's Peerage, Baronetage and Knightage. Dod's Publishing Co., 1909.

House of Lords Companion to the Standing Orders. HMSO, 1976.

The Red Paper on Scotland. Edinburgh University: Student Publications Board, 1975.

Roll of the Lords Spiritual and Temporal. HMSO, 1977.

Titles and Forms of Address. Adam and Charles Black, 1976.

Vacher's Parliamentary Companion. A. S. Kerswill Ltd., 1976–1977.

Whitaker's Almanac. Whitaker, London, 1980.

Who's Who. Adam and Charles Black, 1980.

SELECTED READING

Barnes, Susan. *Behind the Image*. Jonathan Cape, 1974.

Bateman, Michael, ed. *This England*. Penguin Books, 1969.

Bingham, Madeline. *Peers and Plebs*. Allen and Unwin, 1975.

Buck, Phillip, ed. *How Conservatives Think*. Penguin Books, 1975.

Carnarvon, the Earl of. *No Regrets*. Weidenfeld, 1976.

Carr, Raymond. *English Fox Hunting*. Weidenfeld, 1976.

Cecil, David. *The Young Melbourne*. Constable, 1939.

Girardet, Herbert. *Land for the People*. Crescent Books, 1970.

Grant, Francis. *The Manual of Heraldry*. John Grant, 1929.

Guttsman, W. L., ed. *The English Ruling Class*. Weidenfeld, 1969.

Hamilton, Willie, MP. *My Queen and I.* Quartet, 1975.

Harrison, Rose. *My Life in Service.* Cassell, 1975.

Harvey, J., and L. Bather. *The British Constitution.* Macmillan, 1968.

Home, Lord of the Hirsel. *The Way the Wind Blows.* Collins, 1976.

Jenkins, Simon. *Landlords to London.* Constable, 1975.

Lane, Peter. *The Upper Class.* Batsford Ltd., 1972.

Lindsay, Martin, MP. *Shall We Reform the Lords?* Falcon Press, 1948.

Masters, Brian. *The Dukes.* Blond and Briggs, 1975.

Milton, Roger. *The English Ceremonial Book.* David and Charles, 1972.

Mitford, Nancy. *The Pursuit of Love.* New York: Random House, 1945.

———, and Alan Ross. *Noblesse Oblige.* Hamish Hamilton, 1956.

Montagu, Lord. *The Gilt and the Gingerbread.* Michael Joseph, 1976.

———. *More Equal than Others.* Michael Joseph, 1970.

Montague-Smith, Patrick. *Debrett's Correct Form.* Debrett's, 1976.

Morgan, Janet. *The House of Lords and the Labour Government.* Oxford, 1975.

Nicolas, Sir Harris. *Historical Peerage of England.* John Murray, 1857.

Perrott, Roy. *The Aristocrats.* Weidenfeld, 1968.

Pine, L. G. *Ramshackledom.* Secker and Warburg, 1972.

———. *The Story of Titles.* David and Charles, 1969.

———. *Tales of British Aristocracy.* Burke, 1956.

Reid, Ivan. *Social Class Differences in Britain.* Open Books, 1977.

Rose, Kenneth. *The Later Cecils.* Weidenfeld, 1975.

Roth, Andrew. *Lord on the Board.* Parliamentary Profiles, 1972.

Sampson, Anthony. *Anatomy of Britain.* Hodder and Stoughton, 1962.

Sinclair, Andrew. *The Last of the Best.* Weidenfeld, 1969.

Stanworth, P., and A. Giddens. *Elites and Power in British Society.* Cambridge, 1974.

Strong, Roy, *et al.* *The Destruction of the Country House.* Thames and Hudson, 1974.

Sutherland, Douglas. *The Landowners.* Anthony Blond, 1968.

Trevelyan, G. M. *History of England.* Longmans, 1926.

Turner, E. S. *Amazing Grace.* Michael Joseph, 1975.

Westergaard, John. *Class in a Capitalist Society.* Heinemann, 1975.

INDEX

ABOUT THE AUTHOR

SIMON WINCHESTER is a senior feature writer for the London *Sunday Times*. Born in 1944 and educated at Oxford, he has been posted as a correspondent in New Delhi and Washington, and in Northern Ireland— a reporting assignment that won him the award of Journalist of the Year in 1971. *Their Noble Lordships* is his third book. He is married and lives near Oxford.